THE NATIONAL QUESTION IN NIGERIA

In memory of Adekunle Akinola Taylor

The National Question in Nigeria
Comparative perspectives

Edited by

ABUBAKAR MOMOH and SAID ADEJUMOBI
Department of Political Science, Lagos State University, Nigeria

Ashgate

Published by
Ashgate Publishing Limited
Gower House
Croft Road
Aldershot
Hampshire GU11 3HR
England

Ashgate Publishing Company
131 Main Street
Burlington, VT 05401-5600 USA

Ashgate Website: http://www.ashgate.com

British Library Cataloguing in Publication Data
The national question in Nigeria : comparative
    perspectives. - (Interdisciplinary research series in
    ethnic, genDer and class relations)
    1.Nationalism - Nigeria 2.Nigeria - Politics and government
    - 1984-
    I.Momoh, Abubakar II. Adejumobi, Said
    320.5'4669

Library of Congress Cataloguing-in-Publication Data
The national question in Nigeria : comparative perspectives / edited by Abubakar
Momoh and Said Adejumobi.
        p. cm. -- (Interdisciplinary research series in ethnic, gender, and class relations)
        Includes bibliographical references and index.
        ISBN 0-7546-1234-1
        1.Nigeria--Politics and government--1993- 2. Nigeria--Economic conditions--1970-
3. Nigeria--Social conditions--1960- 4.Minorities--Nigeria--Political activity. 5.
Minorities--Nigeria--Economic conditions. 6. Ethnicity--Nigeria. I.Momoh, Abubakar.
II.Adejumobi, Said. III. Series.

DT515.842.N35 2001
966.905'3--dc21

00-054327

ISBN 0 7546 1234 1

Printed and bound in Great Britian by
Antony Rowe Ltd, Chippenham, Wiltshire

Contents

List of Tables

List of Contributors

Wale Adebanwi is a Lecturer in the Department of Political Science at the University of Ibadan. He specialises on the press in Nigeria politics.

Said Adejumobi is a Senior Lecturer in the Department of Political Science of the Lagos State University, co-author and co-editor of several books, articles and chapters in reputable journals and books, Adejumobi specialises in political economy and civil-military relations. More recently he has been writing on issues of youth and federalism and he currently co-ordinates several research works.

Mark Anikpo is a Professor of Sociology at the University of Port Harcourt. He took his doctorate degree from University of Cambridge. Author of several books and articles, Anikpo was until recently the Acting Vice Chancellor of the Enugu State University.

Ibrahim Baba Gana is a Lecturer in sociology at the University of Maiduguri. He specialises in political sociology and rural sociology.

Zen M. Faleiye is a Principal Librarian at the Federal University of Technology, Akure. Faleiye did her graduate studies at Indiana University, Bloomington.

Unyierie Angela Idem is a Linguist. She studied Applied linguistics at the University of Edinburgh where she wrote a doctorate thesis on second language phonology. She taught at the University of Uyo. She now lives in the United States of America.

Abubakar Momoh is a Senior Lecturer in the Department of Political Science at the Lagos State University. He specialises in political theory and political economy.

Cyril I. Obi is a Senior Research fellow at the Nigerian Institute of International Affairs. He specialises in the area of the political economy of oil in Nigeria. He is widely published on issues of oil, environment and urbanisation.

Osarhieme Benson Osadolor is a Lecturer in the Department of History University of Ibadan. A widely published historian, Osadolor is an expert on the history of the Benin Kingdom.

Eghosa E. Osaghae is a Professor of Political Science at the University of Ibadan. Osaghae specialises on Federalism and Comparative politics. Osaghae has many books and articles in reputable journals to his credit. He was a Professor and Head of Political Studies at the University of Transkei, South Africa.

Yima Sen is a social worker and political activist. Sen did his graduate studies at the University of California, Los Angeles. He has held several political and international appointments including with the United Nations. He is currently into consultancy.

Eskor Toyo is a most distinguished Professor of Economics, and was until recently a Professor at the University of Calabar. He has since retired. Arguably the leading Nigerian Professor of economic theory and econometrics, Toyo has been a consultant to many governments in Africa and many international organisations and groups. Above all, Toyo is best known as a revolutionary political activist and advocate of the working class.

Preface

The inspiration for this book came in the aftermath of the annulment of the June 12, 1993 presidential election by the Nigerian military junta under the leadership of General Ibrahim Babangida. The annulment itself led to popular struggles and a mass exodus of people across the country such as was never witnessed since the Nigerian civil war from 1967- 1970. All kinds of interpretation were given to the annulment but the most dominant and recurring of them all was that the election was annulled because Moshood Abiola, the winner of the election, was a southerner and that the Hausa-Fulani, through the military, wanted to perpetuate themselves in power. Coming on the heels of the protracted struggles of the Niger Delta people, particularly the oil-producing minorities who have been agitating and struggling for autonomy and control over their resources, such a claim became a popularly accepted explanation in discourses within elite circles.

What was worse is that this notion of Hausa-Fulani domination began to concretely affect the politics of the real world of people. Platforms that ordinarily were national in outlook began to witness ethnic division, acrimony and animosity based on xenophobia. Scholars and activists who used to share pan-Nigerian and radical (if not revolutionary) world-view, began to abandon their long held views and attitude to the Nigerian polity. Worried about the implications of this, the Academic Staff Union of Nigeria (ASUU) organised a "State of the nation" seminar in April 1994, just to put things in their proper perspective. Choosing the keynote speaker for the occasion was a problem for ASUU. This was because ASUU wanted a credible person who had not been stigmatised, tainted or consumed by the ethnic jingoism and bias; and who will appeal to people across the divide. There were very few people left, ASUU discovered. It eventually settled for Mokwugo Okoye.

The deliberations at the conference were quite instructive and inspiring. It was after the conference that Sani Kabir approached us to do a focussed and scholarly conference on the theme of the national question. He enthusiastically agreed to support the conference, morally and financially. The proposed conference never took place due to certain factors. However the authors onerously contributed to the initiative – this is how this book was conceived. The book is however not a mere political response but also an academic response to the crises and challenges the Nigerian nation-state has been facing in recent years.

In respect of the outline of the book, in chapter one Momoh tries to identify the core philosophical and theoretical issues that underline the discourse on the national question, worldwide. He then examines the specific ways in which the national question manifests in Nigeria and raises fundamental questions bothering on received philosophical assumptions and theoretical formulations on some of the issues. He offers alternative ways of conceptualising the challenges posed by the Nigerian social reality.

Chapter two, Osadolor undertakes an excursion into Nigeria's history and shows that clearly there have been sore areas and grey points in Nigeria's history that have undermined the corporate existence and sovereignty of the country. He shows how various constitutional mechanisms have failed to solve the national question.

In chapter three Anikpo contends that Nigeria's politics since inception has been based on the principle of domination by the three majority ethnic groups. This for him justifies the struggle of minority groups. He contends that the Nigerian social structure needs to be understood in relation to the provision of basic social services. In this context class relations intercept the ethnic to shape the social structure and this generates politics that have deep implications for the national question.

Toyo persuasively argues in chapter four that the revenue allocation is central to all talks about the national question and that injustice in the allocation of revenue is important to the understanding of the national question in Nigeria. He uses historical, constitutional, political and economic variables to underscore his point. He then lays bare the basis for the persistence of the skewed revenue allocation formula and the way out.

Obi attempts to deal concretely with the major source of Nigeria's revenue- oil. He relates this to the demands and struggles of the oil-producing minorities of the Niger-Delta. He avers that at the heart of the crisis is the rentier nature of the Nigeria economy and its location within the orbit of the global capitalist accumulation process. This process has impact on (under)development and hence the intensification of inter-ethnic group relations. He concludes by calling for policy orientation that is transformative and that is focussed on the needs of the people, particularly the oil-producing minorities.

Sen tries, in chapter six, to debunk several myths and notions about the Middle Belt. He asserts that there is an internal colonial master in the Belt, basically Hausa-Fulani. He shows how this group was historically empowered. Whilst he agrees that the Middle Belt minorities of northern Nigeria have genuine demands, he however feels that many of the elite from the area who champion their cause do so for their own ends. He concludes by stating that the Middle Belt people share certain needs and demands with the rest of the oppressed people of Nigeria and that these provide a basis for unity and a common front for struggle.

In chapter seven Baba Gana provides original insights into some minority groups of northern Nigeria that are seldom focussed in the discussion of minorities. He shows us how a group of minorities in northern Nigeria are reconstituting themselves in the exercise of power and domination as a result of the creation of states, which has led to the emergence of new social forces and configurations. Quite intriguing is the way Hausa and Fulani and other hitherto dominant ethnic groups in the politics of the old Bornu State became minority in the new Yobe state that was carved out of it. The political realignment based on ethnic origin has far-reaching consequences for the state.

Adejumobi demonstrably proves in chapter eight that the military is central to the understanding of the crisis of federalism and the national question in Nigeria today. According to him, the military has lost its professional integrity, it has become ethnically-based, inept, incompetent, corrupt and a source and context of expression of primordial identities. Military rule , he argues, has exposed the military even more as a source of the current crises of the Nigerian nation-state. He concludes that the current return to civil rule and the systematic disengagement of the military offers some hope for the re-professionalisation and rehabilitation of the military.

Osaghae insists in chapter nine that federalism is a solution to the national question. He however states that the reason why previous policies meant to address the federal question failed is because they were applied in a situation of over-centralisation of power at the center, a situation that concomitantly comes with the centralisation of wealth or resources. He contends that although the dynamics of the past had pulled the nation state toward decentralisation through the regional principle; however the dynamics of today show the need for a recourse to the decentralisation principle. He is cautious that this, however, is not a solution for all time as the logic of another trajectory may dictate something different.

In chapter ten, Idem lucidly argues that language and the attachment to it is the most natural basis of ethnic community and solidarity. She contends that just like natural resources, language can be used as an instrument of development, unity and cohesion. On the other hand it can be exploited and used negatively. Idem avers that the reality of ethnic domination through the vehicle of language is quite ubiquitous and threatening. She makes claim about ethnic extinction and the use of the languages of the big three major ethnic groups – Yoruba, Igbo and Hausa in official and social relations. She calls for a just national language policy that is also non-aligned if peace and unity are to reign.

In chapter eleven, Adebanwi traces the role of the Nigerian press historically. He spotlights the role of the press under the military. He argues that the military attempted to gag the press. This led to two tendencies a pro-military press preponderantly from northern Nigeria and an anti-military press preponderantly in the south or more precisely the south west (a.ka. *Ngbati* press). The former was led by the *New Nigeria* Newspaper based in Kaduna and the latter by the "guerrilla journalists" based in Lagos. Adebanwi asserts that while the northern press promoted the religion of Islam, the southern press promoted democracy. He also interrogated the language of discourse in the press. He calls on the journalists and the press to undertake a more sober discourse and have a sense of social responsibility to the people, otherwise the tension in the society will continue to deepen, tearing apart the various peoples.

Chapter twelve ties up the discussion by examining at the national question in a more totalising way.

A.M. and S.A.

Acknowledgements

The idea for this emerged as a result of our perceived dearth in a thorough and scientific articulation of the issues involved in the national crisis in Nigeria.

First and foremost, we thank Sani Kabir for the inspiration in urging us to organise a national conference on the theme of the national question. We appreciate the drive and support of Biko Agozino who took keen interest in the manuscript in his capacity as an Editor of one of the several programmes of Ashgate. We equally appreciate the pressure of Anne Keirby particularly at the time we had technical delay in getting out the camera ready copy. Without her persistent pressures this book may have still remained at the manuscript stage with all the ideas and views contained in it fossilised. We are indebted to Mahmood Mamdani, Julius Ihonvbere and Ebrima Sall for all the encouragement, support and inspiration.

The invaluable and professional assistance and advise of Olawepo Sogo and the tireless effort of Bukola Akintola, Taiwo Alabi and S.S. Whenu are greatly appreciated.

Finally, we thank Titi and Tawa for their understanding and support.

A.M and S.A

List of Abbreviations

AD	-	Alliance For Democracy
ADP	-	Agriculture Development Projects
AFRIGOV	-	African Centre for Democratic Governance
AG	-	Action Group
ANC	-	African National Congress
APC	-	Arewa Peoples Congress
APP	-	All Peoples Party
BCNN	-	Broadcasting Corporation of Northern Nigeria
BPU	-	Biron Progressive Union
BYM	-	Borno Youth Movement
BMMC	-	Bala Mohammed Memorial Committee
CA	-	Constituent Assembly
CAN	-	Christian Association of Nigeria
CBN	-	Central Bank of Nigeria
CIN	-	Council for Ikwere Nationality
COAS	-	Chief of Army Staff
COR	-	Calabar Ogoja River State Movement
DFRRI	-	Directorate for Foods, Roads and Rural Infrastructure
EMIROAF	-	Ethnic Minority Rights Organization of Africa
EBA	-	Egbesu Boys of Africa
ENC	-	Egi National Congress
EWM	-	Egi Women's Movement
GR	-	Green Revolution
IDU	-	Isoko Development Union
INC	-	Ijaw National Congress
INP	-	Itsekiri Nationality Youth Movement
INYM	-	Isoko National Youth Movement
IPM	-	Ijaw Peace Movement
IYC	-	Ijaw Youth Council
JAMB	-	Joint Admission and Matriculation Board
MASSOB	-	Movement for the Realisation of the Sovereign State of Biafra
MBF	-	Middle Belt Forum
MOD	-	Ministry of Defence

MORETO - Movement for Reparations to Ogbia
MOSIEND - Movement for the Survival of Izon Nationality in Niger Delta
MOSOP - Movement for the Survival of Ogoni People
MWSM - Mid-West State Movement
NADECO - National Democratic Coalition
NAECS - Nigerian Army Education Corps
NBPE - National Board for Primary Education
NCNC - National Council of Nigeria and the Cameroon's
NCNC - National Council of Nigerian Citizens
NDIC - National Deposit Insurance Corporation
NEPU - Northern Elements Progressive Union
NGOs - Non-Governmental Organisations
NNA - Nigerian National Alliance
NNDC - New Nigerian Development Commission
NNDC - Niger Delta Development Commission
NNMB - Northern Nigeria Marketing Board
NNPC - Nigerian National Petroleum Corporation
NPE - National Policy on Education
NPC - Northern People's Congress
NPF - Northern Progressive Front
NPN - National Party of Nigeria
NPP - Nigeria Peoples Party
NRC - National Republican Convention
NRDB - Northern Regional Development Board
NRDC - Northern Regional Development Company
NUC - National University Commission
NYCOP - National Youth Council for the Survival of Ogoni People
OFN - Operation Feed the Nation
OIC - Organisation of Islamic Countries
OMPADEC - Oil Mineral Producing Areas Development Commission
OOMPCON - Organisation of Oil Mineral Producing Communities of Nigeria
OPC - Oodua Peoples' Congress
PDP - Peoples Democratic Party
PSP - People's Solidarity Party
RMAFC - Revenue Mobilisation Allocation and Fiscal Commission.
SAP - Structural Adjustment Programme
SDP - Social Democratic Party
SDKP - Social Democratic Party of the Kingdom of Poland

SMM	-	Southern Minorities Movement
SNC	-	Sovereign National Conference
SSSCE	-	Senior Secondary School Certificate Examination
TPU	-	Tiv Progressive Union
TROMPCON	-	Traditional Rulers of Oil Mineral Producing Communities
UMBC	-	United Middle Belt Congress
UNIP	-	United National Independents Party
UN	-	United Nations
UNPO	-	Unrepresented Nations and Peoples Organisation
UPGA	-	United Progressive Grand Alliance
VAT	-	Value Added Tax
WASU	-	West African Students Union
WAFF	-	West African Frontiers Force

1 The Philosophy and Theory of the National Question

ABUBAKAR MOMOH

Introduction

Discourses on the National question have centered on disputations about:

(a)   whether it has its historical origin in the rise of capitalism or not.

(b)   the existence or non-existence of the national question in Africa.

(c)   the relationship of the national question to the issues of power and governance.

(d)   the issue of access to resources and its equitable distribution.

(e)   the role of the toiling masses in their quest for liberation as being cardinal to the resolution of the national question.

(f)   the class basis of the national question.

(g)   the ethno-nationalist basis of solution of the national question.

(h)   a consociational and processual solution of the question and

(i)   a liberal democratic or socialist solution of the national question.

I intend to argue that all of these proposals and propositions put forth are not mutually exclusive neither are they contradictory as such. There is something important in the analytic scheme and explanatory coherence that laces them together. For all this to be meaningful, there is need for a philosophical and theoretical framework that animates the historico-material context for the understanding of the national question in Nigeria.

The cardinal philosophical argument I make is that the national question is basically a problem of the realisation of human essence. To that extent and for that reason, it is something beyond ethnicity (not a denial of it) because there is no such thing as the *ethnic essence*. I shall contend that those talks of oppression, domination, and marginalization all boil down to issues of alienation, inequality and inequity in society. Ethnic explanation cannot capture the totality or ramification of such claims. Objectifying an ethnic claim is different from instrumentalising it.

1

On a theoretical plain I shall contend that the specific ways in which the national question discourse has been captured does not historically connect to or intercept politics with economy, and technocracy with the state as the principal agency. The product of which is "unevenness" in all departments with consequences for ethnic, spatial and ideological categories. My view is that ensuring an organic linkage for all those variables will not deny the claim of oppression of people but will falsify an ethnic resolution of the claim. Therefore, the national question, ultimately, requires to be posed as an ideological question.

A further word on the ethnic-domination thesis. Wherever such things as genocide or ethnic cleansing had occurred in history such as in Germany, Rwanda and Burundi etc. they were always seen as irrational or out of tune with civil mode of governance.

My theoretical point of departure is that the national question in Nigeria is nothing but the (un) evenness in the distribution of or access to power and economy in the context of *deliverables* and what advantage co-ethnics or a fraction of them take of one another in the process. It has little to do with *ethnic domination-qua-ethnic domination*. My contention is that there is no theory of ethnic justice, but of social justice. I caution about the banal and the over-exaggeration of ethnicity as a political agency and urge for a sober sociological analysis that will ultimately problematise the particularisms and universalisms of the multi-faceted dimensions of the national question in Nigeria. My ambition in this chapter is merely to probe by threading the philosophically instantiated benchmarks and contours, which a deeper understanding of the national question should chart.

Four key issues that underline our philosophical claim need to be noted. First, the National question is fundamentally related to the question of rights of nations and peoples particularly in the context of oppression. And, the question why are people oppressed is in the last instance, a political issue. Therefore, ultimately, the national question leaves us with the challenge of political solutions.

Second, ethnic identity, is a *baseline identity* and the major substratum of the national question and residue of oppression amongst co-ethnics; it is a trans-class category and not a non-class category. However, at every point in history, an individual bears multiple identities and those identities that conflate or interact with the ethnic to raise the problems of the national question may have something remotely to do with the ethnic factor in its crude or raw form. In most instances the ethnic is mediated by other variables.

Third, to theorise about the national question in Nigeria we do not need to be reductionist or particularistic by basing our analysis on one moment or trajectory but the entire span of Nigeria and the period both pre-dating and ante-dating the emergence of Nigeria as a nation-state, there is need for a methodological fashion of historical sociology. We need to simultaneously historicise (not historicism) our theory and theorise our history in the process of problematising the national question as a *lived essentialism*. Accordingly, the discourse is people-driven and all the attendant normative variables such as equality, oppression, injustice, rights etc. become useful in the process of analysis.

Fourth, theorising is not a meta-epistemological endeavour with claim to final anchors or artefactual constructs. Since such theorising is about a dialogical process (history in motion) and the concrete struggles of people, we can never seek, neither should we expect once-and-for-all answers for the problems arising from the national question. All we should seek to do is to provide a basis for the scientific and philosophical explanation of the real world and the struggles which people wage in the context of the national question. I then try to theorise the discourses around those struggles in the manner they manifested drawing heavily on the Nigerian example.

Discourse of the National Question

Let me begin with a disclaimer. It will be difficult to find a consensus or a universal definition or enunciation of what constitutes the national question what we interrogate, critique or seek to find explanation, synthesis and resolution for will be merely suggestive. It should be noted that such is the dynamics and fluid character of the question. I will illustrate through this critique that the national question has had changing definitions and shifting meanings over time for different scholars and people.

Marx and Engels, although they did not work out a consistent theory on nations and the national question, they however, expressed clear views about the Irish, Jewish, Polish and Czech questions (Omar, 1986: p.1). It will be erroneous to state that they did not. It is incorrect to assert that because Marx stated that "the proletariat has no country" it then means that Marx supported the abolition of nationality (Lowy, 1976: p.82). On the contrary, Marx developed the national question as part of an overall strategy of proletarian freedom and internationalism. This is why Marx supported the Polish and the Irish, criticised the liberal democratic nationalism of Mazzini in Italy and the national nihilism of Proudhon and his followers.

Engels on his part did support the views of Marx. But he propounds the doctrine of "non-historic nation". This is particularly illuminated in his analysis of the South Slav nations (Czechs, Croats, Serbs, Romanians Slovenes, Dalmatians, and so on) who joined the imperial Austrian and Czarist Russian Armies in the 1848-1849 revolutions and were used to cause the liberal revolution in Hungary, Poland, Austria and Italy (Lowy, p.84).

As Lowy was later to conclude, "The 1984 revolution is the classic example of a revolution that failed because it did not provide a radical solution to the agrarian question and the national question (precisely what made the 1917 October revolution successful". This failure was not because Marx and Engels did not take them into account as they lamented the defeat of the Italians in their bid for unification and warned the Germans that their liberation was hinged on her setting free her neighbouring nations (Mzala, 1988: p.32).

Karl Kautsky who was seen as the heir apparent to Marx and Engels, within the Second International, and a leading expert on the national question however stated that language was the most important factor in the formation of nations and along with Edward Bernstein he supported imperialism and insisted that colonialism was a progressive development. Their views just like those of the Austro-Marxists, Karl Renner and Otto Bauer, amounted to Marxist revisionism. Renner for instance sees, "consciousness and will of belonging" as the most decisive factors in belonging to a nation. They then developed the concept of "national cultural autonomy" which is nothing but a cultural personality devoid of territoriality and politics. Lenin joined the Bauer-Kautsky debate and criticised Bauer for holding an idealistic view of nation with undue emphasis on the ethnic factor, which is the basis of bourgeois nationalism (Mzala, p.34).

It was shortly after that time that Rosa Luxemburg, founder of the Social Democratic Party of the Kingdom of Poland (SDKP), Leon Trotsky, Anton Pannekoek, Josef Stragger and Josif Stalin, among others, joined the debate. I shall only highlight the key issues addressed by three of the most outstanding and often repeated views before going to Lenin's most profound and illuminating critique of the dominant discourses, and his enrichment of the debate.

Luxemburg denounced the clamour of independence for Poland and instead called for closer ties between the proletariat of Russia and Poland. She views the call as a sham utopianism and a "series of sterile national struggles". Her view is that a nation is purely a cultural phenomenon with little political dimension to it and that since Poland is economically dependent on Russia, her independence is hence tied to the independence or liberation of Russia. She saw the quest for national liberation not as liberating the mass of the people from oppression but as opening up room for reactionaries and the *petit bourgeoisie* to take over power.

On his part, Leon Trotsky argues that nations have a right to self-determination hence he supported the struggles of the polish people. For him, there is a relationship between proletariat internationalism and national rights and the destruction of the former will lead to the destruction of the latter hence a destruction of both socialism and the "national interest" (Ibid: p.90). However, Trotsky has two major problems in his conceptualisation of the national question. The first is that while he shows the dialectical relationship between internationalism and nationalism, he is unable to show their differences. One may (and does) not necessarily culminate in the other; several sectors may account for why that is not necessarily so. Second, Trotsky has an economistic and deterministic notion of the collapse or destruction of the nation-state. To him, the emergence of a world economy has led to the submergence of several economies that will necessarily make the nation state to collapse! This kind of argument is currently being invoked in defence of globalisation. On the contrary nation-states or their leaders have turned out to be the promoters of globalisation and the national interest. They claim that globalisation is in the national interest it neither contradicts it nor does it spite it. The argument for the collapse of the nation-state even within classical Marxism is not an economistic one but a political-cum-ideological question. J.V. Stalin defines the nation thus:

> ...A historically constituted, stable community of people, formed in the basis of a common language, territory, economic life and psychological make-up manifested in a common culture (Stalin, 1953: p.307)

Stalin formulated the foregoing position in 1913. Many critics attacked it for being static, market-oriented and for identifying values and variables that are insufficient in characterising a nation state. Above all he equated a nation state with capitalism and made language and psychological factors important determinants. Events such as the emergence of the two nations of Germany-German Democratic Republic and the Federal Republic of Germany, Denmark and Norway contradicted the language issue. And the application of the Leninist and Wilsonian concepts of self-determination to colonial territories of the third World also undermined Stalin's view of the relationship between capitalism, the nation-state and the national question. The contention being that nation-states did not arise merely because of the rise of capitalism or commodity relations.

It should however be conceded to Stalin that his contribution came to fill a void in the context of a raging national crisis within the Russia Social Democratic Party in a context which was dominated by the *Tsarist* regime, during the bourgeois democratic revolution of 1912-1913.

Lenin, it was, who sent Stalin to Vienna to write his famous piece "Marxism and the national question". However the outcome of the piece clearly differed from or even contradicted, in certain respects, Lenin's views on the discourse.

Lenin sees the national question first and foremost as a matter of freedom and hence a political question. He succinctly states:

> The right of nations to self-determination means only the right to independence in a political sense, the *right to free political secession from the oppression nation*. Concretely, this political, democratic demand implies complete freedom to carry on agitation in favour of secession, and *freedom to settle the question of secession by means of a referendum of the nation that desires to secede*. (Lenin, 1975: p.5) (Emphasis added.)

There are three important points that need to be made here. First, Lenin believes that a nation could be oppressed by another nation. But the logical question to ask is, does this imply that Lenin denies class oppression even within the oppressed nations? Far from it, Lenin also does not show which is more important or pernicious, class or a nation's oppression, or whether both carry equal weight. But he also does not deny the fact that both class struggle and national struggle can be waged all at once. This is the basis and secret behind the universal appeal of his view. For Lenin everything is to be defined in the context of existing realities – "concrete analysis of concrete situation".

Second, Lenin's further exposition on the first world war and the issue of the "Defence of the fatherland" in the context of imperialist war, and particularly his notion of "just and unjust wars" clarified the linkage between national liberation struggles and socialism.

Third, the concept of secession or self-determination is not to be automatically activated. It has to be tested among those seeking secession through a democratic means in the form of a referendum. In Leninism, self-determination is not mechanical or sterile cliché to be foisted on the people through warfare or militarism. It is clearly a political decision of an oppressed nation to be taken in a democratic form. In this sense warfare becomes only an instrument of accompanying such a popular wish of the nation.

Scholars such as Nicos Poulantzas, Samir Amin, Dani Nabudere, Wamba-dia-Wamba and Nzongola-Ntalaja have joined the debate on the national question from a radical perspective. Poulantzas attacks the Stalinist viewpoint on the national question as too economistic. One his part, Nabudere, following in the Stalinist tradition, denies the possibility of emergence of a nation-state in colonies and neo-colonies (Nzongola-Ntalaja, 1987: pp. 44-5). This is because, in the typically Stalinist fashion, nation-states are to rise with capitalism and hence there are no capitalist economies in the colonial and neo-colonial countries hence there can be no nation-states in the colonies and neo-colonies.

There are two critical issues that are missing in the debate about the rise of nation states. The first one is that the juridical basis for the delimitation of a nation-state is spirited away for the economic. Whereas it is this juridical aspect that makes the difference between suzerainty and sovereignty. Second, it is not always that nation states arose from internal cohesion and freely entered covenant as it occurred in some parts of Europe. In third world countries many nation-states arose from above the people. The Berlin conferences of 1883-4 are worthy of note in this regard. Third and more important, the qualifications of a nation-state in third world countries fall within the framework of western liberalism and this makes it Eurocentric in essence and in application to Africa. In his seminal intervention using the case of the Arabs, Samir Amin contends and I will quote him *in extenso*:

> Firstly, the nation is a social phenomenon which can appear at every stage of history: It is not necessarily and exclusively a correlate of the capitalist mode of production. Secondly, the nation appears when there exist not only the elementary conditions of geographical contiguity, reinforced by the use of a common language (which does not exclude variants of dialect), but also a social class which controls the central state apparatus and ensures economic unity in the life of the community: this class need not necessarily be the capitalist national bourgeoisie. Thirdly, the phenomenon of nationhood is a reversible process. It can develop and grow stronger or, on the contrary, it can weaken and fade away, according to whether the social class in question reinforces its unificatory power or loses it altogether (Amin, 1978: p.81).

Amin's definition of a nation is all-inclusive and historical; it captures all the phases of human history. The critical issue here is, can the gentes or clans (which are lower phases of human history) make claims of self-determination in the modern sense in which the concept is posed? Is Amin implying the interchangeability of nation and nation-state, of nationalities and citizens?

Nzongola-Ntalaja supports Amin on at least three grounds. First for dismissing the view that a nation-state is contingent upon the rise of capitalism. He argues that, "[T]his does not allow for a full understanding of the phenomenon of nationhood in other parts of the world...." (Nzongola-Ntalaja, 1993: p.12) He further contends that a nation is a social phenomenon connected to economic centralisation and political authority or state power. He further states that:

> This is why there is a dialectical relationship between state and nation in the modern world. The nation either emerges to coincide with an existing state or consolidates itself as a modern nation by creating its own state.
>
> The relationship between the two is mediated through two matrices which constitute the materials framework of institutions and social practices;

The spatial matrix territory and geographic contiguity and the temporal matrix of a shared historical and a cultural tradition.

To Nzongola-Ntalaja both matrices are essential for the existence of nations and for the ruling class in control of the state or economy, to manipulate.

Nzongola-Ntalaja makes four pertinent submissions. First, that nationhood develops according to the level of development of productive forces and the role of the state in material organisation. Second, that in pre-colonial Africa some nations existed that corresponded to varying social formations made-up of people and all kinds of groups. And through myths of origin and ideologies, a national identity was forged amongst them. Third, that indeed colonialism disrupted the process of developing viable nations in Africa. Fourth, that colonialism had a contradictory impact on the national question. On one level, it led pre-colonial nations to fade or disintegrate. On another level it united various African nationalities.

This is what for Nzongola-Ntalaja provides the nexus of nation building and state building, i.e. how do we build a nation-state from several nations? He then proceeds to advance three typologies of the national question in Africa:

(a)   The ethnic nation that corresponded to pre-colonial functions destroyed by colonialism.

(b)   The colonially-created territorial nation, and

(c)   The pan-African nation (Nzongola-Ntalaja, 1987: p.48).

Whilst his first two categories impact heavily on current trends of the national question in African countries, it remains to be seen if the last one has had any much impact beyond the rhetoric of it. It must be added that the current crisis of the national question in Africa was brought about as result of the crisis of nation building which has led to the questioning of the colonially–created territorial nation, through, for instance, involuntary or forcible integration process. But this has led to two contradictions. On one hand, there is the talk about fragility and artificiality of inherited colonial boundaries, on the other hand there is the talk of differences among co-ethnics. The latter case is often made in an *essentialist* manner such that not only makes fetish of difference but that also sees difference as inherently conflictual, dangerous, irreconcilable and eternal.

Wamba-dia-Wamba advances a strong theoretical position about the national question as a political question which will result in the struggle for popular democracy by the masses of the people of Africa, and a struggle against imperialism (Wamba-dia-Wamba, 1991:p.67). Accordingly, he avers:

The national question refers to how the global form of the social existence; characterising the internal multiplicity and the relationship of the society to its environments, is historically arrived at. How is "the orderly exercise of nationwide, public authority" organized? Who is or is not a member of that society? Who is an outsider? How has the social membership been changing? Does every member enjoy the same rights/obligations as those of every other member? How are these rights recognised and motivated? How are competing claims (for self-determination, for example) by diverse groups mediated and made consistent globally? Are there people or groups that are, or feel, collectively oppressed or left out? How are inequalities of uneven development handled; are there groups looked upon and paternalistically administered? (*Ibid:* p.57).

To Wamba-dia-Wamba colonialism united the colonised as well as divided them. It did the former by differentiating the colonised from the coloniser and hence an onerous struggle against colonialism ensured therefrom. It did the latter by splitting up hitherto homogeneous ethnic groups. This created a weak social and political foundation in an independence nation-building process, as the emergent elite did not rectify this Berlin-constructed defects, rather they strove to build on them. This for Wamba-dia-Wamba sung the *Nunc dimitis* of the nation building project. Elsewhere and in a different context he accepts, like Amin and Nzongola-Ntalaja, the existence of the nation state in Africa, Wamba-dia-Wamba however calls for the differentiation of nation states in two ways, almost in the same way as Nzongola-Ntalaja does. First, he differentiates the creation of a nation state on the basis of colonial conquest and second on the basis of a national community predicated upon common cultural origin or mass struggle of resistance against domination. For him this second form of self-determination is horizontal and more organic. This is so because self-determination through such a people's struggle "calls for a real transformation of the colonial state to make it democratic" (Wamba-dia-Wamba, 1995: pp.155-6). However, the rhetorical and yet deeply philosophical questions that Young asked become apt here viz. What are the properties of self-determination?

What is the "Self" that may invoke this claim? Does territoriality, ethno-cultural community, subjective collective self-assertion, or some combinations of these define it? Is self-determination to be exercised only once, at the moment of the covenant, or is it subject to continuous review? Must it be solemnised by some participative act of the human collectivity in question, or may a political movement purporting to speak contractually for a "people" exercise this right? Is there some "critical dates" at which the people entitled to exercise self-determination are fully constituted, with those arriving after excluded from the choice? Does self-determination comport with an unassailable right of separation? Is it circumscribed by some criterion of "viability" of a sovereign unit? (Young, 1991: p. 322)

Beyond these questions, there is something that makes self-determination the basis and context of the struggle of nations (genuinely, ostensibly or seemingly) oppressed people to have a universal appeal. This is partly because the United Nations itself has adopted the principle of self-determination in Article 1 of the UN Charter, while Article 73 has specific provision about non-self governing territories. Although initially directed at colonised peoples, this has in more recent times been applied to nation-states with problems of irredentism and war.

Could the profile of those nation-states serve as a useful guide about whether there is a legitimate basis for the claim over self-determination, that is, whether it is useful to aid a democratic framework of discursion and possible resolution of grey areas amongst nations? Wamba dia Wamba avers that "Constitutional exercises have, ...tended systematically to uphold and "legitimise" arbitrariness"(1995: p.161). His view on Zaire under Mobutu Seseseko is applicable to many African countries today, where the ethnic issue as such is not seen as desirous of critical discussion with a view towards a constitutionally-driven resolution. In many states in Africa, the ethnic category is seen as a cultural residue that is useful not in terms of peace in a nation-state but in terms of crisis and in the mutation and permutation of the geometry of political power. Its operational or consociational implication is often frittered away as politically inconsequential or irrelevant. Put differently the relevance of the measure of the ethnic is measured in its demagoguery. But I fathom that the error comes from an uni-linear reading of the political behaviour of the emergent nationalist elite of Africa. While they make claims of nationalism and even pan-Africanism, a "social conflict" emerged among them relating to competing interests and struggle for power, which made it convenient to subordinate the national project by *instrumentalising* the ethnic project, the latter became an agency occupying a ubiquitous status in statist politics. "They (nationalists) were now divisive of that natural unity, initially empowered by a social unity behind social aspirations, which the whole independence project was supposed to be about". (Davidson, 1992: p.112)

The dual allegiance of commitment both to the nation and nation-state in which the nation was often conveniently used to upstage the nation-state is what resulted in the often constructed notion of the existence of a "primordial public sphere" as against a "civic sphere" in Africa. In my view, this claim over-exaggerates the role of ethnicity in the context of the state as opposed to society and social movement politics in Africa. Indeed, it can be hypothesised that while ethnicity divides the people in society, it unites the ruling class in the context of state power. If indeed, power is about inclusion and exclusion, it means state power will not accommodate forces that undermine it by posing a threat to it. Within the framework of "constitutive rules" state power is often used to eliminate such elite. But even where the ethnic factor is over-played or overwhelms the state it still does not deny the civic outlook of the state. It only makes a definition of the state in Africa more complex. It is easy to see why such characterisation of the state in Africa as patrimonial, criminalised, *Kikuyunalised* (under Kenya's Jomo Kenyatta) could not stand any scientific test.

Doumou may disagree with the foregoing construction. For him, the juridical existence of the African State was decreed by colonialism hence it could not be questioned. So nation-states, *ipso facto*, do exist. But several states in Africa have failed to forge is a sense of nationhood out of the nation-state with several *a-national* socio-cultural formations (1987: p.57). To him, a nation state is meant to forge a sense of nationhood and not "unity in diversity," and to homogenise diversities. While this is permissible as a political project, it is impossible as a cultural project. To Doumou the major limitation of the dominant discourse of the subject matter within Marxist theory is that in its study of dependent societies it over-emphasises "class contradictions" and "abolition of class exploitation". Whereas social conflicts are mediated and intensified by discrimination, inequality and oppression based on ethnicity, language, religion and so on. "…whereas it is precisely this incompatibility between the "project-nation" of the ruling class and the specificities of the social formations that constitutes one of the principal causes of the crisis of the state in the Third world countries" (*Ibid*: p.59).

Again, to pose the issue in this way does not appropriately qualify the "project-nation" in the bargaining and trade-offs they make in their competing claims with other elite in the context of the nation-state. They make the bargaining in the name and on behalf of their various nation-states and not necessarily for their individual nations.

All forms of domination are mediated through certain instruments. Humanity's quest for freedom necessarily translates into a form of reason. But "freedom-quest" also provides conditions for its fulfillment as a truth-related category. The crucial issue in this regard is consciousness. By seeking freedom in this sense, the true conditions for the realisation of humanity are set forth through the transformation of conditions of oppression (Magubane, 1987: pp.39-40). The conditions of oppression recognise a sense of legality and legitimacy for the oppressors – the conditions for struggles against oppression are often deemed illegal thus posing some formal restrictions and constraints. Two things arise here. The first is that, in the context of reason, oppression of nations raises the problem of *human intrinsic worth*. Second, the liberation of nations from oppression by other nations only fulfills one of the many strands of liberation that are possible. It does not deny neither does it provide an iron-glad guarantee against oppression within the new nation.

The implication of the foregoing is that national oppression is not an unproblematic normative category. It needs to be interrogated otherwise it becomes a nebulous phraseology with deep-seated implication for social relations in nation-states. Another issue that arises here has to do with what constitutes national oppression? How do we identify and socially disaggregate forms of oppression of nations and oppression within nations? What do we take in and what do we take out of the omnibus sack? Can we intercept or qualify oppression of nation with any other variable? What distinguishes the oppression of a nation from the privileges of other nations within the nation-state? Put differently, is the oppression of one nation the flip side of the privileges of other nations?

On another level, what should serve as the basis of the (co)existence of co-ethnics? What is the relationship of equity to equality? Do both draw the same jurisprudential and political implications from both conceptual usages? It should be stated that equity ensures fairness, whilst equality facilitates justice.

The role of capitalism or merchant capital in the development of nation-states is only one way a nation-state emerges in history. To hold this for all histories will deny the emergence of nation-sates in Africa. It should also be noted that language and culture might be necessary but insufficient basis for the formation of nations or the struggles of oppressed nations. Furthermore, nationhood, is not a pre-condition for formation of a nation-state and a nation-state does not necessarily strive towards nationhood (*a-national* formation). It needs to be stated that the national question is inevitably about the rights that different peoples share or exercise within a political system. Whether such are seen as privileges or rights naturally accruing to people, is an entirely different issue. Whether such rights are democratically and freely arrived at or accepted; whether such rights include the right to self-determination, will not matter. The crucial point however is that all talk about rights necessarily raises the question of citizenship. But even as citizens the question about how to interpret self-determination is purely a political question and not a juridical one. In this sense, self-determination could transmute or mutate into secession and vice versa. The question then is under what circumstances can we describe self-determination as secession and vice versa? Does our vulgarisation of the term make it frivolous? When is it time to secede and when does a quest for secession become a quest for self-determination? The way the politics of equality and equity, production, distribution and deliverables is played is important to the resolution of this dilemma.

The Nigerian Intervention in the Discourse

Thus far there are two major national conferences worthy of note that have been organised on the national question in Nigeria. The first one was held in August 1986 and the Nigerian Economy and Society (NES) held the second one in 1993. The 1986 conference took a particularly academic and doctrinaire character (cf. Omar, 1986). Whilst the 1993 conference had a heavy ethno-charismatic and cultural dimension. During the latter conference, the national question discourse took a near reductionism character of ethnicity. The same spirit characterised the southern minorities' conference of December 1998, held in Lagos.

It should however be stated that prior to all this, there was a healthy polemical exchange between the Bala Mohammed Memorial Committee (BMMC) and the Ife Collectives about the national and nationality questions in Nigeria, in 1982. In 1992, the *Citizen* magazine organised a national dialogue on the national question with such controversial personalities as Ken Saro Wiwa and Yusufu Bala Usman participating and doing presentations at the conference. In February 1994, the Arewa House organised a national workshop, basically it also discussed the national question. That effort culminated in the publication of the book titled, *Nigeria: The State of the Nation and the Way Forward.* Many of the participants at the workshop came with labels or were stigmatised as ethnicists, hegemons, minority chieftains etc. Such name-calling only permitted stereotyping, labeling, fixations and dogma. It does not allow for a sober and tolerant intellectual and political discussion of the problems confronting the nation-state. Quite understandably, in the context of the annulment of the June 1993 presidential elections and the deepening crisis in the oil-producing areas, the discourse around the national question took a clearly ethno-chauvinistic dimension and political mobilisation was done along that line.

The left interventions in the discourse of the national question in Nigeria started in a more doctrinaire way- how Marxist enough was one's analysis of the national question. Class was the primary – and in some cases the sole determinant – in social analysis everything else was reductionist and mechanical, in certain cases disregarding sociology and history in such analysis. Where class analysis was used it was merely mediated by such "irritant" factors as military, lumpen classes and primordial values. The exchanges between the

BMMC and the Ife Collectives become very instructive in this regard; so also is the polemics between Mustapha and Abba (BMMC, 1982; Socialist Forum, 1983; Mustapha, 1985; and Abba, 1985).

To Mustapha, the national question must emphasise the issues of internal democracy within the nation state and liberation from the stranglehold of imperialism. "This approach, it would seem, is closer to the original Marxist proposition...." (1986: p.82). He further asserts that the national question has two dimensions: (a) it deals with the nature of the relationship between Nigeria and world imperialism and (b) the relationship between various Nigerian nationalities (*Ibid*: p.83). More poignantly and pertinent to this chapter is Mustapha's identification of the contradictions which the national question generates on several levels. Mustapha surmises:

> "...The national question in Nigeria manifests itself in a series of eight contradictions: Nigeria versus imperialism; the contradiction between the majority nationalities i.e. Hausa, Igbo and Yoruba; the North South divide between the three major nationalities on the one hand, and the smaller nationalities on the other; inter-state rivalry between the ... states of the federation; inter-ethnic rivalries in a mixed state for instance between the Nupes and Hausas in Niger state; inter- sectional rivalries within an ethnic group of nationality (sic), as between Kano and Sokoto, or the Egba and the Ijebu; and finally, inter-clan rivalries within a province or district, as is common in the southeastern part of the country" (Mustapha, 1986: p.82).

This definition is quite all-encompassing except that it does not pose other ancillary questions relating to the contradictions of the national question such as the contradiction between the character of the state and the sociological basis of the foundation of the Nigerian nation-state; the contradiction between democracy, secularity and religion; and the contradiction between the claim of rights and entitlements and the claim of privileges. All these certainly have implications for the national question. Although they seem to be secondary contradictions they are however capable of overshadowing the primary contradictions, in certain principal respects.

On his part, Madunagu, a well respected Marxist, notes:

> By the national question we mean the problems that arise from the composition of a nation; that is, problems arising from the nature of the relationship between the *ethnic groups* in a nation state (1997: p.12) (emphasis added).

Ade Ajayi also subscribes to a near similar view when he avers:

The national question is ... the perennial debate as to how to order the relations between the different ethnic, linguistic and cultural groupings so that they have the same rights and privileges, access to power and equitable share of the national resources (Ajayi, 1992).

All these views make ethno-nationalism, whether of the polycentric or ethnocentric type, a central issue in the national question discourse. As Fashina rightly contends, ethno-nationalism (the ideological movement for ethnic and cultural separateness) does not give premium to the common human suffering of all peoples. Indeed, ethno-nationalism may serve as the basis of one group to dominate or be dominated by another such as the case of Tutsi and Hutu in Rwanda and Burundi. Fashina further avers:

I am not denying that there is a national question. I am not denying that there is an ethnic problem.... the national question is not, at the root of ethnicity problem and that it has no ethnic solution.

...The national question is a "concentrated" socio-economic-political question. *The ethnic formulation of the national question masks exploitative processes which go on within all ethnic groups in Nigeria"* (Fashina, 1998: p.93).

It is apt to state that at the present conjuncture in Nigeria it is hardly possible to distinguish between left and right discourses of the national question. This is so because of the heavy ethno-nationalist colouration that underlines such discourses (cf. Soyinka, 1996). But to pose the national question in this way, at the risk of repetition, is to oversimplify the question. For instance, Ake fruitlessly attempts to make a conceptual differentiation between ethnicity and "political ethnicity", without explaining how the reality of "ethnic identity" tempers the questions of justice, rights and equity. He gives the impression that current struggles in Africa are actually waged by "traditional solidarity groups" against the "political monolithism" of the African state (Ake, 1993: p.4).

Indeed many solutions, particularly of the consociational type, have come to see proportionality, federal character, and respect for group rights and ethnic balancing in state institutions and structures as the solution of the national question. But many reflections on those solutions have been critiqued as having failed (cf. Ekeh and Osaghae, 1985; Jinadu, 1985; Ayoade, 1986). As Mustapha rightly asserts, the federal character principle and all such policies failed because they do not urge for "profound social change" (Mustapha, 1986: p.89).

There are two critical issues that are attendant to the national question discourse which Fashina raises viz. politics of identities and minorities in relation to the "internal colonialism thesis". On the identities question Fashina argues:

> Each of us has overlapping identities, some of which may conflict with others: class versus ethnic identity, religious versus ethnic identity, religious versus class identity; identities in pure form are not found in real societies" (Fashina, 1998: p.91).

Religious identity can produce an equally turbulent crisis for a nation-state. Awe argues that it is possible to talk of a "cultural identity" in Nigeria. However this identity is a product of British (Western) values, African traditional values, western religion, African religion, western education etc. She argues that while Africans did not completely abandon their traditional values (even at times resisting the destruction of such values) they did not altogether embrace western values. She cites a very pertinent example of the rise of the African native churches which were inspired by the need to "worship God in the cultural mode of their forefathers" (Awe, 1989: p.25).

Mama points to the psychopathology of the invention of black identity without any conscious effort to study the history and person of the black descendents (1995: p.48). But perhaps ethnicity has assumed the dominant theme in identity discourse because of its transnational and resonating character when compared with one's class (Shah, 1994: p.189). But post-modernism in no small way permitted, a confusing analysis of subjectivity and the "politics of cultural recognition" (Parekh, 1994: p.789). Kymlicka addresses the issue of subjectivity from the point of view of multiculturalism (1995).

The other issue that Fashina addresses is the minority question as a cardinal aspect of the national question. For instance, especially in northern Nigeria, there is talk particularly among non-Muslim minorities about "internal colonialism" (cf. Bonat, 1989, Kazah-Toure, 1999).

Indeed, Ekeh refers to two types of minorities, the ethnic minorities proper, who are isolated from the majorities; and the marginals who are ethnic minorities related and or connected to majority ethnic groups example, the Yoruba of Kogi state, (Ekeh, 1972: pp.95-98). Elsewhere, Ekeh further distinguishes between "political minorities" and "historically dominant minorities". To him, first and foremost, the notion of minorities is a political creation of culturally and historically disadvantaged groups. This for him constitutes the political minorities. The Ogoni, Ijaws and Tiv qualify for this group. While the historically dominant minorities refer to those minorities that since pristine had dominated some majority ethnic groups such as the Ijo over the Igbo (Ekeh 1996: p.42). To him, the "minority Fulani have pressed their historic advantages to enormous power holding at the national level"(*Ibid*: p.39).

On account of this, he urges for a "...search into history for a clearer outline of the basis of political power in Nigeria". On his part, Jinadu distinguishes between a numerical minority (e.g. Ogoni) and a sociological minority (e.g. Hausa, because of their educational disadvantage) (Jinadu, 1985: p.81).

Osaghae in two related studies (1986: pp.152-55; and 1991: pp.239-243) argues about the existence of minorities in Nigeria. However his works only take into account the political aspect of the minority question and not its very complex historicity (as demonstrated by Ekeh). There is also the issue of the sociology of minority and its mixture with other identities in the context of defining power relations in Nigeria. And this is partly the problem with the "internal colonialism thesis". The primary assumption of this thesis is that it is ethnic groups that dominate and in this case, majority groups dominate minority groups. The cardinal questions here are; first, do citizens of the colonising ethnic group live better off than those of the colonised ethnic groups? Do some segments of the colonised ethnic groups collaborate with the colonising ethnic groups to perpetuate domination? Indeed, "[W]hat is called "internal colonialism" is an expression of the uneven distribution of power within the ruling class" (Fashina, 1998: p.102). Other penetrating studies have linked the problem of social relations to the nature of power, the configuration of social forces, the structure of the state and the character of the military and all of these have potentials for conflict (Ekeh, 1989; Ayoade,1996; Momoh, 1996; Gboyega,1997; and Adejumobi, 2000).

The Historical Roots of the National Question in Nigeria

The low and ebbs of Nigeria as a federation are often written about and there is detailed documentation of separatist agitation in Nigeria (Tamuno, 1970; Osaghae, 1991: p.245; and Ayoade, 1996: pp.50-5). But the questions are: first, is there separatist agitation because Nigerians are incompatible and heterogeneous people? Second, is the "1914 amalgamation a mistake"? Third, what are the crucial issues in the (erroneous) representation and construction of Nigeria's historiography? Without going into details, I will contend that, although Nigeria is a heterogeneous society, Nigerians had many things in common in pre-colonial times. Also, I will argue that the answer to the crisis in the federation need not be sought in the ethnic groups that make up Nigeria; but in the character of the colonially-constructed state, in the nature of colonial development policies and the ideological character, in the interest of the emergent ruling classes of Africa, in the nature of politics and the use to which political power is put in Africa.

I concede that Nigeria was a forcible creation. But before the coming of the colonialists Nigerians interacted in several ways with one another. Olusanya (1970; pp.11-13) uses the issues of myth of origin, diffusion of culture through commerce, inter-marriages and so on to show that Nigerians had knowledge of and interacted with one another on peaceful basis. He painstakingly uses materials from Clapperton to explain this. He shows the link between Benin and Onitsha and through the Oba – Obi titles; the links between Benin, Isoko and Urhobos; Benin and Ife through the royalty; Hausa and Bornu; Yorubaland, and the Nupes (*Ibid*: pp.12-13). He quite instructively states:

> "...Ethnic groups that now make up modern Nigeria did not live in isolation prior to British rule. There were trading and cultural contacts. Moreover, wars, which resulted in conquest, over lordship and enslavement, provided further links. There were also movements not only of peoples but also of ideas from one area to another. All this provided the necessary and vital links amongst the various groups. *Thus British colonial rule did not bring together the various groups in Nigeria. It brought them together only in a new and vital way.*
>
> ...The various ethnic groups were now subjected to the same historical experience out of which a difference type of unity, the unity of common subjection was forged. They were subjected to exploitation, to racial discrimination and to some extent to a measure of oppression and injustice. (*Ibid*: p.15) (Emphasis added)

Ola (1970: pp.19-28) uses other examples to reinforce my thesis. He argues that even as a colonial project, the colonial integration of Nigeria started from January 1900 when Tubman Goldie raised the Union Jack in Lokoja and through an instrument of Queen Victoria declared territorial ownership of the coast and southern protectorates under the aegis of the Royal Nigeria Company. Erim (1996: pp.12-13) states that the waterways of Nigeria particularly the Niger river and its main tributary, the Benue, provided natural in-let into Nigeria and thus facilitated trade and deeper cultural interaction. He also shows the organic basis of amalgamation. For instance, he contends, the Lagos colony was expanded in 1861 when it was discovered that "Lagos without the vast Yoruba territory was a mere town upon a sandy island, insignificant in itself". (Ibid: p.13) Erim further contends:

> It is on record that the Etsu of Nupe, for example, sought advise for the Balogun of Abeokuta and the Sultan of Sokoto, the latter of whom was reported to have mediated in the Yoruba civil wars of the nineteenth century (*Ibid*: p.15).

Does this amount to romanticising the "unity" of Nigeria? No. Rather I caution about the haste at which people dismiss Nigeria's unity as either artificial or fragile. Indeed "unity in diversity" ought to have been taken beyond mere political sloganeering. Cultural (dis)unity and/or homogeneity or heterogeneity of nation-states is not the basis for their further unity or disunity. If this were so how can the crisis in Somalia, Rwanda and Burundi be explained? As Mustapha states, the nation building project with its emphasis on national unity only emphasised that "old partners of exclusion and domination were continued; and new ones invented" (1995: p.2).

But beyond that, it should be stated, for instance, that although a Fulani autocracy existed in pre-colonial Nigeria, and it dominated over the Hausa emirates by political and spiritual rule, through the *Sarauta* system, however, the Fulani aristocracy became a subject-aristocracy with the coming of colonialism which imposed indirect rule, and to draw on Mamdani's seminal work, this aristocracy transformed itself by internalising the nuances of modernity. Yet, it still unleashed terror on its subjects, particularly the peasants through a ferocious process of "decentralised despotism" (Mamdani, 1996). In pre-colonial Africa, people defined themselves professionally i.e. as farmers, goldsmith etc or politically e.g. as subjects of political Chiefs. Their ethnic origin and identity were often mediated by those two variables.

In a relatively unknown paper, Osuntokun (1999: pp.3-5) argues that the nature of British administration of Nigeria from 1914 was set on two different paths, not so much because of the so-called indirect rule policy but because of the attitude of the two different Britons who ruled the southern and northern protectorates viz. Sir Hugh Clifford and Lord Frederick Lugard. To him, Clifford was a civilian administration with experience of "civility" from Ceylon, Malaysia etc. He is said to cherish representative democracy and introduced constitutional reforms and legislative councils in Lagos and Calabar in 1923. Clifford, Osuntokun narrates, kept traditional rulers at abeyance claiming that "[H]e was not sent to Nigeria to preserve the antediluvian level of civilization preventing in the country...." (*Ibid*: p.5). On the other hand Osuntokun asserts that Lugard was a soldier with conquistador records in Uganda and northern Nigeria- a product of his military adventurism. That Lugard was an autocrat and hence loved the existing traditional form of rule in northern Nigeria and that he disliked educated southerners whom he often called "trousered niggers" (*Ibid*: p.4). Insightful as these assertions are, they are not sufficient to explain the basis of uneven development between the north and the south. Let us just take one example- educational imbalance. Adamu documents that when education first came to northern Nigeria its beneficiaries where the elite, their children and members of the ruling class (Adamu, 1973: p.42). Indeed, Tukur argues that the toiling masses of the north showed unquenchable thirst for western education for their children; but through colonial activities and the machinations of the traditional oligarchies access was blocked (Tukur, 1990: pp.111-118). Yet, it is this same northern elite who are at the head of current campaign for redress of educational and social imbalances with the south. Whereas, indeed, their privileged status was acquired by deliberate blockage and exploitation of the toiling people of the north.

Cast in the foregoing sense it is easy to see why the northern section of the ruling class can not genuinely be said to represent the interest of the north (This is quite apart from the fact that there is no such thing as "North" whether in the ideological, political, religious or sociological sense). I therefore argue that the marginalised people of the spatially-defined territorial north, minorities, the non-Muslim, the toiling people of Hausa-Fulani origins and so on, also have grudges and claims to make on the Nigerian nation state as the oil-producing minorities of the Niger-Delta.

The National Question: Nation or Ethnic Answer?

As a result of the fiscal crisis of the state, the deepening crisis of militarism, the worsening political crisis in Nigeria particularly after the annulment of the 1993 presidential election, separatist agitation from various groups have been in vogue.

The most popular (not necessarily correct) option has been the clamour for restructuring of the Nigerian federation. The hope being that some states will merge to create bigger states and have greater control over their resources and revenue. The objective being that the federal government should be made weaker (Elaigwu, 1999: p.7).

The second popular option is zoning of political offices in an equitable manner in such a way that power will be diffused to various states and ethnic groups; and one ethnic group will not have more than its fair share.

The third popular clamour is for "power shift". By this it is meant that the north or particularly the Hausa-Fulani "ruling class" (no matter how amorphously conceptualised or understood) have had more than a fair control of political power in Nigeria, hence they should give the south a "chance".

The fourth option is autonomy. It is argued that Nigeria should organise politics around ethnic groups and grant them political autonomy and access to control their natural resources. This is a slightly varied and more complex version of the first option I adumbrated.

The fifth is the self-determination quest. This has not been well shaped as an option. In the crudest form it is conceptualised and understood, (and when pushed to its logical conclusion), as culminating in secession. But groups such as Oodua Peoples Congress (OPC) are already canvassing an Oduduwa republic to be exclusively made up of the "Yoruba nation". It is however clear that while it is possible to talk ontological about a Yoruba nation, there is however no historical antecedent to support this call.

The sixth option is the Sovereign National Conference (SNC), by which various nationalities and interest groups of Nigeria will come together to discuss the future of the Nigerian nation-state and the basis of their relationship in the federation.

Three informed academic interventions have been made. First Elaigwu contends that to ensure "power shift" and rotational Executive (political) power will entail fundamental structural changes in the constitution (1999: pp.6-7). Jinadu ostensibly shares this view. For him, the problem of federalism in Nigeria is not related to the Nigerian constitution but to the behaviour of actors with a concentration on "process rather than structure" (1999: p.20). To him, there are enough provisions in the Nigerian constitution that check arbitrariness of political office holders, guarantee rule of law and protect individual and collective rights of peoples.

On his part, Ihonvbere argues that the zoning principle has generated more problems for Nigerians than it has solved; while "power sharing" has failed to "reassure minorities and marginalised communities", and that the federal character while giving a "veneer of equity" in reality is being manipulated and used by a few (1999: p.6). To Ihonvbere the nationality question is being mismanaged, and trivialised by custodians of state power in order to promote "ethnic entrepreneurs" and political warlords (Ibid: p.7).

A few points need to be made here. Power is not a loaf of bread that can be shared. It is absolute. Also, power cannot shift as the focus and social location of power is in the state, the ideological basis of the ruling class as a sociological category is not rooted in the dynamics of the ethnic group identity but to other material tangibles that are mediated by other variables. In that equation, those who wield, seek or contest power often instrumentalise ethnicity. It should be noted that the institutional or (even) structural relocation and reorganisation of power is not the same thing as its social transformation. For the former to be relevant it needs to be accompanied by the latter.

Second, the problem of Nigeria is not about constitution but about the structures, processes and contexts on which the constitution is rooted and expected to perform or function,. Without any iota of doubt, certain aspects of the constitution are problematic and contentious but its fundamental problems are structural and historical. The Sovereign National Conference (SNC) option which was radical, progressive, dynamic, democratic and representative in the way it was initially formulated or couched by the CD has been reduced to mere ethnic or nationality question, so is the question of the mode of representation in it. Civic and professional identities or values are deemed epiphenomenal in the equation.

Ihonvbere is correct to a large extent when he states that "the character of the Nigerian State continues to be directly responsible for reproducing the country's deepening socio-economic and political contradictions". He continues on a different gear, "the state has been captured and privatised by a tiny fraction of the elite that uses its institutions and resources to terrorise non-bourgeois communities, abuse human rights, loot public funds and mortgage the future of the citizenry" (Ibid: p.3).

The relationship of state and citizens in any nation-state is not seen as a relationship between state and ethnic groups. The relationship is viewed from a civic perspective. The denial of rights therefore poses constitution-centered questions before they are contested politically through the ethnic platform. But I intend to argue that the violation of citizens' rights is a civic violation and not an ethnic violation. The language of the ethnic in this sense sounds anachronistic, contradictory and superfluous. Its relevance is to be sought in the politics of embeddedness or pre-text. In this sense, the text is civic but the pre-text may be ethnic or anything else. As an aspect of embeddedness, ethnicity is very measured, carried out in a low intensity form . It is only its rupturable form that finds demagogic outlets in ethnic cleansing or genocide. The crisis of citizenship raises other issues that relate to the character of the state and its actors and the problem of ethnic identity is symptomatic of citizenship crisis. The intensification of ethnic identity often overwhelms citizenship identity and in some cases both citizenship and ethnic identities often assume the same status with difficulty of identifying which is the primary contradiction or which is the predicate.

Citizenship and the Crisis of the Nation State

All Nigerian constitutions since independence recognise both individual and collective rights. However, it should be noted that collective rights are not given to ethnic groups but to communities or the state. Hence the federal character principle is applied not to Hausa-Fulani, Yoruba or Ogoni but to Sokoto, Kano, Oyo, or River State. The first issue that arises here is the question of the definition of "the common good". This will involve a definition of citizenship in such a way that recognises two identities – individuals and citizens-in a way that one is not sacrificed for the other in a political community (Mouffe, 1995: pp.34-35). But the notion of a "common good" is a communitarian and not liberal or libertarian principle. When it is related to diffused groups or heterogeneous people it has wider appeal because it recognises differences, it emphasises the collective and confers social responsibility on the state.

Ekeh contends that, "colonial ideologies encouraged Africans to identify citizenship with rights, but not with duties" (1978: p.317). Colonialism created a new notion of the public sphere and citizenship that defined who was a citizen, how to acquire the status and what rights went with it (Mustapha, 1995: p.15; Nnoli,1998: p.216 and Ifidon, 1999).

In post-colonial Nigeria, this led to two contending definitions of citizenship. Citizenship by statism and citizenship by indigeneity (Son of the soil syndrome). As Egwu surmises:

> …The notion of "indigeneity" ensures that the rights of Nigerians who live outside of the state ascribed to them on the sole basis of their genetic antecedents are severely curtailed as it contradicts the general provisions on the fundamental human rights of Nigerian citizens (1998: p.11).

The foregoing process has led to the emergence of "dysfunctional citizenship" i.e. the absence of "primary attachment or identification with the Nigerian State". On account of this Ifidon avers :

> The level of citizenship is truly realised as not the mega-state, but the home state or primary group level, where the Nigerian is the subject. Beyond this, a Nigerian is an alien in another state, enduring self-imposed social passivity as a strategy of survival (1996: p.106).

But the point to be noted here is that the use of indigeneity in the definition of citizenship on the basis of biology or paternity is highly circumscribed. The other side of the argument is that indigeneity was not constitutionalised or legitimised by co-ethnics but by the state who alone remains the producer of the contradictions of those skewed ways of defining citizenship. This culture is a carry over of the colonial era where the state consciously created the *Sabon Garis* (stranger settlement) in northern Nigeria and a *Sabo* in southern Nigeria. Most of the southerners dwelling in the north were in the Sabon Garis while most of the northerners dwelling in the south created their *Sabo*.

The state through the constitution, has denied the rights that ought to come with citizenship on the flimsy ground of spatial location. As a result of this, the state disempowered the citizens politically because of spatial relocation. It made social and cultural interaction limited amongst co-ethnics. Above all, it did not permit the exercise of rights in any universal sense since its claims over rights and entitlements have been restricted by a code. I submit that all these have serious theoretical implications for the way we conceptualise the national question in Nigeria.

Whilst it may be true that before the discovery of crude oil, the fiscal policy of the state or revenue allocation had depended on the principle of derivation, it shifted to land mass, population, equity etc. all of which are not directed at addressing the problems of the oil-producing minorities. It is a matter of conjecture whether the same principle could have been applied if, purely on the basis of accident, oil were found in a Hausa-Fulani enclave. After all, Shehu Shagari, then President of Nigeria and a Fulani, forcibly dispossessed the Bakolori peasants (his brethrens) of their land for a multinational corporation, IMPRESIT. Indeed, in the process, several peasants were massacred. What analogy can be drawn from this in relation to the Hausa-Fulani hegemony thesis or domination over Nigeria and the oil-producing minorities?

The oil-producing minorities are bound to interpret things the way they understand them because the issue of rights, citizenship and the common good have not been properly tackled by the state and in the process, the Nigerian toiling people are the worse for it because they are collectively disempowered. Curiously election results in Nigeria have proved that it is the minorities of the Middle Belt, Nigeria-Delta, and south-east who vote at elections, to impose so-called hegemony of the "Hausa-Fulani " or the caliphate. This was the case with the National Party of Nigeria (NPN) in 1979. In 1993, the National Republic Convention (NRC), which is perceived to be a reincarnation of the (NPN) won many gubernatorial seats in those minority states. The current Peoples Democratic Party (PDP) believed to be a party of the "Hausa-Fulani hegemons" also won governorship elections in those minority states. The questions then are why did the southern minorities vote for political parties perceived to be controlled by those who oppressed them? Why did they not vote for a southern -dominated or southern minorities-dominated political party? The answer lies elsewhere, in issues and variables that are not connected to the ethnic factor in the understanding of power. *Ethnicity cannot be both a cause and an effect*. That would amount to a tautology.

But let me summarise the way the power logic has been explained by the dominant groups representing various interests; for the Niger-Delta and oil-producing minority it is oil exploitation and environmental degradation; for the Igbo it is marginalisation, for the Hausa-Fulani it is uneven development, for the minorities of the north, particularly the Middle Belt, it is internal colonialism, for the Yoruba, it is power exclusion. Hence, everybody is demanding empowerment on the basis of one assumption - xenophobia. Different claims have been made on this assumption bothering on exploitation and injustice hence the solutions they proffer and answers they seek are different. For the oil-producing minorities there is the need to control their own economic resources through the granting of political autonomy. For the Middle Belt minorities, it is autonomy from Hausa-Fulani hegemony, for the Igbo it is restructuring of Nigeria and for the Yoruba it is "power shift" through the rotation of executive power. For the Hausa-Fulani, it is equal access to resources and affirmative action as an instrument of empowerment or political access . The goal is to make up for uneven development and imbalances.

There seems to be an emerging but dangerous consensus that the ethnic-nation is the fundamental threat to or issue in the national question in Nigeria today. But if that were true what can be said about religion and the problem of secularity? What fears do non-Muslims entertain with the quest for implementation of Sharia in some states. These kinds of claims are quite reductionist, exclusivist and alienatory. These are on most part not the views of the toiling people of the various ethnic groups. The crucial issue here is what sense do the toiling people make out of all this? What does SNC or restructuring mean to them? It is one point to reflect about how the elite and intellectuals feel about the toiling people, it is however important to know how the toiling people feel about themselves and what meaning they attached to their existence and what they make out of their realities. This is the philosophical thrust of *lived essentialism.* The fundamental question to ask is what does (dis)empowerment mean to the toiling Ogoni of River State and to the Fulani of Sokoto State?

Conclusion

I have tried in this chapter to argue that the national question in Nigeria, nay Africa, is far more complex and complicated than many scholars and politicians are wont to suggest.

I have argued that its philosophical essence is rooted in human nature. However, that in relation to theory, the national question is much more than the ethnic, cultural, linguistic or nation building quest. And that the national question is not applicable to the nation state alone neither can it be reduced to the principle of self-determination. It cannot have a restricted explanation for *moments* in a trajectory without having a scientific understanding of the entire trajectory. Moments may throw up contradictions that could make primary determinants assume the form of secondary determinants and vice versa. It is theoretically and politically incorrect for people to use moments and specific manifestations of the national question to generalise about the national question. The form and content of those manifestations should be analysed and explained in a spatio-temporal way. The analysis should focus on the entire historical conjuncture. The national question, no matter how it is understood, is a democratic question because it is about social and political liberation of a people. Ultimately, the history and application of the concept of the national question to Africa has had changing meanings over time. The goal should be to answer the questions how are people organised and how are they empowered or disempowered? Every other thing revolves around this. My analysis does not deny the national question, not even its ethnic manifestation, but it cautions on what we factor into our analysis for the purpose of theorising.

The second logical question is whose national question are we addressing or put differently, national question for whom – is it the class, culture, religion, ethnic group, nation or the nation-state? We have seen how all of these in the mould of artefacts are being made or destroyed, invented or deconstructed over time. The very volatile nature of Africa has not made this reality a settled matter for philosophical consensus. As such, the terrain still remains contested making theorising highly tentative and fluid; with a lot of fresh insights and events evolving to illuminate multiple taxonomies that have been constructed around it. The national question to use Samir Amin's phrase, "is reversible", so also, in my view, are all its components, culture, language, ethnic group, and even the nation and the nation-state. The examples of Palestine, Israel, Ethiopia, Eritrea and Somalia are apt for the latter case. The attempt in this chapter is merely suggestive and not exhaustive.

References

Abba, A. (1985), 'Some Remarks on the National Question and Radical in Nigeria', (Mimeo).

Adamu, Al-Rashid Haroun, (1973), *The North and Nigerian unity: Some Reflections on the Political, Social and Educational problems of Northern Nigeria* Lagos: *Daily Times.*

Adejumobi, Said, (2000), 'The Nigeria crisis and alternatives Political framework', being a paper presented to the conference on, 'The 1999 Constitution and the National Question in Nigeria', Organised by the Centre for Constitutionalism and Demilitarisation, Lagos, January; 25-6.

Ajayi, Ade, F., (1992), 'The National Question in Historical Perspective', *Text of the Fifth Guardian Newspapers Lectures, Guardian*, Nov. 5.

Ake, Claude, (1993); 'What is the Problem of Ethnicity in Africa?', *Transformation* 22.

Alagoa, E.J., (1986), 'Historical Origins of the National Question in Pre-colonial Eastern Nigeria', Being a paper presented at The National Seminar on the National Question in Nigeria, 'Its Historical Origins and Contemporary Dimension'; held at Abuja, August 4-9.

Amin, Samir, (1978), *The Arab Nation: Nationalism and Class Struggle*, London: Zed Press Ltd.

Awe, Bolanle, (1989), 'Nation-Building and Cultural Identity: The Colonial Experience' in Peter, Ekeh and Garba Ashiwaju (eds), *Nigeria Since Independence: The First 25 Years:Culture.* Vol. VII Ibadan: Heinemann Educational Books Ltd.

Ayoade, A.A., (1986), 'Ethnic Management in the 1979 Nigerian Constitution' *Publius,* Vol. 16, No. 2, Spring 1986.

Ayoade, A.A., (1996), 'The changing structure of Nigerian Federalism', in J. Isawa, Elaigwu and R.A. Akindele, (eds), (1994) *Foundations of Nigerian Federalism 1960 – 1995* Abuja: NCIR.

Bala Mohammed Mohammed Memorial Committee (1982) 'Class, Nationality and History in Nigeria' (Mimeo)

Davidson, Basil, (1992), *The Black Man's Burden: Africa and the Curse of the Nation-State*, Ibadan: Spectrum Books Limited

Doumou, Abdelahi, (1987), 'The State and Popular Alliances: Theoretical Preliminaries in the Light of the Moroccan case', in Peter Anyang' Nyong' O (ed), *Popular Struggles for Democracy in Africa*, London: Zed Books Ltd.

Egwu, Samuel, (1998), 'Democracy at Bay: Ethnicity and Nigeria's Democratic Eclipse; 1986-1995'African Centre for Democratic Governance, *AFRIGOV, Monograph Series* No. 5.

Ekeh, Peter, (1972), 'Citizenship and Political Conflict: A Sociological Interpretation of the Nigerian crisis', in Joseph, Okpaku (ed), *Nigeria: Dilemma of Nationhood*, Greenwood Press.

Ekeh, Peter, (1978), 'Colonialism and the Development of Citizenship in Africa: A study of ideologies of legitimation', in Onigu Otite (ed), *Themes in African Social and Political Thought*, Enugu: Fourth Dimension Publishing Co. Ltd.

Ekeh, Peter, (1989), 'The Structure and Meaning of Federal Character in Nigerian Political System' in Peter Ekeh and E. E. Osaghae (eds), *Federal Character and Federalism in Nigeria.* Ibadan: Heinemann Educational Books.

Ekeh, Peter, (1996), 'Political Minorities and Historically- Dominant Minorities in Nigerian History and Politics', in Oyeleye Oyediran, (ed), *Governance and Development in Nigeria*, Ibadan: Oyediran Consult International.

Erim, O. Erim, (1996), 'Pre-colonial Antecedents of the Foundations of the Nigerian Federation: Theoretical Considerations', in Isawa Elaigwu and Erim O. Erim (eds), *Foundations of Nigerian Federalism: Pre-colonial Antecedents*. Abuja: NCIR.

Fashina, Oladipo, (1998), 'Reflections on the National Question', in Omotoye Olorode and *et al* (eds), *Ken Saro Wiwa and The Crisis of the Nigerian State*. Lagos: CDHR.

Gboyega, Alex, (1997), 'Nigeria: Conflict unresolved', in Williams Zartman (ed), *Governance as Conflict Management: Politics and Violence in West Africa*. Washington DC: Brookings Institution Press.

Ifidon, Ehimika, (1996), 'Citizenship Statehood and the Problem of Democratization in Nigeria', *Africa Development*. Vol.XXI, No. 4.

Ifidon, Ehimika, (1999), 'Social Rationality and Class Analysis of National Conflict in Nigeria: a Histographical Critique', *Africa Development*, Vol. XXIV, Nos. 1 and 2.

Ihonvbere, Julius, (1999), 'Federalism, Power sharing, and the politics of Redistribution in Nigeria'. Paper presented at the International Conference on 'Consolidating Democracy: Nigeria in Comparative Perspective' organised under the auspices of AEGIS, the European Network of African Studies, Portugal, Sept. 21-25.

Jega, M. Attahiru, (1999), 'The Nigerian Federal System: Problems and Prospects' in Lidija R. Basta and Jibrin Ibrahim (eds),' *Federalism and Decentralisation in Africa: The Multicultural Challenge*, Fribourg: Institute of Federalism, Fribourg Switzerland.

Jinadu, L. Adele, (1999), 'Nigeria: Path to Enduring Democracy' keynote address at the Eighth Obafemi Awolowo Foundation Dialogue, Nov. 30 – Dec. 1.

Kymlicka, Will, (1995), *Multicultural Citizenship*, Oxford: Clarendon Press.

Lenin, V.I., (1975), *On the National and Colonial Questions: Three Articles*, Peking: Foreign Languages Press.

Lowy, Michael, (1976), 'Marxists and the National Question', *New Left Review*, No. 96.

Madunagu, Edwin, (1997), 'The National Question, The Power blocs and Popular democratic transformation of Nigeria: Provisional: Thesis and Propositions', being a paper presented at the National Seminar on Abacha's Transition. Organised by the Cross River State Council of the Nigerian Union of Journalist (NUJ), in Calabar Dec. 3, 1997.

Magubane, Bernard, (1987), 'South Africa: The Dialectic of Oppression and Resistance', in IFAA *Africa's Crisis*, London: IFAA.

Mahadi, Abdullahi and Monday Mangvwat, (1986), 'Some remarks on the National Question Pre-colonialist Formations: The Case of Nigeria before 1900 A.D'. Paper presented at the 'National Question in Nigeria: Its Historical origins and Contemporary Dimensions', held at Abuja, August 4-9.

Mama, Amina, (1995), *Beyond the Mask: Race Gender and Subjectivity*, London and New York: Routledge.

Mamdani, Mahmood, (1996), *Citizen and Subject: Contemporary Africa and the Legacy of Late Colonialism*, Princeton, New Jersey: Princeton University Press.

Momoh, Abubakar, (1996), 'Popular struggles in Nigeria (1960-1982)', *Working Paper* No. 3, Institute of Development Studies, University of Helsinki, Finland.

Mustapha, Abdul Raufu, (1985), 'Critical notes on the National Question, Practical Politics and the Peoples Redemption Party' (Mimeo).

Mustapha, Abdul Raufu, (1986), 'The National Question and Radical Politics In Nigeria', *Review of African Political Economy*, No. 37.

Mustapha, Abdul Raufu, (1992), 'Identity, Boundaries, Ethnicity and National Integration in Nigeria', paper being presented on 'Ethnic conflict in Africa' organised by CODESRIA, Nov. 16-18, Nairobi.

Mzala, A., (1989), 'Revolutionary Theory on the National Question in South Africa', in Maria van Diepen (ed.), *The National Question in South Africa*, London: Zed Books.

Nnoli, Okwudiba, (1996), 'Ethnic and Regional Balancing in Nigerian Federalism', in R. A. Akindele *et al* (eds), *Foundations of Nigerian Federalism 1960-1995*. Abuja: NCIR.

Nnoli, Okwudiba, (1998), 'Ethnicity, Ethnic Conflict and Emigration in Sub-Saharan Africa', in Reginald Appleyard (ed), *Emigration Dynamics in Developing Countries: Sub-Saharan Africa*, Aldershot: Ashgate.

Nzongola-Ntalaja, Georges, (1987), *Revolution and Counter Revolution in Africa*, London and New Jersey, Zed Books.

Nzongola-Ntalaja, (1993), 'Nation-Building and State Building in Africa', *SAPES Occasional Paper Series*, No. 3.

Ola, Opeyemi, (1970), 'The Party System in the Process of Nigerian Unification', *The Journal of Business and Social Studies*, Vol. 3, No. 1 Dec.

Olusanya, G.O., (1970), 'The Historical Basis of Nigerian Unity: An Analysis', *The Journal of Business and Social Studies*, Vol. 3, No. 1 Dec.

Osaghae, Eghosa, (1991), 'Ethnic Minorities and Federalism in Nigeria' *African Affairs, No. 90.*

Osaghae, E. Eghosa, (1994), 'Towards a Fuller Understanding of Ethnicity in Africa', in Eghosa Osaghae (ed), *State and Civil Society in Africa,* Dakar: CODESRIA.

Osuntokun, Akinjide, (1986), 'The Search for a Common Nationality in Nigeria', paper being read at Seminar on 'The National Question in Nigeria: Its Historical origins and Contemporary Dimensions', August 4-9.

Osuntokun, Akinjide, (1998), 'Backward to the Future: the Political Imperative of a need for Fundamental reappraisal of the Federal Structure of Nigeria', paper presented at the Conference on *Devolution of Power*, held at the Friedeich Ebert Foundation, University of Lagos, 14-15, October.

Parekh, Bhikhu, (1994), 'Discourses on National Identity', *Political Studies* Vol. XLII.

Saro-Wiwa, Ken, (1992), 'The National Question: Confederation is the Answer', in Citizen Annual Dialogue, *Citizen* (Special Edition), Dec. 4.

Saro-Wiwa, Ken, (1994), 'The Constitutional Conference and the National Question', in Abdullahi Mahadi *et al* (eds), *Nigeria: The State of the Nation and the Way Forward,* Kaduna: Arewa House.

Soyinka, Wole, (1996), 'The National Question in Africa: Internal Imperatives', *Development and Change,* Vol. 27.

Stalin, J.V., (1953), *Works*, Vol. 2, Moscow Progress Publishers.

Tamuno, Tekena, (1970), 'Separatist Agitations in Nigeria Since 1914', *The Journal of Modern African Studies*. Vol. 8, No. 4.

The Socialist Forum, (1983), 'Reformism in Nigeria: Possibilities and Limits', in *Socialist Forum* (Special Issue) July.

The Socialist Forum, (1984), 'Reformism in Nigeria: reply to the BMMC's Document on Class, Nationality and History in Nigeria', Socialist Forum Special issue, Jan.

Tukur, Mahmud, (1990), 'The Nature, Extent and Essence of British Social Policy in the Emirates 1900-1914', in Tanimu Abubakar (ed), *The Essential Mahmud: a Selected Writings,* Zaria: Ahmadu Bello University Press.

Wamba-dia-Wamba, Ernest (1991), 'Discourse on the National Question', in Issa Shivji (ed), *State and Constitutionalism: An African Debate on Democracy,* Harare: SAPES Books.

Wamba-dia-Wamba, Ernest (1996), 'The National Question in Zaire: Challenges to the Nation-State project', in Adebayo Olukoshi and Liisa Laakso (eds), *Challenges to the Nation-State in Africa,* Uppsala: Nordic Africa Institute.

Young, Crawford, (1991), 'Self-determination, Territorial Integrity and the African State system', in Francis Deng and William Zartman (eds), *Conflict Resolution in Africa,* Washington D.C: The Brookings Institution.

2 The National Question in Historical Perspective

OSARHIEME BENSON OSADOLOR

Introduction

The period from 1914 to 1998 in the history of Nigeria witnessed severe strains on the corporate existence of the nation. This was because efforts at national integration were not quite successful in transforming the constituent units into national societies with national values and national character apparently because of the low degree of institutionalisation of social-political structures in relation to the centre. The problem of what to do with the country and, how the constituent units sought better understanding led to what became known as the National Question. In which case, the future of Nigeria became tied to the issue of future association of the constituent units with the union. At various times in the over 80 years history from the amalgamation of southern and northern protectorates in 1914 up to 1998, many of the ethnic groups, big and small, did not feel a sense of belonging and made moves to dismember the country. At the core of this stridency of separatist and sub-nationalists agitations was not just the fear of domination but of dissatisfaction with inter-ethnic relations.

In spite of the attempts made through politico-economic and constitutional arrangements to work out on how best to accommodate the competing socio-political and ethno-cultural problems of the various ethnic groups, the national question had not been resolved by the end of 1994. A National Constitutional Conference in Abuja, was however, working out a framework for a redefinition of the basis of the continued existence of Nigeria. Be that as it may, the constraints of defining the patterns of integration which hindered the achievement of shared values, common identity, mutual trust and national consciousness, had their roots in British colonial rule.

Colonialism and the National Question, 1914-1960

What evolved into the Nigerian Union of 1 January, 1914 was the merger by Sir (Later Lord) Frederick Lugard, of southern and northern protectorates under British colonial rule.[1] That development marked the political transformation into a single entity, of states which had lost their sovereignty after the failure of resistance to British conquest of the late nineteenth and early twentieth century. For Nigerians at this time, particularly the educated elites from southern protectorates, the merger was an opportunity for nation-building, albeit, within the context of participation in colonial administration and ultimately, of self-government which made them to look forward to the 'dawn of freedom'. However, the official policy of British Colonial administration was hostile towards Nigerian nationalists whose idea of self-government was in terms of a single and unified Nigerian nation. For instance, Sir Hugh Clifford as Governor of Nigeria denied that the country constituted a single nation. According to him:

> Assuming ... that the impossible were feasible – that this collection of self-contained and mutually independent Native States, separated from one another, as many of them are, by great distances, by differences of history and traditions, and by ethnological, racial, tribal, political, social and religious barriers, were indeed capable of being welded into a single homogenous nation – a deadly blow would thereby be struck at the very root of national self-government in Nigeria, which secures to each separate people the right to maintain its identity, its individuality and its nationality, its government; and the peculiar political and social institutions which have been evolved for it by the wisdom and by the accumulated experience of generations of its forebears.[2]

This opinion was a reflection of the British mind, of lack of faith in the future of a nation they had established through imperial adventures. But Nigerian nationalists put up a strong case, effectively against the European opinion, affirming the peculiar virtues and values of their own society as revealed in its institutions and its historical traditions and thus constructing the intellectual foundations for their claim to the right to manage their own affairs. This, to a large extent, determined the nationalist motivation, objectives and organisation.

While the nationalists made their efforts to build a new nation-state created by colonialism, the colonial situation imposed severe limitations upon the range within which nation-building, albeit, metaphysical could progress.[3] (cf. Osadolor. 1988; Ade Ajayi, 1970; Coleman 1960). Here we face a paradox: the imperial ambition of the British had led to the emergence of a Nigerian nation, yet the colonial administration was determined to oppose its development. This paradox involves an analytical distinction between the aspiration of the nationalists to national self-determination and the British Colonial policy of economic exploitation and extension of the British empire.

The manifestation of British determination to oppose the development of a United Nigerian nation was practically expressed with the introduction of the 1922 Constitution,[4] which came to be known as the Clifford Constitution. The

Nigerian Legislative Council which was established by the Constitution exercised legislative authority over the affairs of southern Nigeria and had a say only in the financial administration of northern Nigeria. In fact, the northern provinces were excluded from the jurisdiction of the Legislative Council and was administered by the issuance of proclamations by the Governor, thereby emphasising that the two regions were different. From 1922 until 1947, the national question which confronted the British about the future of Nigeria was whether the country should remain one. In spite of amendments to the 1922 Constitution,[5] the southern and northern provinces were administered separately without a common law-making body, although the issue of political integration had begun to attract attention.[6]

By the end of the Second World War in 1945, the British seemed to have resolved the issue. Hence, the constitutional arrangement of 1946,[7] which came into effect in 1947, sought to provide a framework for greater interaction between Nigerian peoples. It was for the first time since the amalgamation of the south and north in 1914, that the north was brought into the same legislative authority with the south. "This unfortunate exclusion since 1914", argues K. Ezera, "would seem to be indicative of a hesistancy on the part of British Administration over the crucial question of whether Nigeria was to be governed as a unit or as two separate entities".[8] However, by the time the south and north became integrated politically, wartime developments had affected the nationalist struggle in Nigeria,[9] such that Nigerian nationalists were demanding immediate full self-government. The remark by the governor, Sir Arthur Richards in his inaugural address to the Legislative Council, in which he said that Nigeria was not "yet a sufficiently coherent whole, whether in the political, social or economic sphere, to be capable of immediate and full self-government",[10] ignited discord and acrimony between southern and northern representatives. While responding to the Governor's address, Mallam Abubakar Tafawa Balewa put the case of the northern provinces this way:

> We do not want, Sir, our Southern neighbours to interfere in our development. If the Southern people feel that they are representatives for what they are agitating for and demanding, well they must know that the case of the Northern Provinces is different. We have never associated ourselves with the activities of these people — We do not recognise them and we share no responsibility in their actions ... If the British quitted Nigeria, the Northern people would continue their interrupted conquest to the sea.[11]

As it were, Legislators from the south drew attention to Balewa's speech. Mr. C.D. Onyeama, from the eastern province, felt disappointed:

I am sorry that he said this because I was under the impression that the main reason for this Constitution is to bring the South and the North together .. to make the Northerners and Southerners regard Nigerian interests as one and indivisible ...[12]

In the same way, Mr. T.A. Odutola from the Western Provinces warned that "just as it may be possible for the northerners to attempt to overrun the south".[13] In any case, the northerners left no one in doubt, of their opposition to quicker constitutional changes which the nationalists from the south were demanding. Even in 1948 when the matter was re-introduced during the second session of the Legislative Council in Kaduna, the acrimony between southern and northern legislators gave a foretaste of the dichotomy in the future politics of Nigeria.

In 1949, the colonial government took the initiative in launching the first constitutional conference to discuss the future political development of Nigeria, albeit, the national question. The constitutional conference was unique in the sense that a series of conferences were held, first at village and divisional levels, and then at the provincial level. The various provincial conferences made recommendations which were considered by regional conferences. The views of the regional conferences were considered by a Drafting Committee of the Legislative Council and thereafter, a General Conference was held in Ibadan in January 1950. The resolutions of this conference were debated in the regional houses and by the Legislative Council. The specific task of each of the conferences was to find answers "to a whole series of complex questions", [14] on the future of Nigeria. The conferences enabled Nigerians at every level to participate in putting forward suggestions for the country's new constitution to replace the Richards Constitution that was originally intended to last for nine years. Their particpation was an elaborate and democratic process of adequate consultation and involvement of the people in constitution – making, unlike Sir Arthur Richards who made the mistake of not consulting the opinion of Nigerians over the 1945 constitutional proposals and immediately found himself faced with a spate of bitter criticism from the nationalists.

Although the British Administration accepted the recommendations of the General Conference as endorsed by the select Committee of the Legislative Council, in working out the framework of a new constitution, they ignored the four minority reports signed by some conference members who were opposed to the majority recommendations of the General Conference. The opposition was led by Mr. Mbonu Ojike and Mr. Eyo Ita who jointly signed two minority reports: the first opposing the regional basis of government, indirect election, the establishment of Houses of Chiefs, and the representation of "vested interests"; the second, demanding universal adult suffrage in place of taxpayers' suffrage (which means, the exclusion of women from voting). Dr. Nnamdi

Azikiwe, one of the foremost nationalists at that time, also accused the Ibadan General Conference of having placed less emphasis on the views submitted at the provincial level, and of attaching more importance to those of the regional conferences.[15] At the provincial level for instance, there were calls for the creation of more regions to balance the structure of the emergent nation-state. The views from the provinces also favoured federalism instead of regionalisation. These provincial opinions were ignored at the General Conference; a conference that also failed to examine the fundamental issues on which the south and north were divided. Perhaps, this was because, as Mallam Muhammadu, the Wali of Borno remarked:

> We merely pretend to call ourselves Nigerians ... as soon as there is something to discuss or to consider before us, in five minutes time we automatically take two different strands the North and the South ... I think there is a very strong misunderstanding amongst us all which hinders our unity.[16]

Mallam Abubakar Tafawa Balewa also shared the same view when he pointed out that since the amalgamation of the Southern and Northern Provinces in 1914, "Nigeria has existed as one country only on paper", and that it was "still far from being considered as one country, much less to think of it as being united".[17] As another Northerner put it bluntly during the 1948 Budget session of the Legislative Council:

> ...Many deceive themselves that Nigeria is one ... The presence of unity is artificial and it ends outside this chamber. The Southern tribes ... domiciled in the North do not mix with the Northern people ... and we in the North look upon them as invaders ... Nigerian unity is only a British intention for the country.[18]

Of course, this problem of lack of unity stemmed from the British policy of 'divide and rule'; but the Colonialists leaned more to the north than to the south where the nationalists were very often, confrontational. The 1951 Constitution finally ended up as an attempt by the British to strengthen the political power of the north through their dominance of the Central government. This was why the British Administration rejected the demands for the creation of more regions, and did not also find it necessary to adopt a federal system in a multi-ethnic country like Nigeria. It is not difficult to reach the conclusion argues Obaro Ikime, "that the British who were the umpires at the Constitutional conferences, had some stake in ensuring that the then conservative north dominated the Central legislature".[19] The fact should also be considered that the north had threatened to break away from the federation in 1950 if their minimum demand for equal representation between the north and the south was rejected.[20] "That arrangement and other political developments since independence" as Ikime points out, "have created a political culture in which a particular ethnic group considers that control of Nigeria's Central government is its birthright".[21]

However, when the new Constitution came into effect, it proved unworkable due to manifest deficiences and structural weakness which had been pointed out in the minority reports of the Ibadan General Conference in 1950. For instance, the events after the 1951 elections proved that indirect election was not going to be workable. Dr. Nnamdi Azikiwe won a parliamentary seat in the 1951 elections in Lagos, but was not nominated by the Western House of Assembly to the Central legislature. That incident led to the crisis in the Eastern Region, and in many ways, it was a tragedy for Nigeria's political evolution. From 1952 to 1960, party politics failed to generate national consciousness such that the nationalist struggle became nothing more than a movement to reconcile conflicting aspirations at the level of inter-ethnic, inter-regional and interparty relations. Rather than provide an opportunity for nation-building and national integration, party politics deepened lack of understanding between the two separate parts of the country, and "tended to breed divergence in political outlook, mutual contempt and suspicion".[22] The manifestation of the misunderstanding and tension provoked a series of crises and dramatic events when Anthony Enahoro moved his famous "Motion of Destiny" on March 31, 1953, calling on the House of Representatives to accept as a primary political objective the attainment of self-government in 1956. The motion, as he explained, was to provide representatives from all parts of the country with an opportunity to exchange views on the burning question of self-government, so as to use the central legislature to continue the fundamental struggle for national freedom. Representatives from the northern region opposed the motion as they did not feel themselves ready for self-government. Ahmadu Bello, the Sardauna of Sokoto and leader of the Northern Peoples Congress, moved the adoption of an amendment on the substantive motion, changing "in 1956" to "as soon as practicable".[23] According to him:

> We are fully aware of the implications involved and we want to make it abundantly clear that the destiny of the North is in the hands of the people of the North ... we have embarked upon so many plans of reform and development that we must have time to see how these work out in practice ... We want to be realistic and consolidate our gains ... With things in their present state in Nigeria, the Northern Region does not intend to accept the invitation to commit suicide.[24]

The debate on the amendment motion was 'bitter and tempestuous', and ended only when the NCNC and AG members walked out of the House. Unforunately, after the adjournment of the House, the Northern representatives were subjected to insults and abuses by Lagos crowd, and during the ensuring weeks, they were ridiculed and strongly criticised by the Southern press. At the height of the North-South tension, the AG decided to go on what it described as an "educational tour" of the North. The arrival of the AG delegation in Kano led to a series of riots which lasted four days resulting in the death of fifty people with over two hundred wounded. Shortly after the riots, the Northern House of Chiefs and the Northern House of Assembly passed an eight-point programme, which in effect demanded the dissolution of the federation. It was a lamentation of what they called "the mistake of 1914" merging of the Southern and Northern protectorates. By this action it became glaring that if the North was to remain an integral part of Nigeria, any commitment to the central government would be non-political. To resolve the crisis, albeit, problems emanating from the National Question, the Colonial Secretary, Oliver Lyttleton convened a Constitutional Conference in London from July 30 to August 22, 1953; which afforded delegates from the constitutent units represented by leaders of political parties the opportunity to express their views on the prevalent conditions in the country. A federal constitution was accepted by leaders of the main political parties and it was also agreed that for regions which so requested, internal self-government should be granted in 1956. This solution was not reached easily but it appeared to provide the only feasible answer to the constitutional crisis which was the surface manifestation of deep and unresolved tension that had hindered the fostering of a consciousness of a common national identity.

Although the London Constitutional Conference was completed by a further conference in Lagos in January and February 1954, the series of constitutional conferences held in London and Lagos from 1957 up to 1960 from which new constitutional arrangements evolved to ensure the survival of the Nigerian federation, were mainly attempts to find solutions to the National Question but failed to resolve the problems of the fear of domination. This explains why the ethnic minorities also began to agitate for greater autonomy, with an accompanying demand for the creation of more states within the federation. The 1957 London Conference, for example, gave the assignment of ascertaining the fears of ethnic minorities and making recommendations, to a Commission headed by Sir Henry Willink. The report of the Willink Commission confirmed the fears of the minorities, but since the British government would only create new states or regions on condition that the date of independence be delayed for at least two more years, none of those politicians advocating for independence was willing to accept a delay in achieving independence for fear of losing popularity. This was unfortunate because the attainment of independence on October 1, 1960 did not establish a firm foundation for true unity. The reason, of course, was that inherent in the manner in which the country regained independence were elements of political instability – the result of the preponderance of inter-ethnic suspicions and hostilities.

In essence, colonialism's historical role vis-à-vis the National Question was not so much that of creator of the forces and conditions which tended to fragment the Nigerian nation-state, as it was that of manipulators and exacerbation of those diverse factors which differentiated the country.[25] The arbitrary political boundaries of three regions – North, East, and West, could neither accommodate ethnic diversity nor facilitate integration. Such was indeed the case of Nigeria when independence was attained.

Early Years of Independence and the National Question: Crisis, Conflict and War, 1961 – 1970

In the first decade of Nigeria's post-independence history, the state failed to evolve an indispensable mechanism to mediate and integrate a series of conflicts and contradictions arising from the country's constellation of class, ethnic, economic and social forces. This can simply be explained in the sense that the attainment of independence did not arouse any consciousness as part of the ethos of nationhood. Consequently, harmony, co-operation and unity became remote from social and political life and what became glaring, was inter-ethnic competition and winner-take-all politics in a political environment where opposition was equated with treason. The First Republic witnessed sporadic and, on occasions, near fatal political upheavals and by January 1966, it collapsed. Why was this so? "Over the years following independence", argues Ola Balogun, "political life in Nigeria developed into a cut-throat struggle for power at the federal level".[26] According to him, the reasons for this can only be understood if the nature of political parties in Nigeria and their relation to the country's economy life is fully grasped.[27] In which case, attention has to be focused on the fact that each of the Nigerian political parties developed primarily as an instrument in the hands of the local leadership groups seeking to attain a number of given economic and social ends. The contest for political power was thus primarily a contest for economic survival as a group, and the struggle developed into a naked confrontation in which the rival groups were less willing to respect the outward forms of restraint and conventional rivalry associated with the Western European practice of democracy on which Nigerian political structures had been modelled.[28] These groups addressed their strength mainly to the task of sharing out the meagre "national cake" that could be eked out of Nigeria's economy, instead of seeking to stimulate industrial growth in the country and to create new opportunities for the energies of the nation to fill out into.

It is against this background that the cut-throat struggle for power manifested itself in the political crisis beginning with the Action Group feud and the bloody riot in the Western House of Assembly in 1962 which led to the ultimate declaration of a state of emergency in the whole region by the Prime Minister, Abubakar Tafawa Balewa. The crisis grew to new heights with the arrests, trial and imprisonment of Chief Obafemi Awolowo and other leaders of the Action Group, on charges of treasonable felony. The 1963 census controversy did not help the already charged political situation; or the 1964 federal elections in which there were accusations and counter-accusations of rigging the elections. The Nigerian National Alliance (NNA), with support mainly from the North, was declared winner while the United Progressive Grand Alliance (UPGA), with considerable followership from the south, and which was declared the loser, rejected the election result. In 1965, the Tiv riots in Benue province further charged the atmosphere while the last straw that led to the demise of the First Republic was the October 1965 election in the West. There were allegations of election manipulation and rape of democracy. This triggered anger and vengeance, and by December of the same year, there had been total breakdown of law and order in Western Nigeria: Political violence took the form of *Operation Wetie* in which homes, property and people, of their opponents, were doused in petrol and set ablaze. It was in this atmosphere of chaos and near-collapse of the country's political institutions that a section of the Nigerian Army struck on January 15, 1966.[29]

The coup, though it saved Nigeria from anarchy and disintegration, raised a number of issues about the National Question. This was because of the nature and character of its execution which ended the lives of the Sardauna of Sokoto and Premier of Northern Region, Sir Ahmadu Bello; the Prime Minister, Sir Abubakar Tafawa Balewa; the Minister of Finance, Chief Festus Okotie-Eboh; Premier of Western Region, Chief Samuel Ladoke Akintola, as well as a number of prominent (and mostly northern) army officers. It was planned to be carried out simultaneously in Kaduna, Lagos, Enugu, Benin and Ibadan at 0200 hours on the D-Day. It was only in Kaduna, Lagos and Ibadan that operations were carried out even though in Lagos, Major-General J.T.U. Aguiyi-Ironsi organised a counter move by mobilising the Federal Guards in Dodan Barracks and soldiers of the 2nd Battalion, stationed at Ikeja, to stop the coup plotters. Major-General Aguiyi-Ironsi, somehow, hijacked power from the plotters through an instrument of surrender signed by President of the Senate, Nwafor Orizu on behalf of the civilian regime, proclaiming a hand-over to the military on January 17, 1966.

The pattern of killings in the January coup in which northern political leaders and senior army officers had an unfair share of the casualty figure, and the promulgation of Decree No. 34 of May 24, 1966 by the Ironsi regime which abolished the federal system and created a unitary state, provoked northern elite into believing that the coup was an Igbo plot to take over the country. On the weekend of May 28-30, there were large-scale demonstrations against the military government in the northern cities of Kano and Kaduna. In Kano alone, 50,000 demonstrators bearing placards saying 'No military government without referendum' and 'Let there be secession' delivered protest notes to the Emir of Kano and to the Provincial Secretary.[30] The protest notes alleged that the unification decree opened the way for Igbo imperialism.[31] At least 32 people lost their lives in the riots. Other demonstrations took place in Jos and Zaria. As a result of this development, on June 2, 1966, traditional rulers from the north held a meeting and addressed a memorandum to the military government demanding that no constitutional changes be made without a referendum. The memorandum threatened succession by the north if this warning were not heeded.[32] Riots continued in most of the northern cities, which was to lead to a large-scale exodus of non-northerners resident in the region as they were mostly the victims of attack. The Western Region, however, also threatened succession if the north was allowed to go.

The Ironsi regime acted too late. While a meeting of the Federal Military Government with traditional rulers from all parts of the country was being held in Ibadan from July 28-29, 1966 northern officers successfully staged the second military coup on July 29. In the process, Major General Aguiyi-Ironsi, Lt. Col. Fajuyi who was military governor of Western Region, a number of Igbo officers and soldiers, and some civilians were killed. The July coup represented the north's successful attempt to assert, or reassert its control over the army and through it, the nation. Ola Balogun explains it this way:

> The original intention of the coup had apparently been to arrange for the secession of the Northern Region. The moderating influence of Lt. Colonel Yakubu Gowon and a meeting with top civil servants on 29 July, in the course of which the disastrous economic consequences that secession could have for the North were brought to their attention produced a sobering effect on the coup-plotters. In any case, since they had succeeded in turning the tables and were in control of most of the Federation, there was no longer any real reason to secede. In the end, they agreed to a compromise and renounced their intention to take the North out of the Federation, and Lt. Colonel Gowon assumed control of the army.[33]

The appointment of Lt. Colonel Gowon was challenged by the Eastern military commander, Lt. Colonel Chukwuemeka Odumegu Ojukwu, who asserted that he was prepared to recognise only Ironsi, if still alive, or Ogundipe as Supreme commander. At stake, was national cohesion and stability. The new military leadership was confronted with this problem, and concerned itself with finding solutions to the rage within the Nigerian union that threatened its continued existence as one single entity. This explains why Gowon convened a series of advisory groups, leaders of thought, and consultative assemblies to deliberate and advise on the future of Nigeria. He also set up an Ad Hoc Committee on constitutional proposals, to which each of the regions sent delegations, to discuss the future constitutional and political development of the country. The committee's interim report submitted on September 29 1966, recommended *inter alia*, that Nigeria should continue as a political entity.

Meanwhile, violence erupted again in the north, with renewed massacres of the Ibos, and of retaliatory actions in the south. Although the violence in the north originated from riots, it became quickly uncontrollable "as a result of army mutinies in Kaduna and Kano where troops on the rampage, joined by civilian mobs, attacked Ibo residents in the two cities, looting and burning their properties in some cases".[34] Consequently, many of the Ibo survivors began a mass exodus from the north to the east, to be joined later by their kinsmen and women from the Western and Mid-Western Regions. In October 1966, Lt. Colonel Ojukwu issued an edict ordering all non-Easterners out of his region, stating that he could no longer guarantee their safety. Moreover, when the Ad Hoc Constitutional Committee resumed its deliberations in Lagos on October 24, the Eastern delegates were not authorised by Ojukwu to participate in further constitutional discussions.

In a broadcast of 30 November 1966 entitled 'Towards a new Nigeria' by the Head of the Federal Military Government, the creation of more states or regions was advocated so that no one region or ethnic group should be in a position to dominate the others. He put it succintly this way:

> In the stable Federation, no Region should be large enough to be able to threaten secession or hold the rest of the Federation to ransom in times of national crisis ... But there is no doubt that without a definite commitment on the states question, normalcy and freedom from fear of domination by one Region or the other cannot be achieved.[35]

The principles which guided the creation of new states were stated as follows: no one state should be in a position to dominate or control the Central Government; each state should form one compact geographical area; administrative convenience, the facts of history, and the wishes of the people concerned must be taken into account; each state should be in a position to discharge effectively the functions allocated to Regional Governments; and it was essential that the new states should be created simultaneously.[36] By the time new states were created on May 27, 1967 all these criteria were applied together, such that no one principle was applied to the exclusion of others. In any case, the same broadcast by the Head of State focused mainly on efforts to keep Nigeria as one entity.

It had became obvious towards the end of 1966 that the country was heading towards disintegration as matters steadily worsened. In a last and desperate effort to resolve the national crisis, the country's military leaders had a meeting at Aburi in Ghana from January 4-5, 1967. It was not so much the desire to guarantee the safety of all participants that led to the decision to hold the meeting outside Nigeria but the concern shown by the military leaders in Ghana to help settle Nigeria's inter-ethnic conflicts which was threatening disintegration. The meeting agreed to a return to the Status quo ante 15 January 1966 in so far as the federal structure was concerned, with the following additional measures to reinforce Regional autonomy: The Army was to be broken up into area commands corresponding to each of the existing regions, under the charge of an area commander directly under the orders of each military governor; All major decisions affecting the country were to be taken by the Supreme Military Council collectively, as well as all matters of policy, including appointments and promotions of persons in executive posts in the armed forces, police, civil service and diplomatic service.[37]

The federal Permanent Secretaries, however, strongly objected to the implementation of the Aburi agreements because of what they considered to be the inherent political dangers for the future of the country. This prompted a review of the accord as embodied in Decree No. 8 of 1967. The interpretation of the Aburi agreement by Gowon and Ojukwu resulted in a monumental misunderstanding between the two. By March, Ojukwu promulgated three edicts, which were clear signals of the march to secession, particularly with the Revenue Collection Edict of March 31 which stopped the payment of Federal Taxes in Eastern Region. Although the Federal Government reacted by imposing economic sanctions on the East, Ojukwu went a step further by taking over control of all federal institutions and utilities. On 1 May 1967, Chief Awolowo, the leading political figure in the West, threatened that if the Eastern Region were 'allowed by acts of omission or commission to secede from or opt out of Nigeria', the Western Region and Lagos would follow suit.[38] The efforts of a group of eminent Nigerians which constituted a National Reconciliation Committee, could not help matters.

On May 27 the Eastern Consultative Assembly and Advisory Committee of Chiefs and Elders empowered Ojukwu to declare the secession of the Eastern Region and the formation of a separate Biafran nation.[39] Gowon, in a belated but astute counter-move, decreed a fundamental change in the federal structure with the creation of twelve states on May 27, 1967; which in the process divided the Eastern Region into three states. On May 30, at 2.00 a.m; the Republic of Biafra was proclaimed. The consequences of the development so far, was the outbreak of the Nigerian Civil War,[40] which lasted from 1967 to January 1970. The war was fought largely to determine whether or not Nigeria would continue as a federation according to Gowon's twelve-state scheme, or would split into its component parts in a confederal system, as Ojukwu wanted. The outcome, after two and a half years and between 500,000 and 1,000,000 deaths, represented an enforced military solution to the perennial problem of the proper balance of federalism and the role of elite groupings therein.[41] By implication therefore, the war did not resolve the National Question as it was merely a war of unification by use of force. Among the constituent units or rather, the component peoples, the level of mutual trust and co-operation was still very low to arouse national consciousness as the basis of shared values and common identity. Consequently, the post-war years were tortuous nationhood experiences vis-à-vis the National Question which made it difficult for purposeful national development or put in another way, for the attainment of a national sense of purpose.

Post-War Years: The National Question and Page within the Union, 1971–1994

The national crisis from 1971 to 1994 which threatened the continued existence of Nigeria had its origins in basic economic issues and social conflict. This was due to the centralisation of the economy in such a manner that the federal government became the focus of national economic activity because of increased revenues from crude oil exports in the 1970s, and which were allocated according to different formulas to the states. In 1970, the military administration had suspended section 164 of the Republican Constitution which required the federal government to consult with the regions before altering fiscal arrangements, and subsequent revenue allocation formulas since 1975 have enhanced the economic powers of the federal government.[42] Although, the argument often advanced in support of the varying formulas of revenue allocation has been the issue of equitable geographical distribution of available resources, this resulted in the "sharing of the national cake" at the detriment of accepting common objectives for nation-building.

The resources of the federal government which were referred to as the "national cake" came mainly from oil exploration in the Niger Delta of ethnic minorities.[43] The chronic underdevelopment of the areas of oil exploration led to sub-nationalists agitations because of neglect by the major ethnic groups which have had control of political leadership. By January 1994, when most ethnic groups seemed to have lost hope in Nigeria, a group of southern ethnic minorities advocated a declaration of independence for all nationalities, total commitment to self-determination and mutual agreement on all future associations within the Nigerian territory and union. This development was a reflection of the political furore of the past, and of the National Question which continued to threaten the continued existence of Nigeria.

But the *Nigerian Tribune,* in its editorial, cautioned against such separatist agitations: "To break-up is to ignore the root causes of the National Question but rather, the Constitutional Conference should address the prospects of achieving higher levels of mutual trust, co-operation, shared values, common identity and national consciousness".[44] The paper went further to say that basic to the very core of this nation is the collective effort towards strengthening Nigerian unity and "to offer equality and self-determination to all Nigerian peoples within the framework of a federal structure in which the peoples within each state are accorded substantial measures of self-government".[45]

Since the end of the Civil War, the relationships between the ethnic groups have been uneasy, and on many occasions assumed very disturbing dimensions such as riots, inter-communal clashes with the resultant loss of lives and property. For example, religious riots in Northern Nigeria, came to assume a new dimension in deepening the crisis of national integration. So also, was national politics, in which the military became the instrument of continuing ethnic politics, with the resultant effect of social tension and political acrimony. In 1992, the *Nigerian Tribune* in its editorial warned that the country had reached a point where the problem should be confronted, openly debated and a solution consequently devised.[46] It was not until 1993, after the woeful failure of the political transition programme,[47] in which the future of the country as a single entity was threatened, that most Nigerians began to call for a national conference.[48] The choice which faced Nigeria was either to break up or make up. By the end of 1994, the Constitutional Conference was still debating the agenda for the future of Nigeria.

Conclusion

In the 80 years of Nigeria's history from 1914 to 1994, the state impaired the development of common nationality which increased the disunity of Nigerians. The solution to the National Question therefore, lies not in forced unification but the offer of equality and self-determination along with national integration. The basis of this offer should be justice and righteousness which will enhance the development of a national character and national consciousness.

Notes

1. With the amalgamation, a Nigerian Council which was a consultative body without any legislative or executive authority, was established by Lord Lugard in 1914 as a successor to the Legislative and Native Councils established by his predecessors in Southern Nigeria. See National Archives, Ibadan (hereinafter referred to as NAI) CSO 5/5/28. 22/11/1913, Nigerian Council Order-in- Council, 1913.

2. NAI, NL/D. Governor's Addresses to the Nigerian Council 1919-1920. Sir Hugh Clifford's address was given on December 29, 1920.

3. For details, see O.B. Osadolor, 1988, 'Nigerians in the Colonial Central Legislature: A Study of their Contribution to the Nationalist Struggle, 1923-1960', M.A. Dissertation, Department of History, University of Ibadan, pp.1-25. See also, J.F. Ade-Ajayi, 'African Resistance to Colonialism and the Development of Nationalism in West Africa'. Typescript, Ibadan, 1970; J.S. Coleman, *Nigeria: Background to Nationalism.* Berkeley and Los Angeles, 1960; J.B. Webster, 'Political activity in British West Africa, 1900-1940', in J.F.A. Ajayi and M. Crowder (eds), History of West Africa. Vol. 2, London, 1974; and W.B. Hamilton, 'The Evolution of British Policy towards Nigeria', in R.O. Tilman and T. Cole (eds), *The Nigerian Political Scene.* Durham, 1962.

4. NAI, CSO 5/5/33. 21/11/22. Nigeria (Legislative Council) Order-in-Council, 1922.

5. NAI, CSO 5/5/35. 6/2/1928 Nigeria (Legislative Council) Order-in-Council 1928 making further provision in regard to the Legislative Council of Nigeria; and CSO 5/5/42. 27/11/41 The Nigeria (Legislative Council) (Amendment) Order-in-Council 1941).

6. See for example, NAI, MN/B4A, Sir B. Bourdillon: Memorandum on the Future Political Development of Nigeria. Lagos, 1939.

7. NAI, CSO 5/5/43. 2/8/46 The Nigerian (Legislative Council) Order-in-Council, 1946.

8. K. Ezera, 'Constitutional Developments in Nigeria, 1944-1956: An Analytical study of Nigeria's Constitution-making developments and the Historical and Political Factors that Affected Constitutional Change'. Ph.D Thesis, Oxford, 1957, p.50.

9. The nationalist movement had become a powerful force, with a broader basis of popular support, a more coherent programme, and a more militant strategy than in pre-war wars. It was capable of questioning, in action as well as in words, the constitutional, administrative and economic assumptions of British authority. Several factors helped to bring about this change. For details, see O. Aluko 'Politics of Decolonisation in British West Africa, 1945-1960', in J.F.A. Ajayi and M. Crowder, of Cit.; J.S. Coleman, Op. Cit; chapters 10 and 11; and also, T. Hodgkin, 'Background to Nigerian Nationalism', West Africa, August 4 – October 20, 1951, pp.751-752 and 773-774.

10. NAI, NL/F2 Legislative Council Debates. First Session, March 20, 1947, p.7.

11. Legislative Council Debates. First Session, March 24, 1947, p.212.

12. *Ibid.*, p.215.

13. *Ibid.*, p.238.

14. The questions were published in Legislative Council Debates. Third Session, March 11, 1949, pp.322-323; and also in, O.B. Osadolor, op. cit., pp.92-95.

15. For details, see Legislative Council Debates. Fourth Session, April 3, 1950, pp.506-522.

16. Quoted in Hodgkin, op. cit., p.821.

17. Legislative Council Debates. First Session, March 24, 1947, p.208.

18. Legislaltive Council Debates. Second Session, March 4, 1948, p.227.

19. Obaro Ikime, 'In Search of Nigerians: Changing Patterns of Inter-Group Relations in an Evolving Nation-State', Presidential Inaugural Lecture delivered at the 30th Congress of the Historical Society of Nigeria, at the University of Nigeria, Nsukka, on 1 May, 1985, p.21.

20. B.J. Dudley, 'A Coalition Theoretic Analysis of Nigerian Politics, 1950 – 66'. *The African Review*, Vol. 2 No. 4, 1974, P.532.

21. Ikime, Op. Cit. pp.21-22.

22. O. Adewoye, 'Colonial Constitutions, the Rule of Law and Politics in Nigeria, 1862-1960'. A paper presented at the Seminar on Historical Roots of the contemporary Nigerian Nation held at Durbar Hotel, Kaduna, 3-7 June 1986, p.7.

23. NAI, NL/H2 Debates of the House of Representatives, Second Session, March 31, 1953, p. 991.

24. *Ibid.*

25. See for example, W.D. Graf, *The Nigerian State: Political System in the Post Colonial Era.* London and Portsmouth: (New Hampshire), 1988.

26. Ola Balogun, *The Tragic Years: Nigeria in Crisis 1966-1970.* Benin City: Ethiope Publishing Corporation, 1973, p.14.

27. *Ibid.*

28. *Ibid.,* p.15.

29. There was a spontaneous outburst of rejoicing all over the country with demonstrations of support for the militlary take-over but in the north, reaction was more cautious.

30. Balogun, op.cit., p.27.

31. *Ibid.*

32. *Ibid.*

33. *Ibid.,* p.30.

34. *Ibid.,* p.55. It was now obvious by the army mutiny in Kano that discipline in the army had been deeply undermined by two successive coups, during which the rank and file had been given the bad example of rebellion against constituted order by senior officers.

35. Cited in A.A. Ayida, "The Nigerian Revolution, 1966-1976", Presidential Address delivered at the 13th Annual Confelrence of The Nigerian Economic Society, Enugu, April 1973, pp.5-6.

36. *Ibid.,* p.6.

37. Cited in Balogun, op. wit., p.58.

38. *Ibid.,* p.61.

39. For details, see A.A. Nwankwo, *Nigeria: The Challenge of Biafra.* London; Rex Collings, 1972.

40. For accounts of the Civil War, see A.H.M. Kirk-Greene, Crisis and Conflict in *Nigeria: A Documentary Source-book 1966-1967.* Vol. I January 1966-July 1967 and Vol. II July 1967-January 1970. London: Oxford University Press, 1971; John de St. Jorre, *The Nigerian Civil War.* London: Hodder and Stoughton, 1972; Rex Niven, *The War of*

Nigerian Unity. London: Evans, 1970; Zdenek Cervenka, *A History of the Nigerian War 1967-1970.* Lagos Onibonoje Press, 1972. See also, Robert Collis, *Nigeria in Conflict.* London: Secker Warburg, 1970; Ntieyong U. Akpan, *The Struggle for Secession 1966-1970. A Personal Account of the Nigeria Civil War.* London: Frank Cass, 1972; Frederick Forsyth, *The Biafra Story.* Harmondsworth: Peuguin, 1970 and Ikenna Nzimiro, *The Nigerian Civil War: A Study in Class Conflict.* Enugu: Fourth Dimension Publishers, 1979.

41.   Graf, op. cit., p.43.

42.   See, Federal Republic of Nigeria, Report of the Technical Committee on Revenue Allocation (2 Vols). Lagos, December 1977.

43.   See, K. Panter-Brick (ed), *Soldiers and Oil: The Political Transformation of Nigeria.* London: Frank Cass and Company Ltd., 1978.

44.   *Nigerian Tribune* (Ibadan) Wednesday 9 February, 1994, p.9.

45.   *Ibid.*

46.   *The Nigerian Tribune* (Ibadan), editorial on 'The National Question', Monday 14 September 1992, pp.1 and 11.

47.   See, O.B. Osadolor, 'The Military and the Search for Democracy in Nigeria: Reflections on the Transition Agenda, 1986-1992' in L.A. Thompson (ed), *Democracy, Democratisation and Africa.* Ibadan: Afrika-Link Books, 1994, pp.173-184.

48.   See *The African Guardian* (Lagos) December 27, 1993: January 31, 1994 and February 14, 1994. See also, John F. Clark, 'The National Conference as a Path to democratisation in Africa'. Paper presented at the 35th Annual Meeting of the African Studies Association, Seattle, Washington, 20-23 November, 1992.

3 Social Structure and the National Question in Nigeria

MARK ANIKPO

Introduction

The survival of the modern nation-state is becoming more questionable than ever before. In many parts of the world, especially in Europe and Africa, movements or agitations for the disintegration of existing or erstwhile sovereign national entities have become stronger and more menacing. At the root of the turmoil is an apparent dissatisfaction with or dysfunctionality of the economic and political arrangements that glue these nation states together since many of them are products of unsolicited federalism.

In Africa, for instance, the modern nation-state emerged out of political amalgamations of extremely diverse ethnic groups and class configurations brought together as a colonial necessity. Their continued existence as a sovereign entity has proved to be a precarious balance between the dominant elements of the social structure, namely – ethnicity, religion and class. Social structure here refers to the configuration of social relationships among people (Homans, 1976; Merton, 1976). Where, as in Nigeria, this structure is characterised by instability arising particularly from distorted production and reward systems (Anikpo, 1984), various social groups, usually identified along ethnic, religious and class lines, feel marginalised and cheated in the appropriation of available resources. They embark on agitations for autonomy or a more equitable share of the nation's resources thereby threatening the corporate existence of the nation.

The agitations, threats and general instability raise a number of questions about the nation – its origin, the systems of production and distribution, types of leadership and citizenship, degree of ethnic integration, democratic participation, and religious tolerance, and the defence of justice and all forms of human rights. Collectively they constitute the core of the problematic conceptualised here as the national question. The national question generally seeks to determine the necessity and relevance of the nation-state in the late 20th Century and beyond. For the analysis in this chapter, the emphasis is directed, as indicated earlier, on the dominant issues of the Nigerian social structure which are ethnicity, religion and class. In the first place, how are these elements configured in the Nigerian society? Second, how do the structural configurations impact on the continued existence of Nigeria as a united sovereign nation? And finally, what alternative strategies exist to deal with the national question in Nigeria?

In answering these questions, methodological insights provided by Marxist political economists shall be relied on, which, despite ideological propaganda, remains the most appropriate analytical paradigm for conflict-oriented expositions. Part of this paradigm is a historical approach aimed at revealing, not only the patterns and regularities in empirical events, but also the inter-relationships in the institutional configurations of society which systematically x-ray the national question as the product of contradictions in the existing mode of production.

Dominant Elements of The Nigerian Social Structure

Despite the common notion that social structure refers to the configurations and interplay of social relationships, there are differences of details in its conceptualisation among scholars. Parsons focuses on the identification of these configurations in terms of economic, political, religious, etc and how they relate to one another to produce order and stability in society.

Marx, on the other hand, drew attention to how the interplay of the various components of the social structure determines peoples positions and actions in society. To him the institutional configurations that make up the society fit into two broad structural categories: the infra-structure and the super-structure. The former refers to the economic institution which Marx argued constitutes the major determinant of social action. The latter refers to the political, religious, educational, etc. institutions which are dependent on the former. Marx demonstrated clearly that the interplay between the infrastructure and the superstructure produces a complicated arrangement of society into mainly two social classes on the basis of their ownership or non-ownership of the means of (economic) production. As Ake (1981) also noted, the relationships that produce such classes are inevitably rooted in the economic base of society because man has to eat first before he is alive to play politics, go to church or school.

It is very tempting to reduce the determinants of social structure to only class relations. This is because in a certain sense, class relations connote ethnic relations (see Nnoli, 1980) and religious relations (see Kukah, 1993). Yet, as we have argued elsewhere (Anikpo, 1984; 1991), it is analytically problematic to reduce class to ethnicity or vice versa. The empirical fact is that they co-exist, sometimes overlap, and sometimes reinforce each other. This approach helps to understand why at certain places and times ethnicity becomes an issue where there is an obvious conflict between two contending classes or factions of the same class. In such cases, it becomes important to understand ethnicity as well as class in order to fully comprehend the dynamics of the social structure.

As for religion, it is equally tempting to dismiss it as a class phenomenon, that is, weapon for the domination of the masses by the ruling class. That will also pose analytical problems as it could ignore empirical facts that are relevant to our comprehensive understanding of the national question. In order therefore to avoid a change of theology, the Nigerian social structure will be identified and analysed as the product of ethnic, religious and class relations operating as distinct but interrelated social phenomena.

Historical Perspectives

Before the colonial encounter, there existed in the territorial area that is known today as Nigeria, various ethnic and sub-ethnic groups. They lived and interacted according to their own ecological dictates, cultural accomplishments and historial circumstances. For instance, in the north, following the 1804 jihad of Uthman Dan Fodio, the Hausa, Nupe, Kanuri, and other ethnic groups were infilterated by the Fulani who conquered some of these ethnic groups and imposed their political and religious systems on them.

Down south, the River Niger created natural boundaries for various ethnic groups. In the west a dominant Yoruba ethnic group interacted closely with the Bini, Urhobo, Itsekiri and other minor ethnic units in the region. In the east, the Igbo occupied virtually the entire territory except the Delta riverine section occupied by the Ijaw and the south-eastern tip of the region occupied by the Efik, Ibibio, Yakuur and other minor ethnic units.

Before European colonialism, the interaction between these various ethnic groups was essentially through trade and in some cases, warfare. Otherwise, they existed as autonomous socio-cultural, political and economic units but sharing some cultural patterns in common. For instance, in terms of political organisation,Nzimiro (1975) informs us that monarchical feudal formations existed in the northern parts of the country among the Fulani-Habe emirates, the Habe (Hausa) emirates of Daura, Argungu and Abuja, and the Nupe, Bornu, Igala and Jukun kingdoms. In the southern parts, similar monarchial political organisations existed among the Yoruba, the Bini, Urhobo and Itsekiri chiefdoms; among the Onitsha and other Ogbaru Igbo; the Etubong organisations of the Efik and the chiefly houses of the Izon in the Niger Delta.

Despite these similarities, the Nigerian pre-colonial ethnic groups maintained their respective autonomies in governance and economic exploitation of their resources. Their ethnic identities were reinforced by distinctive myths of origin which informed their religious observances and stratification patterns. Among the emirates of the north, society was structured into different social strata on the basis of nobility, occupation, religion, ethnic group and slavery. It is however the stratification based on nobility that polarises the society into the "Masu Sarauta" (ruling class) and the "Talakawa" (commoners). Again, according to Nzimiro, "the ruling class consisted of those who held vital offices in the state". The "Talakawa" was made up of the peasants, serfs, and slaves who cultivated the land and paid rent to the land owners.

In the Southwest, the Yoruba ringed themselves in the myth of Oduduwa in which the Oba and his aristocratic nobles sustained their oppression of commoners in the belief of divine kingship. The same class divisions and oppression existed in the Benin kingdom and its prototype chiefdoms of Onitsha, Igala, and the Ogbaru Igbo.

The stratification pattern among the hinterland Igbo, Tiv and Ibibio groups was different but no less exploitative. A rigid success ethos placed the strong and wealthy at the apex of the social ladder and legitimised their dominance in the affairs of seemingly democratic communities. Thus in precolonial Nigeria, ethnicity, religion and class prevented the integration of the Nigerian ethnic groups into a nation-state until the Europeans imposed nationhood on them in 1914.

Similar contradictions existed during the colonial era. Arising mainly from the British administrative strategy of "divide-and-rule", the colonial government did little or nothing to erase the divisive barriers imposed by ethnicity, religion and class. Rather, these elements of the social structure were further reinforced as instruments to gain competitive advantage in the new political arena. For instance, western education and christian religion brought into the country by European colonisers flourished differently among the various Nigerian ethnic groups. Those who acquired the education before others used it to reinforce their respective ethnic identities. Similarly, christianity and Islam sharpened further the ethnic dividing lines between the ethnic groups that embraced christianity and those that embraced Islam. In the north particularly, the Islamic religion became a powerful tool for political coercion and ethnic exclusiveness. As Matthew Kukah (1993) clearly shows, during the politics of the first Nigerian Republic, the northern ruling elite,

> cast politcal opposition in religious terms. Those who were outside the
> orbit of the NPC were cast in demonic idioms, they were traitors. The

religious ideals of the Sokoto caliphate had become incarnated within the NPC and its political manifesto.

The northern ruling elite envisioned a monolithic north in political opposition to the south. Consequently, areas in the geographical north that embraced christianity as most of the Middle Belt ethnic groups did, faced severe castigation from the northern ruling elite and strong overtures from the southern elite to embrace a southern christian brotherhood. So intense was the religious factor in politics that it has continued to be a stumbling block toward the emergence of a stable and integrated Nigerian nation.

As the ethnic and religious dividing lines hardened in the colonial and post-colonial Nigeria, so also did the class lines. The colonial class structure began with a racial colouration, the Europeans as the all conquering ruling class and the Nigerians as the conquered labouring class. The contradictions of colonialism necessitated the emergence of a rural-urban dichotomy; the emergence of a petty-bourgeois indigenous class who formed a socio-economic layer between the Europeans and the rest of Nigerians. This group was to metamorphose later into an independent Nigerian ruling class. Unlike the racial overtones that separated the British colonial ruling class from the bourgeoning Nigerian elite of the colonial era, the class configurations of the late colonial and post colonial epochs were interwoven with ethnic alliances which enabled factions of the ruling class to gain competitive political and economic advantages over other contenders. Nigeria's political history is replete with illustrations of factions of the Nigerian bourgeoisie manipulating ethnic sentiments to win political positions.

This recourse to ethnicity by factions of the ruling class generated two problems that are relevant to the national question. The first was the acrimony and distrust it generated among Nigerian leaders and also the attendant spirit of vendetta it planted perpetually in inter-ethnic relations. The second was the confusion it created in the conceptualisation of class and ethnicity. It became almost impossible to draw any dividing line between the two except conceptually. In practice, normally, the intra-class struggle in Nigeria is geared toward the control of the means of production and the appropriation of existing resources. To that extent, we agree with Nnoli (1980) that ethnicity in Nigeria is essentially a class phenomenon. That is to say that if the class question can be resolved, the ethnic prejudices may disappear with it.

In theory however, ethnicity is rooted in the existence of ethnic identities which are primordial. Assuming it were possible for classes to disappear, ethnicity in economic and political competitions may also disappear but ethnic identities will never disappear. Their relevance in inter-group competitions may only be marginalised. But their existence still poses potential threat to complete national integration and as experience in Europe has shown in recent times, could erupt in a more damaging "ethnicity" at a later date.

The Nigerian Social Structure and the National Question

The crisis in Nigeria's social structure has engendered instability in the nation's political economy. It is in the political arena that this instability has manifested most glaringly. Since 1960 when Nigeria became independent, it has recorded eleven Heads of State and regimes. Only three were democratically elected. The others were military regimes that emerged through *coups d'etat* in addition to a military-sponsored interim regime. Three of the Heads of State died through assassinations and one was literally chased out of office. Within the same period, the country also witnessed a 30-month civil war.

In 1966, the government of Sir Abubakar Tafawa Balewa was toppled and Balewa was assassinated in a military coup that brought General Aguiyi Ironsi to power. Six months after, a counter coup toppled Ironsi who was also assassinated. The next government of General Yakubu Gowon spent 8 years trying to heal the political wounds of two devastating military coups and a destabilising civil war. In 1975, another military *coup d'etat* toppled General Gowon and ushered in the regime of Generals Murtala Mohammed and Olusegun Obasanjo. The assassination of Murtala Mohammed early in 1976, brought Obasanjo in as the Head of State. After three years, he voluntarily handed over political power to a democratically elected civilian President Shehu Shagari who succeeded in holding the fragile federation together for the four years of his first term of office. He was re-elected in 1983 in an election that re-enacted all the ethnic, religious and intra-class acrimony that has put a permanent question mark on the future of Nigeria as a nation. Barely three months into his second term of office, Shagari was toppled in another military coup that brought Generals Muhamadu Buhari and Tunde Idiagbon to power in December, 1983. They did not last two years because in August 1985, they were toppled in yet another military coup that ushered in the regime of General Ibrahim Babangida. For failing in his promises to hand over power to a democratically elected civilian regime, Babangida fell out of favour with Nigerians particularly for his unexplained act of annuling an election he spent millions of the country's money to organise. He was disgraced out of office after installing a sham civilian regime under Chief Ernest Shonekan in August 1993. Shonekan's interim regime lasted only till November 17, 1993 and was toppled by yet another military general in the person of Sani Abacha. General Abacha died in office and was replaced by General Abubakar

Abdulsalam who in turn handed over power to President Olusegun Obasanjo.

This obvious instability in the political system becomes even more bizzare when seen in the context of the ethnic, religious and class overtones associated with it. For instance, out of the eleven Heads of State, seven were Hausa-Fulani; three were Yoruba and one (a ceremonial President) was Igbo. The ethnic implications of this imbalance are many. The other ethnic groups, particularly the minorities who have never had a Head of State feel marginalised and aggrieved. They are bound to question their membership of the Nigerian nation. The religious implication is also clear. All the seven Hausa-Fulani or northern Heads of State except General Yakubu Gowon were muslims. The muslims have therefore had more Heads of State and the christians feel uncomfortable with this and are resentful of the dominance of the muslims in national politics. In class terms, we also see the factionalisation of the Nigerian ruling class into political and military elite groups. The military as a faction of this ruling class has certainly had the upper hand since it has produced seven of the Heads of State as against three for the civilian politicians. As a faction of this ruling class, the politicians feel cheated and have cause to question the legitimacy of the military in governance. These resentments also engender distrust and a sense of betrayal which are inimical to national integration.

The instability in the social structure is also manifest in all aspects of the Nigerian economy. Despite enormous deposits of mineral resources and a large expanse of land for agricultural food production, political instability arising from inter-ethnic and class acrimonies have resulted in ineffective policies and total failure in harnessing the economic potentialities of these two key areas. The following illustrations may be useful.

Ever since petroleum production took over from agriculture as the mainstay of the Nigerian economy, government policies on oil production have shown a disregard for the plight of the oil-producing communities. Government legislations on land use have been in favour of oil companies and members of the Nigerian ruling class. Large tracts of land are alienated from rural peasant producers without adequate compensation. Several oil producing communities have been devastated by the massive pollution that accompanies oil production. After several years, the apparent insensitivity of government and oil companies to the plight of the oil producing communities has given rise to violent conflicts between these communities and oil companies on one hand and the communities and government agents on the other. These conflicts reached alarming proportions between 1991 and 1993 when the Umuechem and Ogoni communities in the Rivers State challenged both the oil companies and government agents; demanded adequate compensation for the destruction of their lands and threatened to secede from the Nigerian federation. The disaffection of the Ogoni towards the Nigerian nation is a typical example of the frustration felt by many ethnic groups in Nigeria over the ruling class manipulation of the economy to serve its members' interests thereby engendering instability in the economic and political systems.

In the area of agricultural food production, successive Nigerian governments have attempted to introduce rural development programmes aimed at raising food production and addressing the development imbalance between Nigeria's rural and urban areas. None of these programmes has succeeded in achieving these objectives. Consequently, the social relationships existing between Nigeria's rural and urban dwellers threaten the very foundations of Nigeria's nationhood. A long-standing rural neglect in development planning had created an exodus of able-bodied and educated labour force from the rural to the urban areas. This tended to concentrate the economically and politically dominant members of society in the urban areas thereby reinforcing the polarisation of society into two unequal classes. The dominant urban based class had used its vantage hold on the state apparatus to exploit the politically powerless rural dwellers and entrenched a permanent conflict of interest in the relationship between the two groups.

The Food Crisis

By far the most disastrous agricultural policy of the immediate post-colonial Nigerian government was the colonial hangover of emphasising cash crop production to the detriment of food crops. It led to the steady decline of food crop production and the attendant intensification of hunger in the country. It also created the well known paradox in which Nigerians produced what they did not eat and ate what they did not produce, through massive food importation from Europe and America.

The importation of food later assumed extra-ordinary proportions during the oil boom era of the 1970s and early 1980s as it intensified corrupt private accumulation of capital by strategically placed state officials and their allies. Yet, it did not stop the intensification of hunger and poverty among Nigeria's rural majority. The imported food was not only too expensive for many average Nigerian families, it also impeded the production of similar crops in the country as the producers inevitably lost their customers. For instance, the massive importation of rice stiffled its local production because rice farmers could not compete with the new rice merchants.

Olatunbosun (1975) notes that the failure of the food importation strategy was the major factor that forced a rethinking in the area of local food production. Emphasis on rural development gradually shifted to food production.

OFN

The 1976 Operation Feed the Nation (OFN) programme by the Obasanjo regime was an outcome of this rethinking and new emphasis on food production. So also was the emergence of the Agricultural Development Programmes (ADPS). Available records show that this rethinking was basically superficial. According to Olatunbosun (1975), the overall impact of the efforts to improve agricultural food production was increasing food shortage resulting from inconsistencies and contradictions in policies that recognised the importance of increased food production but denied the means of social reproduction to the food producers, (see also Anikpo, 1985). Despite all the fanfare on ADPs and OFN, none made an appreciable change in the food situation. Nzimiro (1985) maintains that the OFN which, as an agricultural scheme, was meant to stimulate the growth of food by individuals and corporate bodies, turned out to be a collosal waste of time and resources. The scheme was controlled and directed by the bureaucratic bourgeoisie whose sole interest in the OFN was the huge financial rewards they reaped from clandestine deals with businessmen. Nzimiro (1985) also reveals that some of the government officials who propagated the project later retired and became consultants to the very same government. Huge consultancy fees were paid to them for reproducing ideas that never worked in a preponderantly peasant society.

The criticism of the OFN by Forest (1985) raises another dimension of policy failure in Nigeria's rural development efforts. He points out that the "Operation Feed the Nation was a hurried political initiative launched in the middle of the farming season by a military regime that was anxious to secure support from urban groups and students." The students who were involved in the scheme were only interested in the ninety six Naira paid to them at the end of the month and for the Ministry staff, it was just a wage employment. The point here however is to underscore the fact that rural development policies and programmes in Nigeria are usually *ad-hoc* in nature because the governments usually embarked on specific programmes as a matter of political expediency. They establish programmes to address specific pressing practical problems such as food scarcity, disruptive rural-urban migration, acute unemployment and declining productivity. We had noted elsewhere (Anikpo, 1989) that the problem with embarking on rural development vigorously only when a crisis is apparent is that it tends to be too specific, lacking meaningful integration with other national development programmes. Moreover, it tends to be short-lived since, as a child of circumstance, it tends to disappear when the circumstance that gave rise to it disappears or is removed from the national priority list.

A corollary, and indeed consequence of the *ad-hoc* factor in the country's rural development policies and programmes is the consistent element of rural exploitation for urban benefit. Every step taken by the government turns out to be a design to deal with urban-based rather than rural-based problems. Fertilizers and improved seeds are distributed to rural farmers in order to produce more to feed the nation. Roads are constructed in order that food could be evacuated from rural production centres to the urban areas or that urban-based state officials can drive to their villages more comfortably. This is why in many cases, a supposedly rural development project becomes more harmful to a community than useful (see Anikpo, 1984). An effective rural development policy must transcend this urban bias (overt or covert) and place the rural inhabitants as the primary beneficiaries of its programmes.

Green Revolution

The Green Revolution (GR) agricultural programme of 1980 also failed to achieve its stated objective of ensuring food self-sufficiency for Nigeria. It failed as a result of similar bureaucratic excesses that stiffled the OFN and therefore needs no further elaboration here.

DFRRI

It is also appropriate to mention the Directorate for Food, Roads and Rural Infrastructure (DFRRI) which the Babangida administration established in 1986 as an integrated rural development programme to deal with the shortcomings of earlier programmes.

The establishment of DFRRI was the organisational panacea to the government's determination that "rural development will move away from past narrow sectoral preoccupation with the generation of food and fibre surpluses to the overall formulation of a national rural development strategy as rural development holds the key to agricultural transformation and national food security," (1986 Budget Speech). The administration was thus poised to pursue what it described as a "vigorous rural development policy aimed at strengthening the economic viability of the rural areas to ensure adequate and continuous food production and distribution" (1986 Budget Speech). Nobody has given the DFRRI pass mark yet since it was scrapped by General Abacha.

State Creation and the Permanent Shadow of Ethnicity

More than any thing, the instability in the Nigerian social structure the distrust and suspicion that characterise ethnic, religions and class relationships, and the threat to the corporate existence of Nigeria as a nation, are epitomised in the perennial agitations for state creation in Nigeria. Because of its centrality in the national question, it is given elaborate consideration in this analysis. Nigeria was split into three regions in 1947 by the Arthur Richards Constitution. Some writers use this date as the beginning of state creation in Nigeria. Some other writers take the date further back to 1914 when the southern and northern protectorates became parts of the same country as decreed by Lord Frederick Lugard. There are equally those who even go as far back as 1883-84 when the colonising European powers sat in Berlin and drew arbitrary boundaries of their territorial possessions in Africa (Ellah, 1983).

For most part of Nigeria's political history, the three region structure has made a more lasting impact but because it predated Nigeria's independence we shall not regard it as an exercise in state creation. Moreover, nobody requested or struggled for the creation of the three regions. It was an imposition by colonial powers and what we consider here as state creation in Nigeria came in the aftermath of the regionalisation exercise.

By 1954, the agitation for Nigerian's independence had already forced the British colonial government to take certain actions aimed at decolonisation. Such actions as the introduction of representative government at the centre by elected regional representatives and the revision of existing electoral laws had convinced many political observers that Nigerian independence was merely a matter of time. It was at this time that ethnic minority protests which had been on in some parts of the country since 1906, became more audible and began to transform into political movements for the creation of states. As Ukpana Okpu notes, after the constitutional conference in 1953 decided that Nigeria should become a federation composed of three regions with residual powers, ethnic minority groups expressed fears about their future in such regions and at the resumption of the conference in 1954, demanded to have their own states. He further contends that the increased wave of agitations was fuelled by four major developments:

(a)   the establishment of three regions in 1947;

(b)   the formation of ethnic organisations by the majority ethnic groups – the Ibo State Union, the Egbe Omo Oduduwa, and the Northern People's Congress;

(c)   the formation of Nigeria's three major political parties – the NCNC, the AG and the NPC;

(d)   the prospect of independence.

The agitations by minority ethnic groups for state creation was generally based on fears of marginalisation and domination by the majority groups. Although these fears were expressed in political terms, they were indeed rooted in the socio-economic inequalities that characterised the relationship between the different groups. Capturing political positions had become the only strategy for appropriating economic resources. Communities that had people in the central or regional governments attracted more government amenities, more jobs to their indigenes and more opportunities to excel in competitive endeavours. That was what all the politics was about. It was a crude game of numbers. The larger ethnic groups dominated the politics and thus economics of their regions. The ethnic majorities controlled the parties and hence the politics. To be from an ethnic minority group, in the existing political scheme, was decidedly a political and economic disadvantage. Those who found themselves in such situations usually struggle to avert permanent marginalisation.

Independence in 1960 tended to intensify the struggle for resource appropriation through political manoeuvres. The three regions became enclaves for the majority ethnic groups - Hausa, Igbo and Yoruba. Through the political parties they separately controlled, they not only reinforced their controls over these regions, but they also tried to gain control of the central government in Lagos. Each regional ethnic majority fought hard to ensure the political unity of its territory and at the same time connived with agitators from the other regions to ensure a break up of those other regions into smaller states. Yet, all the Premiers of the three regions had in 1957, agreed to a memorandum addressed to the delegates from ethnic minority areas to the creation of new states on the following principles:

(a)   the wishes of the people of the area should be determined by plebiscite;

(b)   the creation of new states should be consistent with the principle of viability;

(c)   the component units of the new states should be geographically contiguous;

(d)   no ethnic group should be divided into new states except with the wishes of a two-third majority of the said group determined by a plebiscite.

This agreement was in recognition of the enormous pressure which the movements for state creation had put on the various regional governments. It was also recognised as a strategy to allay ethnic minority fears of domination. As indicated earlier, the pressure from these political movements for state creation intensified after independence and the number of such groups were increasing. The major movements at the time were the Mid-West State Movement (MWSM) in the west, the Calabar Ogoja-River State Movement (COR) in the east, and the United Middle Belt Congress (UMBC) in the north. Shortly after the inauguration of the COR state movement at Uyo in 1954, a separate movement for the creation of a Rivers State was initiated by the Rivers chiefs. In the pre- and immediate post-independence era of Nigerian politics, it was considered political suicide for any region to allow a new state carved out of its territory. The eventual emergence of these states and more owed more to the internal contradictions of the Nigerian political economy than to goodwill policies that recognised the rights of the minority groups to have their own states. Thus states were forcefully created either out of political acrimony as in the 1963 creation of the Mid-West Region; or out of war strategy as in the 1967 creation of the twelve states; or out of expediency as in the 1976 creation of nineteen states; or even out of spite as in the 1987 creation of twenty-one states, or, as in the 1991 creation of thirty states, out of egomania. Let us examine them one by one.

Creation of the Mid-West Region (1963)

Ukpana Okpu (1977) provides us with a useful account of the political gymnastics that culminated in the creation of the first post-independence state in Nigeria. Although all the political parties, NPC, NCNC and AG were opposed to the creation of any state within their power base, they, except for the AG, secretly encouraged minority movements in the other regions. The AG, as Okpu put it, "remained in the forefront of ethnic minority agitation for more states in the Northern and Eastern Regions". It was an open and deliberate campaign policy and succeeded in getting both the UMBC and COR state agitators as political allies. The other parties waited for their opportunity to retaliate. The opportunity came when after the 1959 elections, NPC and NCNC formed a coalition federal government. To both parties the AG was a common enemy and they decided to give Awolowo a dose of his own medicine. Firstly, the federal government, as a result of a crisis in western Nigeria and in the deliberate attempt to destabilise the AG financially so as to stop it financing the UMBC and COR groups, instituted an inquiry into the financial transactions between the Western Nigerian government corporations and the AG as a party. Secondly, the FG gave overt support to the Mid-West Movement and by 1963, the mid-west region was carved out of the erstwhile western Nigeria.

The creation of the mid-west region therefore did not conform with any of the principles being debated as the appropriate basis for creating a state. It was created primarily to spite the AG and teach Awolowo a political lesson. Thus, it did not assuage any ethnic minority yearnings and it was only a matter of time for these minority fears to surface again in the new region.

Creation of the Twelve States (1967)

On 30th May, 1967, two historically significant events occurred in the country. On that day Emeka Odumegwu Ojukwu announced the secession of Biafra from the Nigerian federation. In Lagos, Yakubu Gowon announced the restructuring of the country into twelve states. Two issues arise here. The first is, why twelve states? The second is, why the exercise at that particular time?

On the first issue, Gowon had perhaps relied on existing recommendations on state creation in Nigeria. Francis Ellah (1983) has reflected on the appropriate criteria for state formation in Nigeria and drawn a comparison with other countries whose constitutions and circumstances are similar to those of Nigeria, e.g., India, USA and West Germany.

> India with a population of about 500 million has 14 states; the USA with roughly 200 million has 50 states and West Germany with 56 million has 10 states. Based on the proportions of states to overall populations in India, the USA or West Germany, Nigeria could have 3, or 25 or 20 states in that order.

Ellah also recalls Gowon's declaration in November, 1966 that based on the principle *inter alia* that no one region or ethnic group should be in a position to dominate the other and no region should be large enough to be able to threaten secession or hold the rest of the federation to ransom in times of national crisis, Nigeria should be divided into not less than eight and not more than fourteen states." These figures approximate those earlier suggested by Azikiwe and Awolowo. In his "Political Blueprint For Nigeria", Zik had proposed that Nigeria should be divided into eight nationalities (i.e. states). In 1953, Awolowo had equally submitted that if Nigeria should be carved out into states, there should be nine states in all made up of four in the north, two in the west and three in the east. It is indeed interesting that earlier suggestions on the number of states into which Nigeria should be divided were between eight and fourteen states. Therefore, in creating twelve states in 1967, Gowon must have been influenced by earlier arguments on states creation. There were six in the north and six in the south. A less critical observer would argue that there was a lot of objectivity on the state creation issue at this time.

However, the apparent objectivity that may have guided the 1967 exercise becomes questionable when one considers the timing of the state creation exercise. Observers were quick to see it as a tactical manouvre to undermine the survival of Biafra. In that respect it achieved its objective. Since this latter reason was the major objective for creating the states, as soon as the war ended, the agitation for more states resumed more vigorously than ever.

Creation of the Nineteen States (1976)

It was obvious by 1970 that by creating twelve states, new minorities had also been created. Some former minorities had become majorities in their new states and were vehemently resented by the new minorities. It was also obvious that all states received equal share of the federal revenue allocation. Politicians saw the political and economic gains which they could make if states were created for their own ethnic or sub-ethnic groups. Since the military was in power and politicians really had very little to politik about, they diverted their energies to the political agitation for more states.

Gowon was overthrown in 1975. The new Murtala/Obasanjo regime needed to gratiate itself with the Nigerian political agitators. In August 1976, General Obasanjo set up the Irikife Panel to look into the question of creating more states in Nigeria. Following the Panel's report, seven new states were added to the previous twelve to turn Nigeria into a federation of nineteen states. Again, the motive behind this new exercise was hardly genuine. It lacked the objectivity to make it permanent. Hence, hardly had the exercise ended than those who were not favoured renewed their demand for their own states.

Creation of Twenty - One States (1987)

On Wednesday, January 12, 1983, the *National Concord* (quoted by Ellah, 1983) reported the drama at the National Assembly where several state seeking groups had gone to persuade the Assembly committee on state creation to shortlist their states. From Sokoto State came a delegation led by the State's Deputy Governor, Alhaji Muhammadu Buchaka, with a ten-man team. He vowed that he would not return home until the National Assembly agreed to recommend the creation of Kebbi State out of the present Sokoto State. The assurance was eventually given by the Speaker of the House of Representative Chief Edwin Ume-Ezeoke.

Another group representing the National Union of Izon Youth from Bendel State wondered why they were not allowed to join their kith and kin in the

Rivers State. Yet another group from Edda Local Government in Imo State wanted to be merged with Abia State and not Ebonyi State as proposed in the report.

Another group of agitators was from the proposed Anioma State who did not want Onitsha people in their proposed state. The report also mentioned the groups for Abia State and for Aba State. It is interesting to note that it did not mention the Enugu (Wawa) State group.

The movement for the creation of Enugu (Wawa) state had not recovered from the disappointment of not getting the state in 1976 despite its powerful submission to the Irikife Panel. The leadership had almost lost its cohesiveness as they split into two opposing political parties, the NPN and the NPP.

Before the Shagari regime could do anything about creating more states, it was swept out of office by Buhari and Idiagbon. They, in turn, were not able to create any new states by the time they were overthrown by Babangida in 1985.

The Babangida regime was equally bombarded with the requests for more states. Most of the complaints focused on the acrimonious relationship that had arisen between the ethnic and sub-ethnic groups occupying the same state. The case of the "dichotomy" politics in the then Anambra State must be mentioned as a typical example of that acrimony. At a more general level however, the argument revolved around the injustice in allowing the north to have more states than the south; in squeezing all the Igbo people into two states while the Yorubas are located in five states, etc. The thinking was that since the states received equal shares of the federal resources, the per capita share per state was unequal. The bigger states therefore needed splitting to let them have a fair share of the national wealth or "cake".

In August 1987, Babangida announced the creation of two more states - Katsina and Akwa-Ibom to bring the number of states in Nigeria to twenty one. If Babangida pleased Katsina and Akwa-Ibom indigenes by this exercise, he drew more anger from the groups whose hopes he had dashed. Particularly among the Igbo people they felt horrified that they had become minorities in a former region where they constituted an overwhelming numerical majority. For the Enugu State movement, it was a terrible tragedy. Many people were already poised for the celebration of a new Enugu State. The failure to create the state was extremely vexing. For them and others in a similar predicament, the exercise of state creation must be revisited.

The States Bonanza of 1991

For reasons that are yet to be fully determined, President Babangida again in 1991 succumbed to the state creation pressure. In a surprising move, he created nine extra states bringing the total to thirty. It was Indeed a bonanza. Many of the state agitators got their states, including Enugu state. Yet, even as the celebrations were going on in many places, new agitations were surfacing leading to the creation of more states in 1996, showing that perhaps the issue of state creation in Nigeria may never end as long as the objective is either to meet political expediencies or to assuage ethnic minority protests. Nigeria is reported to have more than 250 ethnic groups. To create states on the basis of ethnic representation is to create 250 states.

The Constitutional Conference established by General Sani Abacha in 1994 included the issue of state creation in its deliberations. The Committee on State Creation headed by Dr. Peter Odili, after what it described as careful consideration of petitions, recommended another fourteen states for Nigeria. All that it shows is that the issue of state creation continues unabated and reflects the instability in the Nigerian social structure. General Abacha succumbed to the agitation for more states by creating additional states bringing the total to thirty-six states.

Conclusion

The Nigerian social structure is the product of the interplay between the institutional configurations of society. It manifests empirically in the ethnic, religious and class relationships that inform the stability or instability of the Nigerian nation. Historical experience in Nigeria shows that the configuration of these relationships has engendered distrust and acrimony among various contending groups in the Nigerian society and hence poses a threat to the corporate existence of the nation.

It was clear from 1947 when the three regions were constitutionally created by the colonial government, that it was aimed at moderating the major ethnic influences that played noticeably on the Nigerian political scene. The north was for the Hausa/Fulani, the west for the Yoruba and the east for the Igbo. Each group was to use whatever strategies and resources at its disposal to gain control of the central government through the instrumentality of its controlled political party - the NPC, The Action Group (AG) or the NCNC respectively. The guiding constitution was modelled on the British parliamentary system.

The inherent error and contradiction in this federal structure was that none of the three regions was ethnically monolithic. Each contained, coexisting with the major ethnic groups, a multiplicity of other ethnic groups of varying sizes. These minority groups naturally wished to maintain their ethnic identities. Thus, they saw the existence of these major groups as a threat to their specific interests in self-determination. The fear of domination was of course real because federally owned wealth was shared among the three regions and there were tendencies to concentrate development projects around the seat of political power. Moreover, the majority of the dominant classes in these regions was drawn from the major ethnic groups thereby creating intra–class conflicts at both regional and national levels. The combination of ethnic minority fears and intra-class conflicts produced political tensions which reverberated along all the levels of governance - regional and central. It culminated in the creation of the Mid-West as the fourth region in 1963.

That seemingly politically expedient exercise has turned into a cancerous agitation that casts a permanent shadow of ethnicity in the Nigerian political system. Its class and religious pillars pose a permanent threat to the survival of Nigeria as a nation.

From the perspective of the social structure, the national question in Nigeria is the question of equity in sharing resources among the various ethnic and social classes that make up Nigeria. The contradiction arising from the existing inequalities generate instability in the social structure and sustain the national question. Given the persistence of these distabilising forces, Nigeria seems to be presented with only two options. It is either a violent revolutionary intervention to redress these inequalities objectively or a breakup of the Nigerian nation.

References

Ake, Claude (1985), (ed), *Political Economy of Nigeria,* London and Lagos, Longman.

Anikpo, Mark (1985), 'Rural Development in The Third Republic: Preconditions for National Integration In Nigeria' (Conference Proceedings of the Nigerian Anthropological and Sociological Association', NASA).

Anikpo, Mark (1991), *Trade, Class and Ethnic Identity,* Enugu: ABIC Publishers.

Castells, Manuel (1977), *The Urban Question: A Marxist Approach,* London: Edward Arnold Publishers.

Coleman, James (1976), 'Social Structure and Theory of Action,' in Peter Blau (ed), *Approaches To The Study of Social Structure*, New York, The Free Press.

Ellah, F. J. (1983), *Nigeria and States Creation,* Port Harcourt:, Ellah & Sons Publishers.

Forrest, Tom (1985), 'Agricultural Development in Nigeria. 1900-1979', in *Rural Development In Nigeria. 1900-1980*, Zaria. Department of Political Science, Seminar Papers, Vol. 2.

Frank, Gurpider (1966), 'The Development of Underdevelopment', in *Monthly Review*, No. 8.

Helleiner, Gerald (1966), *Peasant Agriculture. Government and Economic Growth In Nigeria,* Illinois: Richard Irvin Inc.

Heyer, Judith. Pepe Roberts and Gavin Williams, (1981), (ed), *Rural Development in Tropical Africa*, London: Macmillan Press.

Homans, George (1976), 'What Do We Mean By Social Structure' in Blau (ed).

Kukah, Matthew (1993), *Religion, Politics and Power in Northern Nigeria:* Ibadan and Lagos: Spectrum Books.

Marx, Karl (1936), 'A Preface To The Critique of Political Economy' in Karl Marx, *Selected Works.* Vol. 1. New York: International Publishers.

Nzimiro, Ikenna (1985), *The Green Revolution or the Modernisation of Hunger,* Oguta: Zim Publishers.

Okpu, Ukpana (1977), *Ethnic Minority Problems In Nigeria: 1960-1965,* Uppsala: ACTA Universitatis.

Parsons, Talcott (1937), *The Structure of Social Action*, New York: McGraw Hill Book Company.

4 Revenue Allocation and the National Question

ESKOR TOYO

Introduction

Mao Zedong once said that for thought to be relevant to life, it should deal not with errors in books, but with errors in men's heads. We are about to launch out on a bookish disquisition on revenue allocation. Our discussion intends to be principally informative and relates to the outcry about revenue allocation associated with the wide demand for a 'sovereign' or 'constitutional' conference following the exit of the Babangida regime.

This conference, as seen by many, has on the top of its agenda the resolution of the national question. Allegations fill the air about domination of 'the south' by 'the north' of the rest by the Hausa-Fulani, and of the minor ethnic groups by the major ones. Fumes of anger pour out about the alleged injustice done by the present arrangements to states in general, to oil-producing states in particular, and to oil-producing areas by an excessively powerful Federal government thought by some to be manipulated by a certain section of the country. We have heard demands for a secession clause in the Constitution, for a weaker federation, for confederation and for power sharing. There naturally follow demands for new revenue allocation schemes in which the Federal government will be less favoured or 'spoilt' with excess money or made less inviting to prospective dictators or hegemonies.

This is the background to the present discussion. This chapter addresses the importance of a revenue allocation as a constitutional issue, revenue sources, the general and Nigerian allocation principles and the Nigerian practice, the question of justice or injustice in the Nigerian allocation, the causes of repeated acrimony over revenue allocation, and the importance of national direction in the revenue allocation issue.

It also emphasises that it is important to be informed about the actual situation, to be clear what to do with Nigeria, and to have a clear idea of how one wants the country to move in the twentieth century and the requirements of such motion.

Federalism and Revenue Allocation

People who emphasise the diversity of Nigeria ignore the fact that Nigeria was administered unitarily by British colonialists up to the 1950s and that it is in recognition of the country's ethnic, historical and cultural diversity that the Nigerians who led her to independence opted for the federal form of government. Moreover, Nigeria's federalism started in the 1950s with what is technically a 'strong' federation, namely, one in which the federal government is vested with the residual powers. In the 1979 and 1989 constitutions, the federation became technically a weak one-with the residual powers vested in the states.

Owing to intense ethnic attachments, mediocrity and power rivalry among Nigerian bourgeois leaders, Nigeria's Constitution making has been an unfinished business. In 1959, 1963, 1979 and 1989, the country had new Constitutions and another constitution making in 1994 which partially produced the 1999 Constitution.

Sources of Revenue

To be clear about revenue allocation we need to have an idea about the sources of government revenue. Apart from borrowings – which have to be repaid – government revenue comes from direct taxes, indirect taxes, and earnings from rents (including royalties) and interest and profits from government investments. Direct taxes are those that fall on incomes directly. They are taxes on personal incomes from wages and salaries, allowances, rent, interest or dividends as well as taxes on business profits. Indirect taxes fall on income and wealth through the things that people buy or own. There are customs and excise taxes as well as taxes such as stamp duties, licences, taxes on business premises, and capital gain taxes.

As far as sources of revenue are concerned, the constitutional provisions are such that some sources belong to Federal, State and Local Governments separately.

In discussing revenue sources and allocation in Nigeria, it is preferable to base ourselves on what the 1989 Constitution prescribes. This is for three reasons. First, military rule is a dictatorship. Nothing compels it to deal with revenue matters as prescribed by any Constitution. Secondly, the 1989 Constitution states a constitutional assembly thinking and the fundamental law on the matter which a post-Babangida civilian regime was supposed to follow. Thirdly, agitation for revenue division in Nigeria does not show awareness of what the 1989 constitutional provisions are. There is need for this awareness.

The revenues from other sources are collected by the Federal or State government and distributed to prescribed levels of government. For the Federal Government, the Constitution provides:

> 'Revenue' means any income or return accruing to or derived by the Government of the Federation from any source and includes (a) any receipt, however described, arising from the operation of any law; (b) any return, however described, arising from or in respect of any property held by the Government of the Federation; (c) any return by way of interest on loans, and dividends in respect of hares or interest held by the Government of the Federation in any company or statutory body (Nigeria Constitution 1989, Section 160(8).

The same section of the Constitution provides:

> The Federation shall maintain a special account to be called 'the Federation Account' into which shall be paid all revenue collected by the Government of the Federation, except the proceeds of he personal income tax from the residents of the Federal Capital Territory, Abuja (Nigerian Constitution, 1989, Section 160(1).

Thus apart from personal income tax collected from the Federal Capital Territory at Abuja, the Federal Government is enjoined not to retain as its own revenue from any of the already specified revenue sources collected by it. There is the first revenue allocation formula.

According to Item 67 of the Exclusive Legislative List (see Appendix 1), the Federal Government is responsible for the "taxation of incomes, profits and capital gains, except as otherwise prescribed by the Constitution." (Section 161 and Part II (D) of second schalme of 1989 Constitution). Concerning the States, the Constitution provides three sources of revenue:

(a) taxes imposed by the National Assembly and collectible and retainable by the states,

(b) stamp duties imposed by the State Assembly, (part II (1) of the Second Schedule of the 1979 Constitution) and

(c) share in the Federation Section 160(4) Account. (1989 Constitution)

The taxes which may be imposed to the benefit of states are taxes on capital gains and on incomes or profits of persons other than companies (company income taxation is by the Federal Government) as well as taxes on documents and transactions by way of stamp duties. (Part II (D) (9) Second Schedule of 1979 Constitution. Concerning the Local Governments, there are three sources of revenue, namely,

(a)   taxes fees, and rates which the House of Assembly of the State may make laws to enable local governments to collect,

(b)   direct share from the Federation Account, (Section 160(2) of 1989 constitution)

(c)   a share of the 'Local Governments Account' of the State "into which may be paid such funds to be applied for joint purposes as may be prescribed by the state or the National assembly. (Section 160 (5) and (6) of 1989 Constitution)

It can be seen from Appendix 3 that local governments can collect taxes and rates from items (b), (c), (d), (e), (f), (i), (j), (k), and (l) in that appendix.

Thus with regard to States, as the taxes imposed by the National Assembly to the benefit of the States is to be allocated to them on the derivation principle, considering the nature of these taxes, each State will be buoyant in revenue to the extent of the personal income of its inhabitants and the amount of unincorporated business done in it.

Table 1 shows the sources of federally collected revenue from 1988 to 1992. It will be observed that oil revenue dominated the sources to the tune of 72 to 83 per cent. One is, therefore, virtually talking of oil revenue. The other tiers of government are in the same position, being heavily dependent on oil revenue allocation from the Federation Account.

Table 1   Sources of Federally Collected Revenue 1988-1992

(₦ million)

Sources	1988	1989	1990	1991	1992	As Percentage of Total				
						1988	1989	1990	1991	1992
Oil Revenue	19,831.7	39,130.5	55,215.9	60,315.5	115,391.7	71.9	81.9	79.1	76.6	83.2
(i) Petroleum Profit Tax	6,814.4	10,598.1	13,136.6	10,053.6	17,793.0	24.7	22.2	18.8	12.8	12.8
(ii) Rent, Royalties and NNPC Earnings	13,017.3	28,532.4	42,079.3	50,261.9	85,990.7	47.2	59.7	60.3	63.9	62.0
(iii) Accretion of Oil Revenue Surplus Account	–	–	–	–	11,608.0	0.0	0.0	0.0	0.0	8.4
Non-Oil Revenue	7,763.3	8,667.8	13,362.2	18,325.2	23,225.3	28.2	18.2	19.2	23.4	16.8
(i) Company Income Tax	1,550.8	1,914.3	2,997.3	3,827.9	5,417.2	5.6	4.0	4.3	4.9	3.9
(ii) Customs and Excise Duties	5,672.0	5,815.5	8,640.9	11,456.9	16,054.8	20.6	12.2	12.4	14.6	11.6
(iii) Federal Government Independent Revenue	540.5	938.0	1,724.0	3,040.4	1,753.3	2.0	2.0	2.5	3.9	1.3
Total Federally-Collected Revenue	27,595.0	47,798.3	69,788.2	78,640.7	138,617.0	100.0	100.0	100.0	100.0	100.0

Note: The data is provisional
Source: Central Bank of Nigeria, *Annual Report and Statement of Accounts*, 1992, Table 4.2

Table 2   Allocation of Federally Collected Revenue 1988-1992

(₦ million)

	1988	1989	1990	1991	1992	*In Percentage of Total* 1988	1989	1990	1991	1992
Total Federally-Collected Revenue	27,595.0	47,798.3	69,788.2	78,640.7	138,617.0	100.0	100.0	100.0	100.0	100.0
Less										
(i) Statutory Allocation to State Government (Net)	8,332.7	10,091.1	13,509.7	15,905.1	17,403.3	30.1	21.1	19.4	20.2	12.6
(ii) Statutory Allocation to State Government (Net)	2,727.1	3,399.3	7,680.0	10,764.8	16,488.0	9.9	7.1	11.0	13.7	11.9
(iii) Transfers of Stabilisation Fund (Net)	—	8,208.1	8,411.1	21,600.3	34,665.7	0.0	—	12.1	27.1	25.0
(iv) Balance on Oil Surplus Surplus Account	—	—	—	—	2,485.6	0.0	—	—	—	1.8
Federal Government Retained Revenue	15,525.0	25,893.6	39,033.0	31,774.5	63,564.8	56.3	54.2	55.9	40.4	45.9

Note: The data is provisional
Source: Central Bank of Nigeria, *Annual Report and Statement of Accounts*, 1992, several years

Table 3   Statutory Allocation of Revenue to State Government

State			Percentage of Total	
	1991	**1992**	**1991**	**1992**
	(1)	(2)	(1)	(2)
Abia	217.6	462.1	1.4	2.7
Adamawa	217.2	598.7	1.4	3.4
Akwa Ibom	615.9	688.8	3.9	4.0
Anambra	652.3	472.5	4.1	2.7
Bauchi	638.3	664.1	4.0	3.8
Bendel	500.7	–	3.1	0.0
Benue	554.8	584.7	3.5	3.4
Borno	704.6	612.4	4.4	3.5
Cross River	517.1	535.9	3.3	3.1
Delta	251.6	535.1	1.6	3.1
Edo	201.8	486.9	1.3	2.8
Enugu	230.2	594.4	1.4	3.4
Gongola	422.9	–	2.7	0.0
Imo	768.3	566.6	4.8	3.3
Jigawa	234.4	583.0	1.5	3.3
Kaduna	505.5	593.3	3.2	3.4
Kano	946.3	804.2	5.9	4.6
Katsina	608.5	643.4	3.8	3.7
Kebbi	183.2	486.9	1.2	2.8
Kogi	197.6	550.9	1.2	3.2
Kwara	539.1	502.4	3.4	2.9
Lagos	1,348.9	624.4	8.5	3.6
Niger	542.9	513.9	3.4	3.0
Ogun	526.4	565.5	3.3	3.2
Ondo	608.2	641.8	3.8	3.7
Osun	276.3	591.5	1.7	3.4
Oyo	836.0	630.8	5.3	3.6
Plateau	538.9	613.7	3.4	3.5
Rivers	725.1	549.8	4.6	3.2
Sokoto	794.5	700.4	5.0	4.0
Taraba	–	457.3	0.0	2.6
Yobe	–	547.9	0.0	3.1
Federal Capital Territory	–	–	0.0	0.0
Total	**15,905.1**	**17,403.3**	**100.0**	**100.0**

Source: Central Bank of Nigeria, *Annual Report and Statement of Accounts,* 1992, p.65

Table 4   Statutory Allocation of Revenue to Local Government

			Percentage of Total	
State	1991	1992	1991	1992
	(1)	(2)	(3)	(4)
Abia	163.9	432.9	1.5	2.6
Adamawa	161.4	472.8	1.5	2.9
Akwa Ibom	373.6	630.0	3.5	3.8
Anambra	375.0	396.1	3.5	2.4
Bauchi	413.5	658.9	3.8	4.0
Bendel	218.9	–	2.0	0.0
Benue	365.7	488.8	3.4	3.0
Borno	417.5	563.7	3.9	3.4
Cross River	311.4	378.9	2.9	2.3
Delta	159.0	466.7	1.5	2.8
Edo	132.1	346.9	1.2	2.1
Enugu	169.6	514.0	1.6	3.1
Gongola	225.6	–	2.1	0.0
Imo	455.5	534.8	4.2	3.2
Jigawa	172.8	518.9	1.6	3.1
Kaduna	370.9	523.8	3.4	3.2
Kano	567.4	877.0	5.3	5.3
Katsina	388.4	672.4	3.6	4.1
Kebbi	140.5	408.7	1.3	2.5
Kogi	157.2	445.8	1.5	2.7
Kwara	338.1	347.3	3.1	2.1
Lagos	818.1	493.1	7.6	3.0
Niger	351.3	463.7	3.3	2.8
Ogun	322.9	436.0	3.0	2.6
Ondo	398.5	699.5	3.7	4.2
Osun	208.4	612.6	1.9	3.7
Oyo	505.3	630.1	4.7	3.8
Plateau	386.0	620.8	3.6	3.8
Rivers	348.4	579.7	3.2	3.5
Sokoto	505.3	798.9	4.7	4.8
Taraba	140.4	238.9	1.3	2.0
Yobe	137.2	378.3	1.3	2.3
Federal Capital Territory	565.0	768.0	5.2	4.7
Total	**10,764.8**	**16,488.0**	**100.0**	**100.0**

Source: Central Bank of Nigeria, *Annual Report and Statement of Accounts,* 1992, p.66

Table 5 Federal Government Expenditure (Capital and Recurrent) 1988-1992

(₦ million)

	1988	1989	1990	1991	1992	Percentage of Total*				
						1988	1989	1990	1991	1992
Administration	7,676.4	8,888.0	9,460.1	10,298.8	11,415.0	27.7	21.7	15.5	15.3	10.6
General Administration	4,755.4	5,586.3	5,521.3	5,717.2	6,568.1	17.1	13.6	9.0	8.5	6.1
Defence	1,720.1	2,219.3	2,285.2	2,711.7	2,677.1	6.2	5.4	3.7	4.0	2.5
Internal Security	1,200.9	1,082.4	1,653.6	1,869.9	2,169.8	4.3	2.6	2.7	2.8	2.0
Economic Service	3,350.0	5,345.3	5,099.4	4,448.4	4,634.2	12.1	13.0	8.3	6.6	4.3
Agric. & Natural Resources	742.9	1,885.0	1,856.2	1,427.7	1,245.1	2.8	4.6	3.0	2.1	1.2
Industry	766.3	834.7	903.9	628.1	540.1	2.8	2.0	1.5	0.9	0.5
Construction	693.6	491.0	630.4	406.8	998.1	2.5	1.2	1.0	0.6	0.9
Transport and Communication	695.5	848.3	534.7	690.4	697.5	2.5	2.1	0.8	1.0	0.7
Others	451.7	1,286.3	1,030.2	1,295.4	1,153.4	1.6	3.1	1.7	1.9	1.1
Social and Community Services	3,840.2	6,074.9	5,492.0	4,168.6	5,334.7	13.9	14.8	9.0	6.2	5.0
Education	1,786.4	3,399.0	2,819.1	1,553.3	2,414.2	6.2	8.3	4.6	2.3	2.2
Health	578.2	798.8	823.2	771.3	1,240.5	2.1	1.9	1.3	1.1	1.2
Housing and Others	1,475.3	1,879.1	1,849.7	1,844.0	1,671.0	5.3	4.6	3.0	2.7	1.6
Transfers	12,883.0	20,720.1	41,097.6	48,613.9	68,328.3	46.4	50.5	67.2	72.0	63.4
Public Debt Service	11,345.5	19,308.1	39,545.1	46,014.4	65,777.3	40.9	47.1	64.6	68.1	61.1
(i) Internal	4,338.9	6,145.0	8,689.3	10,680.2	25,015.6	15.6	15.0	14.2	15.8	23.2
(ii) External	7,006.6	13,163.1	38,855.8	35,334.2	40,761.7	25.2	32.1	63.5	52.3	37.8
Pensions and Gratuities	961.4	700.6	744.8	792.8	791.6	3.5	1.7	1.2	1.2	0.9
Others	576.1	711.4	807.7	1,806.7	1,971.6	2.1	1.7	1.3	2.7	1.5
Add. Extra Bud. Expenditure	–	–	–	–	18,011.1	–	–	–	–	16.7
TOTAL	27,749.6	41,028.2	61,149.1	67,529.7	107,723.3	100.0	100.0	100.0	100.0	100.0

Note: *The Percentages are added by us
** Percentages do not add up exactly to 100 because of sounding

Source: Central Bank of Nigeria, *Annual Report and Statement of Accounts*, 1992, Tables 4.3 and 4.4

Table 6   Application for Shares in National Oil and Chemical Marketing Company Ltd. During Privatisation

State	No. of Applications	No. of Shares	Value
Akwa Ibom	2,413	2,265,622	2,531,244
Anambra	17,824	9,498,105	18,996,210
Bauchi	344	715,312	1,430,624
Bendel	9,144	6,602,783	13,205,566
Benue	1,176	1,615,584	3,231,168
Borno	878	1,194,104	2,388,208
Cross River	935	626,626	1,253,252
FCT	21	15,587	31,174
Gongola	2,213	1,942,191	3,884,382
Imo	18,021	8,159,511	16,319,022
Kaduna	660	1,784,766	3,569,512
Kano	1,550	3,449,458	6,898,916
Katsina	748	718,250	1,436,500
Kwara	4,089	3,238,748	6,898,916
Lagos	7,435	19,946,333	39,892,666
Niger	988	676,594	1,353,188
Ogun	11,471	6,849,431	13,698,862
Ondo	6,146	4,086,363	8,172,726
Oyo	11,006	7,162,011	14,324,022
Plateau	664	1,033,369	2,066,738
Rivers	2,996	1,797,770	3,595,540
Sokoto	1,944	1,697,920	3,295,840
Total	**102,666**	**85,076,428**	**170,152,856**

Source: Third Progress Report of the Technical Committee on Privatisation and Commercialisation, *The Presidency*, Lagos, 1989, p.6

Allocation: Ground Rules

In general, revenue in a Federal Government system is allocated following the principles of responsibility, derivation and population. By 'responsibility' is meant fulfilling the responsibilities imposed on each tier of government by the Constitution and by law makers following the Constitution.

It is sometimes thought that the exclusive and concurrent lists in the Constitution impose responsibilities on the federal and state governments. This is not correct. These lists permit National and State Assemblies to make laws on certain matters. Actual governmental responsibility depends on what a government wants to do for which it seeks legislation.

Appendix 1 shows the Exclusive Legislative List. On these matters only the National Assembly may make laws for citizens and governments to obey. Actual power for the Federal Exclusive to act on these matter is given by Section 5 (1) of the Constitution. It says:

> Subject to the provisions of this Constitution, the Executive powers of the Federation (a) shall be vested in the President and may, subject as aforesaid and to the provisions of any law made by the National Assembly, and exercised by him either directly or through the Vice-President or Ministers of the Government of the Federation or other officers in the public service of the Federation, and (b) shall extend to the execution and maintenance of this constitution, all laws made by the National Assembly and all matters with respect to which the National Assembly has for the mean time power to make laws.

Similarly, the executive powers of a state are vested in the Governor who may, subject to the provisions of any law made by a House of Assembly, exercise it directly, through the Deputy Governor, or through the Commissioners or other officers in the State's public service.

Consequently, even though it is in the exclusive list, Federal Government may abandon the railways, so that only the National Assembly can legislate on matters concerning it. On the other hand, a Federal Government may decide to open new railways, aided by laws made by the National Assembly. In short, the Executive list is an enabling list, in principle giving the Federal Government legal powers to act on the subjects listed. It is not a list which imposes on the Federal Government what to do or not do, and how much to spend or not spend on the matters listed.

One observation that cannot escape attention is that the Exclusive Legislative List in the Nigerian Constitution seeks mainly controlling and regulatory powers for the Federal Government. It is difficult to deny that on the matters listed there only federal institutions should exercise jurisdiction, bearing in mind contemporary problems and the actual situation in Nigeria.

Appendix 2 is the Concurrent List. It will be observed that the aim of this list is to delimit what the Federal authorities may do in respect of the items therein. For instance, the fact that the Federal Government may take actions relating to higher and post-primary education as specified in that list does not mean that the Federal Government must take any action or that a State Government may not take any action. The word 'may' recurs throughout.

It is noteworthy that the subjects on which the development of the standard of living depends most, namely, (a) industrial, commercial and agricultural development, (b) scientific and technological research, and (c) university, technological and post – primary education, are on the concurrent list. Let us note also that residual matters, that is, matters not in the exclusive or the concurrent list, are left to the states. Technically as already observed, a weak federation is defined as one in which federal powers are limited, and powers beyond these limits belong to the States. The Nigeria federation is, therefore, a weak one.

Appendix 3 lists the functions of local governments as in the Constitution. It is for running their administrations and for performing the functions which they are empowered to perform that the revenue collectable in the country is shared among the three tiers of government.

Let us now turn to the allocation procedure. The Constitution empowers the Federal Government to retain only the personal income tax collected from residents of the Federal Capital Territory at Abuja. All other revenues collected by the Federal Government are to be paid into the Federation Account.

As to allocation from the Federation Account, the Constitution says (Section 160(2) of 1989 Constitution):

> Any amount standing to the credit of the Federation account shall be distributed among the Federal and State governments, and the Local Governments in each state. On such terms and in such manner as may be prescribed by the National Assembly.

Further, subjection (3) and (4) of section 160 of the 1989 Constitution provide:

> Any amount standing to the credit of the States in the Federation Account shall be distributed among the states on such terms and in such manner as may be prescribed by the National assembly.

So far as we have seen, for the Federation account, states are entitled to certain revenues – capital gains tax, taxes on incomes of persons or profits of enterprises other than companies, and stamp duties – which do not come from their share of the Federation Account. The Constitution enjoins that revenue from these sources should be distributed among the States on the principle of derivation. Such tax or duty can only be imposed as prescribed by the National Assembly. If a Federal agency collects it, it should give it to the State from which it derives. Section 161 of the Constitution says that where under an Act of the National Assembly tax or duty is imposed in respect of any of these matters, "the net proceeds of such tax or duty shall be distributed among the states on the basis of the principle of derivation." According, section 16 (a) provides:

> Where such tax or duty is collected by the Government of a State or other authority of the state, the net proceeds shall be treated as part of the Consolidated Revenue Fund of that State.

Section 161 (b) provides:

> Where such tax or duty is collected by the Government of the Federation or other Authority of the Federation, there shall be paid to each state... a sum equal to the proportion of the net proceeds of such tax duty that derived from that state.

Concerning Local Governments, we have seen that they have their independent sources of revenue, namely local taxes and rates. In addition, however, they receive their own direct share of the Revenue Account and grants from the State Government. They may also receive grants from the National Assembly. Sections 160 (4-7) provide thus:

> Any amount standing to the credit of Local Governments in the Federation Account shall be allocated directly to the Local Governments concerned on such terms and in such manners as may be prescribed by the National Assembly. Each State shall pay to the Local Governments in its area of jurisdiction such proportion of its revenue (excluding the sums received from the Federation Account) on such terms and in such manner as may be prescribed by the National Assembly . Each State Government and Local Governments in the State shall be paid such funds to be applied for joint purpose as may be prescribed by the State or the National Assembly. The amount standing to the credit of the Local Governments in the Local Governments account shall be distributed among the Local Government on such terms and in such manner as may be prescribed by the House of Assembly of the State.

It will be observed that at the Federal level, the revenue passed into the Federation account is allocated as prescribed by the National Assembly. On the state level, the revenue credited to local governments in the Local Governments Accounts is allocated to the local governments as prescribed by the State Assembly. Section 160 (8) of the Constitution enjoins that in exercising their powers in these matters, 'the National Assembly and the House of Assembly of each State shall... act after considering the report of the Revenue Mobilisation Allocation and Fiscal Commission (RMAFC)'.

This commission is one of fourteen 'certain Federal Executive Bodies' established under section 151 of the Constitution. They include the Code of Conduct Bureau, the Council of State, the Federal Civil Service Commission, etc. among the functions of the RMAFC defined in Section 26 of the Third Schedule of the Constitution are 'to monitor the accruals to and disbursement of revenue from the Federation account; to review from time to time the revenue allocation formulae and principles in operation to ensure conformity with changing realities; and to advise the federal, state and Local Government on fiscal efficiency and methods by which their revenue can be increased'.

The foregoing citations make clear that revenue sources are allocated by the Constitution, that the principle of deviation is recognised, and that the bulk of the revenue in the country is supposed to be allocated by the National Assembly and the State Assemblies as advised by the RMAFC.

Allocation: Proportion

As we have already remarked, mineral oil revenue dominates federally collected revenue to the tune of 72 to 83 per cent. This is unfortunate, for instead of thinking of the principles of revenue allocation, and how the country's revenue may best be increased, Nigerians are drawn into the static framework of debating how 'fairly' to allocate revenue which is practically from one natural source, oil, and also from foreign investment and activity.

The actual allocation of federally collected revenue during 1988 to 1992 is shown in *Table 2*. We see that in that period the percentage share of the Federal Government ranged from 55.9 to 40.4 with a tendency to fall, that of the states from 30.1 to 12.6 with a declining tendency, and that of Local Government from 7.1 to 13.7 with a tendency to rise.

It is clear that the percentages used for allocation to States and Local Government changed from year to year. In 1991 the Federal, State and Local Governments were supposed to receive 50 and 15 per cent respectively of federally collected revenue. In 1992, the respective percentages were supposed to be 48.5, 24 and 20. In 1994 the State and Local Governments were expected to be allocated 24 and 20 per cent respectively of the 86.3 billion Naira was expected to accrue to the Federation Account. In 1994 the new tax, value-added tax (VAT), was expected to bring in a handsome yield and of this 80 per cent was to be allocated to the States.

Although the States have sources of current revenue, independent of the

Federation account, *Table 7* shows that these sources contributed only 18 to 21 per cent of the current revenues of states in the 1988 – 1990 period. The position in subsequent years is known to be the same. The detailed allocation of revenue from the Federation accounts in 1991 and 1992 is shown in *Table 3* and the allocation to Local Governments States in those years in shown in *Table 4*.

Question of Rationale

As we have seen, in a Federal set-up revenue is normally allocated in consideration of the responsibilities of the various tiers of government, derivation and population.

If we look at responsibility, as we have observed, there is no subject in the exclusive list which ought to be left to the states. There is also no area in the concurrent list that the Federal Government should not participate in regulating, controlling or developing.

Table 7   Dependence of States on Statutory Allocation

(₦ million)

				Percentage of Current Revenue		
	1988	**1989**	**1990**	**1988**	**1989**	**1990**
Current Revenue	10,360.1	11,502.1	16,516.5	100.0	100.0	100.0
(i) Statutory Allocation	8,181.3	9,899.8	13,509.7	79.0	86.1	81.8
(ii) Internal Revenue	2,178.8	1,602.3	3,006.8	21.0	13.9	18.2

Note: The percentages are added by us

Source: Central Bank of Nigeria, *Annual Report and Statement of Accounts*, 1990

Table 6 shows the distribution of Federal Government capital and recurrent in the years, 1988 to 1992. We see there that Federal expenditure is concentrated on vital federal services. Even things as important as agriculture and natural resource preservation and development and manufacturing, mining and quarrying together received only 5.6 per cent in 1986, this declined to 4.5 per cent in 1990, 3 per cent in 1991 and 1.7 per cent in 1992.

Even if federal expenditure were concentrated exclusively on areas where the Federal Government must operate, such as defence and internal security, it would not be able to save much revenue for distribution to other tiers of government. To show this, we present *Table 8*, which is extracted from *Table 5* and which shows proportions of Federal Government expenditure on areas which are entirely unavoidable.

The Table shows that if the Federal Government were to abandon all its other services except the ones listed in it, it would still need as much as 70 per cent or more of the total it spends. In some areas, such as education and health, the Federal Government is far from doing enough as matters stand. This is reflected in *Table 5 and 8*. The proportion of Federal expenditure devoted to debt services alone, which in the 1990s come to more that 60 per cent of total Federal expenditure, should be observed. As can be seen from both *Table 5* and *8*, the Federal Government is squeezing vital areas in order to be able to service debts. Yet unless the debts are repudiated they have to be serviced. We have been looking at selected vital areas, but no rational consideration would conclude that the Federal Government can and should abandon its services in the other areas.

Let us turn to the principle of derivation. We have seen that this principle is indeed applied. The scope of its application is defined by the 1989 Constitution. Is this scope rational? We argue that it is.

Table 8   Federal Government Expenditure in Selected Areas 1988-1992

	(Percentages)				
	1988	**1989**	**1990**	**1991**	**1992**
Defence	6.2	5.4	3.7	4.0	2.5
Internal Security	4.3	2.6	2.7	2.8	2.0
Transport and Communication	2.5	2.1	0.8	1.0	0.7
Education	6.4	8.3	4.6	2.3	2.2
Health	2.1	1.9	1.3	2.7	1.6
Public Debt Service	40.9	47.1	64.6	68.1	61.1
Pensions and Gratuities	3.5	1.7	1.2	1.2	0.9
Total	65.9	69.1	78.9	80.3	71.2

Table 1 shows that practically, the Federally collected revenue came from petroleum profit tax; the rent royalties and earnings of the Nigerian National Petroleum Company income tax, and customs and excise duties. Federally

independent revenue is a very small source.

For this reason the Mineral Ordinance, the Crown Lands Ordinance and the Public Land Acquisition Ordinance were passed and all the land in northern Nigeria was moved by the Nigerian government, for a similar reason.

The question arises concerning which of the main resources can be handed over to states on the principle of derivation. Under British colonialism minerals belonged to the Nigerian government and its regions and provinces. The basic reasons for this were three. First, expatriates controlled the activities of the companies that were actually mining minerals. Secondly, the revenue from royalties and the taxation of these companies could help enormously to open up a very underdeveloped country where the tax paying capacity of the indigenous inhabitants was extremely low. Thirdly, the colonial government wanted to avoid sectional or private claims to land, minerals and waterway standing in the way of the development of the country. It, therefore, decided to own the minerals and to have the right to take any land for public purposes. All these reasons for the ownership of minerals by the Federal Government apply today with as much force as during colonial rule. Besides, it is the Nigerian government that had to create and created all the ports, major roads, railways and postal and telecommunication links that made mining activity possible. It was entitled to a share in the income of the companies.

The foregoing reasons apply also to company income tax. The substantial companies existing in Nigeria are expatriate. Appropriate national conditions have to be created for them. Their earnings are a vital source of government revenue in an economy that is very much underdeveloped and had a poor national tax base. The Federal Government deserves compensation for its role in creating the infrastructure which the companies use. It is an important argument that what we need to create is a national market and not a segmented one.

The principle of derivation should actually apply to taxes on income and wealth arising from the activities of the population of an area and not expatriate activity which is not theirs or renter income from minerals or forests which they did not create. It is for this reason that it was correct to apply the principle of derivation to taxes on cocoa, palm produce, groundnuts, cotton, rubber and the like in the 1950s and 1960s. Income from these activities comes from the work of the local people of the area. Mineral royalties or taxes on the activities of expatriate companies of Nigerian companies that operate nationwide is a different matter.

As per the 1989 constitution, the derivation principle still exists, and it applies to items to which it should apply by economic logic. The real problem is not any abrogation of the derivation principle but the fact that taxable income from the activities which derivation rightly applies and used to apply has stagnated whereas both Federal and State expenditure has greatly expanded, having been boosted enormously by the explosion in oil exports in the 1970s.

Table 9   Comparison of Government Revenue Sources

Percentage of	Federal (£000) 1963/64	Federal & State (£000) 1963/64	1992	Federal (N=million) 1992		Total
	(1)	(2)		(3)		
Oil Revenue						
(i) Petroleum Profit Tax	-	-	17,793	-	-	14.0
(ii) Rent, royalties and NNPC Earnings	-	-	85.991	-	-	67.7
Non-Oil Revenue						
Individual direct Taxes		2,028	10,1061	-	8.5	
Company Income Tax	5,409	5,409	5,417	8.9	4.6	4.3
Customs and Excise	45,295	91,110	16,055	74.2	76.8	12.6
Independent Revenue	8,298	11,983	1,753	13.6	10.1	1.4
TOTAL	61.030	111,601	127,099	100,00	100.0	100.0

Note: Independent Revenue is derived from interest, royalties rents and Profits
Source: Federal Office of Statistics, Annual Abstract of Statistics, 1966, and Central Bank of Nigeria, Annual Report and Statement of Accounts, 1992

Table 9 shows that in the 1960s mineral oil revenue was not even important enough to be listed separately in the government accounts. Then both the Federal and the Regional governments depended to the tune of around 75 percent on customs and excise taxes formed no more than 12.6 per cent of Federal Government revenue.

Let us now turn to the population principle. This principle is adopted because of the responsibility of the Federation to all its citizens. Population is responsible for the fact that Imo, Kano, Lagos, Oyo and Sokoto states consistently received larger allocations compared with, say, Edo, Kebbi and Kogi states. This is true of the allocation to the Local Governments in the states as well. These facts are shown in *Tables 3* and *4*.

Question of Justice

The contention is often heard that existing allocation is unjust. This position is taken on three grounds. The first is that oil producing activity destroys the land and fishing grounds available for use in the oil-producing areas, depriving the people there of their means of livelihood. The second is that oil itself is a wasting asset. As exploitation in Nigeria also wastes the natural gas resource available along with oil, some years from now, these resources will no longer be available and the populations of the areas where they occur would have lost a rich source of potential development for good. The last is that when oil was not available, revenue was allocated to the states on the principle of derivation. It is often alleged that the supposed abandonment of this principle occurred because the oil is found very largely outside the territories of the major ethnic groups, or that it is due to the conspiracy of the non-oil-producing states.

We shall deal first with the last allegation. We have already seen that the derivation principle has not been abandoned and that it applies to tax revenue to which it did and should apply. The fact that oil leads to ecological losses for people in the oil-producing areas is an indefensible case for adequate compensation. It is widely observed that the compensation as currently paid are far from sufficient to offset the losses. However, while the people of the actual oil-producing areas are entitled to such compensatory payments, the whole state where oil is found is not so entitled, since the inhabitants of such a state other than in the oil areas lose nothing.

The argument about oil being a wasting asset is cogent, but again rightly applies to the people whose land and fishing grounds are adversely affected by oil activities. Despite the derivation of oil from these areas, in terms of development, they are conspicuous by the lack of attention paid them by the oil firms and the Federal Government. It is unfair, it is rightly urged, to use revenue from these areas to develop, say, Abuja, Lagos and Kano, while the area is neglected.

The arguments about non-compensation and developmental neglect necessitate the setting up of a special fund and agency for dealing adequately with these matters. They do not justify a change in the general allocation arrangements which will permit the handing over of petroleum revenue to oil areas embracing states whose governments may pay no more attention to the compensation and development of the people of the oil-producing areas than now do the oil companies and the Federal Government. The same argument applies to mineral-producing activities generally.

It must be pointed out, however, that the argument that the people of the oil areas be adequately compensated for loss and that their development be adequately attended to is at bottom a humane, or socialist one. It is based on the general case against exploitation of the people, inequality or uneven development. On capitalist grounds there is no case for compensation, and there is no basis for insisting on developing the people of an area from which resources are taken.

The oil companies neglect the oil areas that they despoil and destroy because this is what capitalist firms do all over the world. Capitalism is a system in which capitalists shift losses to society or the weak in order to enhance profits. The question of environment and what economists call 'externalities' (Koutsoyianis, 1978: pp.541-549; and Russell and Wilkinson, 1979: pp.375-387) have become acute in Europe and North America because of the ruin and the carefree exhaustion of society's natural resources brought about by capitalist activity (Panayotou, n.d.).

This point deserves a little more attention. If it is capitalism that Nigerian leaders will continue to build, the oil areas have no argument except it is based on the reversal of this course. Regarding productive property, orthodox capitalist economic theory either assumes that people are simply 'endowed' with the property they happen to own at any time or that capital comes from the saving of the capitalist (Green, 1977: pp.21-35). In that case, either we do not enquire into how people come by property or whatever the evidence, we assume it to arise from their own abstinence from consumption.

Moreover, capitalist theory is oblivious of the social cost of capitalist activity, because it is an individualistic theory in which the firm is doing very well if it simply minimises its own costs to boost its own profits, whatever happens to parties external to it.

We know, however, that under capitalism, property is possessed by the process of *dispossessing* peasants and the society as well as by accumulating at the expense of workers and the society. We know also that the process by which capital is accumulated inflicts costs on other individuals and society which capitalists cannot bother about because their goal of activity is simply profit.

Economic justice consists in making the whole of society own the property on which the lives of its members depend and making the individual who works alone for a living own the property on which his life depends. Economic justice consists also in not allowing privilege or bargaining power position which permit anyone exploit another.

The argument for justice has to be generalised and not restricted to the oil case. After all, coal, tin, etc. were used for developing Nigeria in general and, in accordance with the capitalist logic of capitalist colonialism, no one cared for the social cost and injustices of resource exploitation. Similarly, if the development of capitalism continues, more communities will suffer in future and the oil areas will never have the compensation they deserve.

It is true that it is unjust from the human standpoint to impoverish the people of an area or deprive them of natural resources in the area in which they have settled, in order to develop capitalists elsewhere. However, capitalist logic is the law of the jungle. Each one grabs what he can.

Behind Redivision Cries

There are three basic reasons why the issue of revenue allocation recurs. The first is that Nigeria was originally administered as a unitary polity. The second is the uneven development of the country and people's general anxiety about the future in a grabbing system. The third is the ambitions of the grabbers and the politicisation of these ambitions. What are the roots of continual dissension?

Since Nigeria was first administered as a unitary system, the question of how to share revenue tends to recur, especially as the society is not standing quite still, so that income-producing endowments change over time and regimes and leaders come and go with little or no legitimacy (Toyo, 1994: p.22-26). The country which British colonialism left was unevenly developed. The whole country was underdeveloped, but some areas were less developed than others. Some parts of the country had the benefit of towns, roads, post offices, electricity, hospitals, secondary schools, etc. while other areas did not. Since the whole population is now very conscious of the effects of roads, post offices, hospitals, schools, factories, etc., there is an intense concern for not being ignored or left behind. This is so at the regional, state and local levels.

Table 6 presents indicators that reflect the extent of uneven development already existing in the country. In this illustration, which is typical of the pattern of application for the shares of the privatised companies, if we exclude the Federal Capital Territory of Abuja, the difference in the aggregate values of share applied for state by state range from about 1.2 million Naira in the case of the Cross River State to about 40 million Naira in the case of Lagos state. There is not doubt that to have a peaceful or united country such gross inequality has to be removed. A thoughtful allocation of the oil revenue and a judicious and productive use of its share by the Federal Government are among the ways of doing so.

The third cause of the vitality of revenue allocation is primitive capitalist accumulation. This is the process by which capitalism actually grows in any country. What may be called the first generation of capitalists acquired money capital by the transfer of income from non-businessmen to the businessmen. This happens through unequal exchange which favours middlemen of various sorts; through the monetisation of land and its transfer to money owners; through inflationary processes by which non-traders are deprived in favour of traders; through government contracts and direct or indirect loans; through infrastructural investments and subsidies to business enterprises; through the sale of government property which the businessmen themselves could not have developed; and through peculation which involves the appropriation of government property or income by fraud and other venal practices.

Primitive accumulation is a ruthless grabbing process with no rules. The accumulators are forever at one another's throat. 'The nation' is seen by them as a cake to be shared or a carcass to fight over as well as a battle ground for the sharing battles. Government is a theatre of power-sharing contest and manipulation. Revenue re-allocation is one of the bones of contention in the political and economic contests of the accumulators who claim to represent regional, ethnic and state interests. A lot of ethnic chauvinism in general and revenue allocation chauvinism in particular is the result. There is much ethnic or regional talk about 'injustice', 'deprivation' or marginalisation'. What is true is the masses everywhere want progress and desire equality, but more often than not the chief agitators for so-called 'justice' when it comes to power and revenue sharing are the perpetrators of injustice. It is not ghosts that practise injustices in Nigeria; it is real bourgeois persons with material bourgeois ambitions, and they do so in all ethnic areas.

The power-sharing contestants in the name of 'justice' have claimed that the Federal Government is too powerful and the states too weak. Such a claim is urged when no distinction is made between the Federal Government as defined in the various Constitutions of Nigeria and the Federal Government under military rule. Military rule is necessarily unitary and centralised. Out of thirty-three years of independence twenty-four have been taken up by military and the military authoritarianism continues. Federalism had not been given the chance to operate for more than two brief periods in Nigeria. It had been frustrated both by the vandalism of bourgeois primitive accumulation and its politics and by military opportunism or praetorians. The authors of the revenue allocation provisions in the 1989 Constitution approached the matter democratically, realistically and dynamically. The approach is democratic because the allocation of the bulk of revenue receipts is done by the National Assembly for revenue deposited in the Federation Account and by the State Assembly for Local Governments in the case of the revenue in the Consolidated Revenue account of the state. The National and State Assemblies are supposed to be democratically elected. The approach is realistic because it enjoins the National Assembly and the State Assemblies to seek the information and advice of the technical body for the purpose set up by the Constitution, namely, the Revenue

Mobilisation Allocation and Fiscal Commission.

The approach is dynamic because it recognises that the same formula cannot be used at all times, since circumstances change. This is one reason why revenue allocation has to be a continuing exercise rather than a once and for all affair. This also is one reason for setting up the RMAFC in the first place and for requiring consultation with it. It is the reason, moreover, for providing that the National and State Assemblies should explore new revenue possibilities as circumstances change and for giving the RMAFC the task of research and advice in this regard.

Revenue allocation can only be fruitfully looked at in the context of a united country. In this context, the provisions must be credited with being thoughtful.

Direction and Resource Use

The question of whether Nigeria is to continue to develop capitalistically or otherwise cannot be postponed until one had decolonised, developed, democratised or unified the country, for the basic issues of decolonisation, development, democracy or unity are tied up with the answer we give to the question of the overall social direction.

If Nigeria is to continue to develop capitalistically, the following are the implications. In respect of decolonisation and development, it should be understood that the *underdevelopment* of existing underdeveloped countries is not the same thing as low level of modernisation. It involves a situation in which this low level arises from a particular international division of labour stemming from the incorporation of the underdeveloped countries in the system of world capitalist imperialism with the many consequences of this (Jenkins, 1977: pp.132-147). It involves a situation in which underdevelopment is not only a level of existence of so-called underdevelopment indicators, not only an international situation, but also a process.

It is the process in which the underdevelopment situation perpetuates itself through certain forms of capital accumulation and the politics associated with them. In other words, it is a self-reproducing phenomenon.

It is in the interest of advanced capitalist countries which dominate the capitalist world economy that the conditions defining underdevelopment should remain, hence the emergence of colonialism and policies to perpetuate it. So long as capitalism and its neo-colonial manifestation continue, the mineral oil will never benefit principally the people of the areas where oil is found. Development implies as one of its definitive aspects the modernisation of productive forces. In terms of productive forces, modern development is industrialisation. Industrialisation involves the establishment and mastering of the production processes of basic machine-using industries, namely, machine making, iron-and-steel, non-ferrous metallurgy, power, chemical, and construction material industries. It is more beneficial to use the resources of the country integrally for such a development than to fight over the use of it for the importation and consumption of goods produced by modern economies.

One point that needs to be stressed here is that the stand-point of the power sharers is static. If the correct industrialisation direction is adopted the oil revenue will have its potentially great effects on the development of productive forces in industry, agriculture and export. In this way the non-oil revenue base will be revolutionary and enormously enlarged.

This is the really reasonable solution. Europe, Japan and even the oil-rich United States of America have enormous taxable non-oil income and wealth because of their industrialisation.

Table 10 shows the main current revenue sources of the Federal Government of the U.S.A. in 1986 and the proportion of receipts contributed by each source.

Table 10   Receipts of the U.S. Federal Government 1986

Source	Per cent Distribution
Individual Income Taxes	45.52
Corporation Income Taxes	9.12
Social Insurance Taxes and Contributions	36.08
Excise Taxes	4.45
Customs Duties	1.60
Miscellaneous Receipts	2.44

Source: Statistical Abstract of the United States, 1987

Individual income taxes and social insurance taxes and contribution together accounted for 81.6 per cent of the revenue, the same percentage as mineral oil revenue to the Nigerian Federal Government in 1992, Which was also 81.7 per cent as shown in *Table 9.*

It is clear that proper industrialisation will develop the country and her states and the Local Government Areas rapidly and, correspondingly, their tax bases. The basic industries can be much more easily created by the Federal Government. For their creation the Iron Ore deposits are as important as oil.

It follows that Nigeria should use oil earnings to offset the neocolonial handicap, but this is not the way power sharers view the matter. Their static cake-sharing outlook and their parasitism paralyse the country over which they struggle. We have in consequence instead of development an unwarranted vicious circle of underdevelopment in a country naturally well endowed.

In terms of democratisation, capitalism is not really a democratic system. It is a system where those who can grab money have the real power and those who can grab power use it to accumulate money. In essence we have in capitalism the dictatorship of those with money power. Therefore, there can never be any democracy in the ultimate sharing of the wealth and income effect of oil exploitation, or the exploitation of any other mineral resource in Nigeria, so long as the direction of motion is capitalistic.

Unity is valuable for development which can benefit not only Nigerian citizens but also the people of Africa and men and women of African descent who suffer from many disabilities. However, unity implies the absence of exploitation and the eradication of inherited inequalities. Both requirements are contradicted by capitalism. Because it is exploitative, it promotes disagreements, rancour and conflicts rather than unity. Because it is self-centred and oriented on private profits, it leaves historically inherited social inequalities unattended to.

Suppose one takes the non-exploitative course, then the use of the oil revenue can play a unifying rather than divisive role. It will play that role if it is used by a people-oriented and fully democratic government that genuinely seeks to develop the people everywhere - including first and foremost the people in the oil producing areas. Working people will be satisfied with living comfortably or at least having their basic needs met. They will be satisfied when they see that a consumate effort is being made in this direction and that there is no parasitism. It is the injustices generated by a parasitic course and parasitic leadership that is responsible for the frustrations felt over the allocation of oil or any other substantial revenue.

Conclusion

As we said at the beginning, the main purpose of this discourse is to inform in order, hopefully, to save society from the often costly consequences of error. Naturally, we could not refrain from drawing conclusions warranted by the findings of our factual investigation. If federalism will really be practised in an authentic way, if the provisions of the 1989 Constitution are given a chance, if oil revenue will be used to industrialise the country thus creating the potential for a large and expanding non-oil revenue, and if a humane, genuinely democratic and non-exploitative course is followed revenue allocation will be removed from acrimony. The first requirement is a people-oriented leadership. What has to end immediately is a parasitic leadership that believes in a predatory society. Such a society contradicts the growing humane conscience of contemporary times which is the product of growing education, interdependence and knowledge. It is thus filled with frustration and crisis prone.

References

Green, Francis and Nore, Peter (1977), (eds), *Economics: An Anti-Text.* The Macmillan Press.

Jenkis, Rhys (1977), 'Underdevelopment' in Green, Francis and Nore, Peter (1977) (eds), *Economics: An Anti-Text.* Macmillan Press.

Kousoyianis, A. (1978), *Modern Microeconomics.* The Macmillan Press, London: Second edition.

Panayotou, Theodore, Green Markets (n.d.), *The Economics Sustainable Development.* The Institute For Contemporary Studies, San Francisco, Califonia, U.S.A.

Russell, R.R, and M. Wilkinson (1979), *Micro-Economics.* New York and Toronto.

The 1979 Constitution of the Federal Republic of Nigeria with Amendments.

The 1989 Constitution of the Federal Republic of Nigeria with Amendments.

Toyo, Eskor (1994), *Crisis and Democracy in Nigeria.* Zaria: Ahmadu Bello University Press.

5 Oil and the Minority Question

CYRIL I. OBI

Introduction: An Historical Overview

Long before oil became the economic mainstay and fiscal basis of the Nigerian state, the Minority Question in Nigerian politics had fuelled separatist tendencies' (Tamuno, 1970; Osaghae, 1986) among the diverse (more than 250) ethnic nationalities that made up the country. Thus, the emergence of the minority question is organically linked to the creation of Nigeria as a colonial state (Mustapha, 1986; Nnoli, 1978) by British imperialism. Nigeria's forcible integration into the international capitalist system became more pronounced after the creation of the three regions in the mid-1940s. The imposition of colonialism as a political form of subordination facilitated the arrest of competing indigenous pre-capitalist modes of production in Nigeria. As pointed out elsewhere:

> The political economy of British Imperialism had the following effects: the creation of a centralised stateform for diverse groups of peoples with equally diverse cultures, historical experiences and stages of development; the manipulation of these diversities by the British to prevent any form of unity or national integration, thus preserving the contradiction between the colonial state and the 'new' Nation. (Obi and Soremekun, *forthcoming*).

The contradiction between the colonial state and the 'new' Nigerian nation articulated itself, not only in the form of inter-group relations, majority-minority group relations, but more fundamentally over the political contestation for access to resources within the colonial political economy. Capturing the connection between the creation of the colonial state and the evolution of ethnic nationalities, Ikime observes, that:

> ... Nationalities began to identify themselves as such first in the context of the colonial state, and then in the context of the Nigerian multinational state, as they were forced by changing circumstances of history to act politically in defence of their perceived interests vis à vis the interests of other competing groups. (Ikime, 1986)

The politicisation of inter-ethnic group relations often referred to as the national question,' is tied to the social relations spawned by the mode of colonial capitalist accumulation and the inequalities sown between ethnic groups by the differential rate of capitalist penetration. In terms of the patron-client relations that sustained this mode of peasant expropriation, and unequal trade, the majority ethnic groups using the advantage of demography and 'acting politically', were able to marginalise the other competing minority ethnic groups within the framework of the three regions: Northern, Eastern and Western. Since each of the three regions in Nigeria coincided with a majority ethnic nationality, it established a basis for future distrust, fear of domination and instability in the Nigerian federation.

Due to the relative scarcity of resources available to Nigerians under colonial rule, the effects of regionalism and the manipulation of the factors of language, culture and religion, the premium on the monopoly of power by dominant groups at the expense of smaller ones grew, and with it, the tendency for the losers to want to opt out of a 'contract of perpetuity in inequality', and that of the winners to prevent their exit. In order to protect themselves, the minorities sought self-determination through the creation of autonomous regions or states based on ethnic identity or the institutionalisation of equality, social justice and equity as the tenets of inter-group relations within the context of Nigerian federalism.

According to Akinyele (1992), minority protests in Nigeria since 1900 had always been centred on the issues of self-determination, equity, representative bureaucracy and accelerated or even development. While minority agitation appeared uncoordinated it nonetheless had an early regional character. In the northern region, it took the form of the agitation of the ethnic minorities of southern Zaria, and the Middle Belt (the Tiv in particular) while in the West, it involved the non-Yoruba, ethnic minorities (Edo, Ishan, Urhobo, Itshekiri, Western Ibo, Etsako) and that of the east comprised the Efik, Ijaw, Ogoja and other non-Ibo ethnic nationalities. Their agitation became more organised in the decade before independence when the minorities formed political movements to demand for states of their own:

> Three important movements emerged to champion the interests of the minorities. These were the Calabar Ogoja-Rivers State Movement in the Eastern Region, the Benin-Delta State Movement (later changed to Midwest) in the Western Region and the Middle Belt Movement affecting the Northern Region. (Olusanya, 1980: p. 541)

As a result of the activities of these organisations, the minority question could not be sidetracked during the constitutional talks on the transfer of power from Britain to Nigeria in the second half of the 1950's. As such, the Willink Commission was set up to inquire into the fears of the Minorities about Majority domination, what could be done to allay such fears, and what constitutional checks could be designed to forestall future domination of minorities in an independent Nigeria. In 1958, the Willink Commission in its report did confirm the use of physical force by the Majority ethnic group-dominated political parties (who were in power at the regional level). It also among other things reported that 'no regional government secure in the majority would pay attention to criticism or attempt to meet the wishes of the minorities.' It however doubted if the creation of states could resolve the minority question.

Rather than resolve the minority question, the Nigerian nationalist elite anxious to step into the shoes of the departing colonial authorities and Imperial Britain decided to sweep the complaints of the ethnic minorities under the carpet. This was typical of the Patron-client networks, that had been built up between Britain and the 'Big-three' ethnic groups during colonial rule. Thus, the minority question was buried under constitutional niceties and a clause providing that a state could be created if it met the requirement of a two-third majority in the Federal legislature and was approved by a simple majority in two regions. In this way, the minorities were placed at the mercy of the ethnic majority groups in independent Nigeria. That way their 'freedom' could only come through the 'benevolence' of the numerically superior and politically dominant majority groups. With specific regard to the Niger delta, provision was made for the creation of a Nigeria Delta Development Board to allay the fears of the minorities there, and attend to their peculiar developmental needs. However, after independence in 1960, the board never took off and the people continued to suffer under the yoke of the dominant regional group.

It was therefore hardly surprising that minority discontent and agitation found expression in the politically volatile First Republic. As Ikime recalls;

> In the struggle and acrimony the small groups came in for little consideration. In the early years of independence our leaders played the game in a manner which far from fostering a spirit of commitment to the newly independent state, produced considerable alienation on the part of the many groups that felt cheated both politically and economically. (Ikime, 1986)

Thus, in the 1960s some of the minority groups resorted to violence in the political contest against majority hegemony, and domination. In all cases rather than assuage the fears of the minorities, the regional and federal governments either 'resorted to the use of state violence and repression', (Obi and Soremekun, 1993) or sought to buy out leading activists or figures in the minorities movement with 'tantalising crumbs of office without their ethnic groups necessarily benefiting as groups'. The use of armed troops and police to quell the Tiv rebellion and the abortive Delta Peoples Republic secessionist bid were entirely in character with intergroup political relations in the First Republic. As part of the strategy of narrowing the political base of the opposition party the Action Group which was in power in the Western Region, the Northern Peoples Congress controlled federal government (the NPC also controlled the Northern Region) and National Council of Nigerian Citizens controlled Eastern Region colluded to carve out a state for the minorities of the West, and named it the Midwest Region. The AG on its own part built bridgeheads into the minority areas of the north and east by supporting states' creation movements (and opposition parties) in those regions, and causing considerable discomfort to its political rivals.

The fear of regional ethnic hegemons and the resort to force by the Minorities in their quest for self-determination grew as the political crisis of the First Republic deepened. In February 1965, a UMBC activist Isaac Shaahu, was openly reported as advocating for Tiv secession. (Tamuno, 1970). A year later, Isaac Boro, Sam Owonaro and Nottingham Dick, all Ijaws, led an abortive attempt to forcibly secede from Nigeria and create a Delta Peoples Republic. According to Tamuno:

> They feared that the establishment of the Ironsi regime, strongly supported
> by Ibos, prejudiced the long standing demand for the creation of a River
> State, an agitation which had begun seriously in the late 1940. (Ibid)

The minority question also featured during the political crisis that eventually grew into the Nigerian civil war. Shortly before the outbreak of hostilities in 1967, Gowon who had come to power at the federal level a year earlier, replaced the four regions with a twelve-state structure. The minorities of the Eastern Region, got two states thereby satisfying to some extent their age-old quest for self-determination, while at the same time weakening Ojukwu's base in his secessionist bid. Since this period also coincided with the period when oil exports were beginning to have an appreciable impact on the country's balance of payments profile, the oil producing minorities of the Niger delta aligned with the federal side to stave off 'Biafran' claims to the oil fields, hoping to seize the opportunity to gain access to the oil wealth as sons and daughters' of the delta.

When the Nigerian civil war ended in 1970s the oil minorities discovered to their chagrin, that the over-concentration of power and resources at the centre (Obi and Soremekun, forthcoming) provided whoever held power at the federal level the capacity to control and transfer resources, in this case oil wealth, from the minorities to the majority ethnic nationalities. In spite of the creation of states and the onset of an oilboom, the ethnic minorities discovered that the locus of power had merely shifted from the old regions to the federal government which was still dominated by the 'big three.' Thus the calculation of the oil minorities faction of the Nigerian ruling class that the creation of states meant that the majority ethnic groups were now excluded from direct access to their oil wealth, and they, who owned the land, would now have exclusive control of the oil turned out to be totally wrong. By the enactment of Decree 51 of 1969, the Federal government legislated the monopoly of the collection and sharing of all oil revenue to itself. (Obi and Soremekun, forthcoming) The monopoly was further extended by Decree 9 to include all off-shore oil revenue from oil wells located in the coastal waters adjoining the oil producing minority states. The implication of this development is well captured by Williams when he notes that:

> ... The dependence of the oil producing states for their very existence on Federal Military power and the defeat of Biafran claims to the oilfields, enabled the Federal Government to appropriate an increasing share of oil revenue and control the allocation of the remainder to the states. (Williams, 1981)

In order to concretise its monopoly of oil revenues the Federal Government changed the basis of the Revenue Allocation formula from Derivation (which had benefitted the hegemonic nationalities in the old regions) in favour of the principles of equality and the population of states (Obi, 1988; Onah, 1983) (which again benefitted the big ethnic nationalities), thereby shutting off, and alienating the oil producing minorities from any direct access to oil – the new wealth of the Nation.

> Clearly, the new principles were a response to the change in the shift of the wealth of the Nation from agriculture to oil, and the desire by the hegemonic faction of the Ethnic Majorities to continue to retain the larger chunk of national revenue. These moves further marginalised the oil-producing ethnic minority states who saw in these changes in inter-governmental revenue sharing in Nigeria, a ploy to deny them the benefits of the oil produced from their ancestral lands and waters and perpetuate their marginalization and exploitation within the Nigerian nation. This served to exacerbate contradictions between the oil-producing nationalities and majority nationalities in Nigeria.(Adedotun, 1991; Obi and Soremekun, forthcoming)

The immersion of oil in the minority question has brought the struggle of the oil minorities to the fore of the national question in Nigerian politics. This is not an attempt to deny or downplay the role of other minorities in their struggles for self-determination, democracy and social justice in Nigeria. What one intends to do in this chapter, is to focus primarily on the oil minorities due to their strategic linkage with oil, and the growing intensity of their struggle, what it portends for the nation-state project in Nigeria. This has become more relevant in a context where oil is both the mainstay of the economy (accounting since the 1970s for over 80 percent of government revenues and 90 percent of Nigeria's foreign exchange earnings), and the fiscal basis of the state. Oil is also central to the rentier state's capacity to reproduce its brand of patrimonialism, perpetuate its monopolistic political practices and oil-based accumulation. This brings out clearly the strategic importance of the oil economy to the national question and the ongoing struggles between those who control and reap the gains from oil, and those whose access to it has been blocked.

The economic and debt crisis whose immediate (but not fundamental) roots lie in the collapse of global oil prices in the late 1970s and early 1980s exposed the fragile economic basis of the Nigerian nation and its unity. Militarism, the worsening of the economic situation and shrinking oil revenues have caused increased tensions and the worsening of relations between the oil Minorities and the federal government:

> With the deepening of economic crisis, continued devastation of the oil-producing environment, and increasing federal expropriation of oil rents, have grown calls by the Minorities for a redress in the distribution of oil rents and inter-nationality relations within Nigeria. Thus oil, and the distribution of oil revenues between and among the diverse Nationalities that make up Nigeria in a manner that is just, equitable and fair has become a central issue in the on-going struggles over oil. The oil minorities have become united around the issues of: equity, fairness, justice and the right to self determination in the struggle against federal (and by implication majority nationality) hegemony and appropriation of oil revenues. (Obi and Soremekun, forthcoming)

These struggles have reached an unprecedented pitch since 1990 in the form of massive protests in the Niger delta, the emergence of a new brand of community activism and militancy led by pressure groups and popular movements, the emergence of very vocal spokespersons and groups of the oil minorities who have not only acted nationally, but have also taken their case to international fora. (Obi, 1997; 1999) These groups have drawn up Charters of Demands and Bills of Rights insisting on the right to self-determination, a derivation-based redress in Nigeria's fiscal federalism and adequate compensation for and restoration of the oil producing environment whose devastation by the producing companies strikes at the very core of the people's basis of existence and livelihood. Also, there have been demands for the restructuring of the Nigerian federation 'on the basis of the principles of true federalism'. (Obi and Soremekun, forthcoming)

With the deepening of the National crisis and the shrinking of national oil revenue, the response of the Federal Government to the legitimate demands of the oil minorities has ranged from attempts to co-opt leaders of the struggle, to offering some tokens of 'development' the use of state violence and repression (such as the establishment of Oil Minerals Producing Areas Development Commission, OMPADEC, in 1992, and which has collapsed, and the more recent attempts at setting up a Niger Delta Development Commission, NNDC, in 1999). Most fundamental is the perpetuation of the marginalisation of oil minorities from political and economic power-at-the-centre, and the dependence of oil producing states on the federal government which more than ever before guards its monopoly of oil rents.

What the preceding has shown is that so far, reforms in Nigeria's federal experiment have failed to address the oil minority question. More than ever before, the oil factor has sharpened the contradictions in majority-minority relations, with adverse implications for the nation-state project in Nigeria. It also should be noted that oil manifests in strong terms the centrality of the economy from: who gets what, when and how much, and to the national question. One cannot but agree with the position that the present situation of inequality of access (Osuntokun, 1986) to the national oil wealth by the constituent nationalities of Nigeria can only lead to distrust, fear, more intense struggles and further crises.

The Conceptual Issues

The conceptual issues include the minority question, the national question and the state-rentier economy nexus. In dealing with these, there is need for a materialist interpretation of social reality and a holistic treatment of the various factors in the development of society. (Aina, 1989) Through it, the conceptual issues become well grounded in terms of their analytical fusion of economics, politics and social consciousness (Obi and Soremekun, op.cit) which when applied to our subject-matter explains the material basis of the minority question, the social forces at play, and how the contradictions thrown up by oil and the minority question are expressions of the oppressive character of class relations in Nigeria and the dialectics of a state assuming an increasingly rentier character.

The Minority Question

The minority question is one of the results of 'the bringing together of diverse nationalities and economic modes at various levels of development by the 'Nigerian' colonial state'. As Madunagu asserts, such minorities became so in the double sense. (Madunagu, 1982) Firstly, they were a minority in relation to the three dominant ethnic nationalities (Hausa-Fulani, Yoruba and Igbo) and secondly, all of them combined constituted a minority in relation to the three dominant nationalities put together. Their status was further reinforced by the centralised form of political control institutionalised by the colonial state, in which "the dominant ethnic group in each region emerged as the most favoured in the colonial patrimonial system. The dominant ethnic group used its advantaged position in the patrimonial system to ensure its monopoly of the regional cash crop base. This made the group amenable to the 'divide and rule' tactics of the colonial administration. It also engendered a feeling of suspicion and rivalry between the regions, and the fear of domination and exploitation within the regions: between the powerful dominant ethnic groups and the marginalised and dominated ethnic minorities. Apart from the inequity in political terms, the minorities lacked a strong economic base. With economic and political power firmly in the hands of the dominant ethnic groups and their British patrons, the ethnic minorities were effectively sidelined, or left with the crumbs from the high-table of the colonial accumulation.

As has been asserted elsewhere, ethnic majority-minority relations must not be reduced to an unmediated or unilinear process:

> It should be however be pointed out, that the domination of minorities was not undifferentiated (that is, only a small faction of the 'big three' actually participated in the actual domination). While the minorities also had a small faction which collaborated with the hegemonic factions of the 'big three'. This trans-national ruling class coalition was often expedient, and contradiction-riven by inter-nationality, inter-regional and intraclass cleavages. (Obi, 1997b)

What we are dealing with, is in reality intra-ruling class relations (defined in terms of ethnic nationalities) , at one level, and inter-class (defined in terms of democratic participation and rights) relations at another level. Both levels merge at certain conjunctures: when due to the growing demands for legitimacy or as part of the strategy for capturing or competing for political power the ruling class faction of an ethnic nationality group mobilises the people through the manipulation of ethnic sentiments of solidarity and loyalty, language, religion, political interest and historical experience. Such cross-class alliances are often transitory and expedient, and do breakdown if the expected political goods are not delivered.

In the decade before independence, the ethnic minorities intensified the struggle to ensure their freedom from further domination by the hegemonic ethnic majorities. In response to these demands, and partly informed by the desire to protect its long term interests in a stable independent Nigeria, the colonial government set up the Willink Commission to investigate the basis of such fears. (Olusanya, 1980) The Commission, as noted in the preceding section confirmed that some of the fears of the minorities were well placed, but the colonial government and its patrimonial clients, subordinated this to their own interests, through the instrumentality of constitutional guarantees for the protection of minority rights. Unfortunately, after independence in 1960, these constitutional provisions failed to arrest their fears, and violent struggles broke out in the regions against majority ethnic group domination. Specific cases of such struggles were the Tiv riots, and restiveness among the Ijaw, the Yoruba in Kabba and Ilorin and the Igbo in Asaba and Aboh divisions'. (Falola, 1988)

One salient feature of the highly regionalised politics of the First Republic was the fact that members of the majority ethnic groups could become minorities outside regions where they were clearly in the majority. The instances that readily offer themselves are the Igbo of the (predominantly Yoruba) Old Western region (and later midwest region) and the Yoruba of the (predominantly Hausa-Fulani) old western region. However, some of these contradictions have been addressed, but, it must be said that in spite of the creation of states, the regional poles of Nigeria's political compass continue to play a significant role in intra-ruling class politics.

Certain economic developments had an impact on the nature and dynamics of the minority question. The most significant of these till date has been the replacement of agriculture by oil, as the basis of capitalist accumulation and state reproduction in Nigeria. By 1965, the export-based cash crop economy fell into a crisis resulting from a fall in global commodity prices. This, adversely affected the regions as centres of political and economic power, deriving from their dependence on cash crop exports. Thus, the governments of the north and western regions ran budget deficits as a result of the collapse in expected foreign exchange earnings. The result of this crisis as noted by (Falola, 1988) was that the regions began to look to the federal government for aid.

In real terms, by the mid-1960s the economic basis of regionalism had begun to wane. While the global prices for cash crops collapsed, export earnings from oil, a hitherto insignificant factor in the Nigerian economy, rose. Since the oil was produced mainly from the ethnic minority areas of the Niger Delta, it directly placed them on a collision course against the majority ethnic groups who sought access to, and control of the new wealth of the Nigerian nation. Thus the minority question became immersed in the greasy cauldron of oil politics: with the oil minorities entering another phase in the historical struggle against majority-nationality hegemony.

Intra-Minority Contradictions

One of the secondary contradictions in the minority question in Nigeria is the seldom discussed, but significant issue of intra-minority conflict and oppression. Minority-on-minority oppression often arises in circumstances when one minority ethnic group becomes a 'majority group, in relation to another minority group, within a defined political space'. At this level of the minority question, the 'dominant' minority group seeks to replicate the forms of oppression at the majority-minority or federal level in the attempt to monopolise power, resources and lucrative public offices at the state or local government level. The contradictions in intra-minority ethnic relations are often exploited by the majority groups to prevent the formation of a broad minority front against majority ethnic group hegemony. Intra-minority conflict seems to have deepened with the creation of states. Although these states seem to have provided the minorities with access to the centre, it has also provided the ethnic hegemons with more states and monopoly of oil wealth. Thus we continue to witness two levels of the minority question: in terms of majority–minority oppression, and intra-minority nationality oppression. Recent examples of the latter can be found in the minority states and have tended to assume more violent forms in the oil minority states.

The National Question

The national question in Nigeria revolves around the contradiction between the *Nation* and the *State*. It can be conceptualised in terms of the urgent need to work out modalities and reach a broad consensus for a just and equitable basis through which the diverse nationalities in Nigeria can unite, and pursue a common destiny of national development as Nigerians. For this reason it impinges on the issues of democratic space and Nigeria's peripheral position in the international market economy system. This in turn has consequences for the current struggles for the holding of a Sovereign National Conference (SNC) directed towards arriving at a commonly agreed, mutually beneficial, just and equitable basis of social and political relations between and within the various nationalities that make up Nigeria. Due to the highly militarised terrain of the

Nigerian political process, even as the country basks in the wake of a newly-won democracy following the handover of power to an elected government on May 29, 1999, the struggle for democracy is far from being over. The hegemonic faction of the political class having donned the toga of new democrats, is using cooptative tactics to block any attempt to resolve the national question. The new democrats are keen to secure the hegemonic ruling class coalition, and prevent the possibility of an alternate decentralised nation-state project coming on board, and 'destroying' the political basis and legitimacy of the post civil 'national' ruling class.

Our notion of the national question not only draws attention to the high stakes of the current contest for national power, and the dangers it portends for Nigeria, it is also informed by the following assumptions:

(a) that the national question cannot be separated from the manner of the creation of Nigeria by British colonial capitalism;

(b) that the present upsurge in calls for a re-examination of the national question are organically linked to the crisis of structural adjustment in Nigeria, which has benefitted the unproductive, but politically powerful 'few', and alienated and dispossessed the majority, fuelling increased struggles between and within social groups/classes for a larger share of shrinking oil rents;

(c) that the resolution of the national question must necessarily commence outside the structures of dependent (rentier) capitalism and monopolistic practice; and

(d) that the democratisation of all facets of political and economic life is central to the resolution of the national question.

While there is a school of thought that had earlier postulated that the minority nationalities of the oil producing areas were too few to threaten the hegemony of the majority ethnic nationalities, (Asiodu, 1980) the fallacy of that position has been borne out by current developments. The central element or cementing factor between the *Minority* and *National Question* is oil. And it operates at two levels within Nigeria: the struggle for access and control of oil resources between all nationalities, and the struggle, compensation, and access to oil resources by the oil producing minorities on the basis of their ownership of the oil bearing lands and waters, the desire to end their expropriation by 'outsiders', and on the grounds of justice, equity and environmental integrity. Apart from the internal struggles, there is an external factor: the foreign oil multinationals which firmly control oil production in Nigeria, and have increasingly become the object of protest and attack by the restive oil communities. The linkage between oil and the minority question throws up specific contradictions which hold immense significance for oil-based accumulation and the fortunes of the oil-dependent state.

The State-Rentier Nexus

The state-rentier nexus is hinged on the notion that monopoly oil-based accumulation spawns undemocratic forms of production and political relations which directly feed into the Nigerian crisis. (Obi, 1994) Apart from being the fiscal basis of the Nigerian state, oil has provided the surplus with which the Nigerian state has reproduced itself and provided the impetus for the process of class formation and reproduction. Since the end of the Nigerian civil war in 1970, oil has remained the most crucial element for the continued integration of Nigeria into the global economic system through the pursuit of oil-based transnational accumulation.

At the external level, the Nigerian state is subordinated to the oil multinationals who mine, produce and market its oil internationally. It depends on the oil multinationals for the realisation of its share of the surplus accruing from transnational oil-based accumulation. This not only curtails the autonomy of the Nigerian state, but beholdens it to the oil multinationals; without whose activities it cannot collect oil rents. Thus, the Nigerian state is obliged to provide all necessary conditions, if need be by force, to remove any obstacles that may threaten, or in any way put at risk, the operations of the oil companies. At the internal level, the rentier nexus has created a social context where (politicised) ethnicity has become one of the modalities for mediating class relations and class rule. It is therefore necessary to examine the concept of a "rentier" and its relevance in this context. According to Beblawi (1987):

> A rentier economy is thus an economy where the creation of wealth is centred around a small fraction of the society, the rest of society is engaged in the utilisation of this wealth. The respective roles of the few and the many can hardly be overstated in the concept of the rentier economy.

> The state in a rentier economy becomes the sole collector and distributor of externally earned oil rents. Due to the monopoly character of oil-based accumulation, the rentier nexus spawns exploitative and anti-democratic social relations:

> The 'economic power', thus bestowed upon the few would allow them to

seize 'political power', as well.

In political terms, therefore, the economic power of the few (who either are strategically located in the state or have links with state office holders) translates into an authoritarian core, which is often sustained by a series of patron-client networks terminating at the feet of a grand patron, or involving the brutal repression of contending/oppositional groups. (Obi, 1994)

Applied to the Nigerian context, there is no doubt that the transformation of the process of accumulation from one based on cash crop to oil exports, hold certain implications for a rentier nexus: the government at the centre has been relatively, 'overdeveloped' (vis-à-vis the other tiers) immensely strengthened by its monopoly of oil rents which in turn has fed into centralising tendencies that are intolerant of marginal/minority interests. The state's lack of control over oil production has reinforced its distributive role, leading to a winner-take-all approach to politics, while its dependence on oil multinationals renders it vulnerable, and amenable to external manipulation. Thus, the state in the rentier context pursues an unproductive and patently patrimonial form of capitalism. The state-oil rentier nexus has had very destabilising consequences for Nigeria's ethnic politics. As discussed in the section on the historical overview, the majority ethnic groups were able to act politically, to retain the larger share of the 'national cake' in spite of the change from four regions/cash crop economy to 12,19,21, 30 and 36 states/oil-based economy. This has led to a deterioration of majority-minority relations on the grounds of access, inequality/inequity over-centralisation of power, and environmental degradation.

With the deepening of the Nigerian crises and the adoption of the Structural Adjustment Programme in 1986, there has been a sharpening of contradictions between: the oil minorities and the Nigerian state, between the oil minorities and the oil companies, between the oil minorities and the ethnic (non-oil producing) majorities and within the oil minorities themselves. In sum, oil, has acted as a catalyst in the aggravation of the minority question in Nigerian politics, as the various groups intensify their struggles for a shrinking share of oil in a context where the rules are mainly determined by force and the power over oil.

Oil and the Minority Question

As can be gleaned from the preceding paragraph, oil has sharpened the contradictions in Nigeria's ethnic politics. In spite of the overwhelming contribution of the oil minority areas of the Niger delta to federal revenues, they have been excluded from direct access to oil revenues, except through federal (and ethnic majority) benevolence. Apart from being marginalised, despite the creation of states, the oil minorities have been made to bear the full environmental consequences of oil production, which threaten the very basis of their survival: land and water. Thus, the historical conditions which created the minority question in Nigeria have been given a new and militant impetus by the crisis in oil-based accumulation, state and class relations.

The oil factor was inserted into the minority question, with its discovery in Oloibiri in the Niger delta, an area inhabited by people of minority ethnic origin in 1956. Since the oil was produced in that ethnic minority area of the Eastern region, it became a factor in the ethnic-based and regionalised politics of the First Republic. By the mid-1960s oil exports began to increase, while the traditional cash crop exports shrank as a result of the crash in global prices for agricultural cash crop exports. Since the fiscal basis of the regions was cash crop exports, they began to witness economic difficulties, with the north and western regions running budget deficits. (Falola, op.cit) This had several consequences: the growing profile of oil in replacing cash crops as the new wealth of the nation made it a locus of struggles between and within the national ruling class, its regional factions, and between them and the oil minorities who had historically resisted majority-nationality domination. It also led to the weakening of the regions who now looked up to the Federal Government for aid, while the oil minorities attempted through the instrumentality of the oil leverage to assert their own autonomy and throw off the regional hegemons.

> With the growing contribution of oil to national revenue (and the decline of the contribution of cash crop exports) there emerged an intense struggle between the regionalist bourgeoisie of the three regions for the control of oil, while the Delta minorities sought to use the leverage offered by oil to assert their autonomy. (Obi and Soremekun, forthcoming)

In this way, oil became a potentially explosive element in the minority question. The oil minorities from this point sought to protect their oil wealth from the ethnic majority groups. As early as 1966, an unsuccessful attempt was made to create a Niger Delta Republic. Although the attempt was crushed and its leaders failed, it led to a new consciousness at the federal level that access to representation and power by the oil minorities could no longer be totally blocked; moreso as they were the key to the new source of national wealth and federal power. Thus when the four regions were replaced with twelve states in 1967 the minorities got some states of their own. The oil minorities in the eastern region got two states (Rivers and South Eastern States) giving them some measure of access to power and resources with the federal framework. However this was overshadowed after the civil war by increased centralisation of federal fiscal and political power which retained the larger chunk of the national cake, in the hands of the 'big three' (particularly the victorious Western and Northern ruling class factions).

The point that comes out clearly from the foregoing is that in spite of the shift from cash crop exports to oil exports, the character of accumulation has remained monopolistic, divorcing the producer from his product, within a context defined by dependent patrimonial capitalism. Oil, rather than being a lubricant of inter and intra ethnic harmony and cohesion, has brought out in pronounced form the contradictions inherent in Nigeria's highly centralised federalism. It has also shown the links between monopolistic oil-based accumulation, anti-democratic fiscal federalism and political practices by the militarised Nigerian state, and how all this has fed into conflictual relations between the various factions of the highly divided, but 'united' ruling class.

At the height of the oil boom in the mid-1970s the minority question seemed to have cooled considerably. The increase in the number of states to nineteen from twelve broadened the political space available to the various nationalities. However in the case of the oil minorities they had to wait until the late 1980s and early 1990s for additional states to be created for them. The Cross River State (former South Eastern State) was split into Cross River and Akwa Ibom, Bendel State (former Midwest State) was split into Edo and Delta State, while Rivers State much later had Bayelsa state excised from it. What is clear is that states creation for the oil minorities has not translated into self-determination nor has it put an end to their marginalisation from the centres of economic and political power spawned on oil rents. This fully explains why, in the wake of the deep-seated Nigerian economic and debt crises in the 1980s, the struggles of the oil minorities acquired more vibrancy and militancy.

With lesser and lesser amounts of oil revenues accruing to the country as a result of the collapse of global oil prices, and a resultant oil glut, there has been an intensification of struggles between the factions of the ruling class over shrinking oil rents. The ruling class faction of the oil minorities with its ambivalent attitude towards the erstwhile regional hegemons: that of opposition at the local level and collaboration at the centre through the avenues provided by states creation, have come under immense pressures to openly side with popular forces protesting the domination of 'their' oil by the nationally preponderant ethnic group factions and foreign oil multinationals. Even the oil minorities faction of the political class has been aggrieved by its loosing out at the centre in terms of decreasing oil rents and patronage, and is therefore pushing for a derivation-based redress in Nigeria's fiscal federalism which would enhance its legitimacy and stem class struggles from below. (Obi and Soremekun, op.cit)

Recent developments clearly indicate that the oil-minority question interface is increasingly threatening the stability and cohesion of the Nigerian federation. The current economic crisis and a decade and a half of military dictatorship and abuse of power, have excercebated the existing ethnic cleavages in Nigeria's politics and class relations. Following the annulment of the June 12, 1993 Presidential elections by General Ibrahim Babangida, these ethnic cleavages have become lines of distrust, and even conflict, provoking the popular interrogation of the viability of the Nigerian nation-state project, and raising the spectre of possible disintegration. Under an embryonic and more militant leadership thrown up by the historical conjuncture, the people of the Niger delta have sought through mass action to achieve self determination as well as the right to an equitable share of the proceeds from oil, and compensation for the destruction of the environment. The militant forces of the oil minorities have thus had to contend with a desperate and repressive Nigerian state, determined to protect the exclusive monopoly of (shrinking) oil rents as well as its foreign partners, the oil multinationals. (Obi, 1998) describing the current plight of the Nigerian oil minorities, Ake opines:

> It is well known that our oil wealth has become a nightmare for the people of the oil producing areas. Demands for fair treatment and environmental protection have always elicited firm refusal, more repression and state violence, . What is not so well known is how much worse the nightmare has become recently. (Ake, 1994)

Apart from the effort of the Military Government to suppress agitation by the oil minorities, it has offered a few carrots to the people, especially the oil minorities ruling class faction. During the Babangida years, the Federal Government established the Oil Minerals Producing Areas Development Agency (OMPADEC) (Gbadamosi, 1992) headed by a chief executive of Niger delta origin, to address some of the problems and contain the struggles of the militant organisations of the oil minorities. Due to the high premium placed on political power as the sole guarantor of the monopoly of, and access to oil rents, the political space has been further constricted by the hegemonic forces of the political class. This has placed the oil minorities further at the disadvantage in the "pyramid of power and patron client networks spawned on oil rents". (Obi, 1994) The neocolonial national ruling class confronted with the spectre of a diminished oil rents base has clearly become desperate in excluding the people from governance. It has had to contend with the organised and militant groups of the oil minorities, particularly MOSOP, which have increased in number and strength (Obi, 1999).

Table 11   Main Oil Minority Rights Pressure Groups since 1990

1.   Movement for the Survival of Ogoni People (MOSOP)
2.   Ijaw National Congress (INC)
3.   National Youth Council for the Survival of Ogoni People (NYCOP)
4.   Council for Ikwere Nationality (CIN)
5.   Southern Minorities Movement (SMM)
6.   Movement for Reparations to Ogbia (MORETO)
7.   Ethnic Minority Rights Organization of Africa (EMIROAF)
8.   Ijaw Peace Movement (IPM)
9.   Ijaw National Congress (INC)
10. Ijaw Youth Council (IYC)
11. Itsekiri Nationality Patriots (INP)
12. Movement for the Survival of Izon Ethnic Nationality in Niger Delta (MOSIEND)
13. Chikoko
14. Egbesu Boys of Africa (EBA)
15. Isoko Development Union
16. Organisation of Oil Mineral Producing Communities of Nigeria (OOMPCON)
17. Isoko National Youth Movement (INYM)
18. Bayelsa Forum
19. Egi Women's Movement (EWM)Urhobo Study Group
20. Egi National Congress (ENC)
21. Ogba Solidarity
22. Urhobo Study Group
23. Urhobo Progressive Union
24. Traditional Rulers of Oil Mineral Producing Communities (TROMPCON)

Sources: *Author's Fieldwork*

Of all these groups, MOSOP, and more recently Chikoko, IYC and MORETO have effectively mobilised the people against the pollution of their environment by oil companies, to demand the payment of royalties and reparations for oil exploited and damages inflicted on the fragile delta ecosystem and which directly threaten the peoples basis of livelihood. MOSOP in 1993 brought the plight of the oil minorities, particularly the Ogoni, to national and international attention. Its leader, Saro-Wiwa hinged the arguments for MOSOP's struggles on some basic issues: "the need for social justice for minorities, equity in power sharing in Nigeria, compensation for environmental devastation and the restoration of the environment, payment of economic rents to oil producing areas, human dignity and self-realisation." Through militant and popular action MOSOP disrupted oil operations in Ogoniland, joined the national-democratic struggle, and carried its case to the United Nations, the Unrepresented Nations and Peoples Organisation (UNPO), as well as other global fora. Its struggle brought it face to face with the Nigerian state whose earlier attempts at buying out the MOSOP leadership or exploiting the intra-oil minority cleavages to whittle down MOSOP's militancy and influence failed, and paved the way for brutal repression. The MOSOP example gave impetus to the spread of militancy to other parts of the Niger delta, with mobilised villagers and youth blocking oil installations, disrupting oil operations and seeking to protect their rights as oil minorities. In order to stem the rising tide of militant struggles for self determination and an end to the exploitation of oil companies, nine leading MOSOP activists including Saro-Wiwa were arrested, detained and hanged (on murder charges) in November 1995, while MOSOP was driven underground and the whole of Ogoniland placed under a tight military occupation. The siege spread to other parts of the delta, but it has not stopped protesting villagers from blocking, and disrupting the operations of the oil companies as a way of drawing attention to their plight, and forcing the state-oil business alliance to attend to their demands. In other oil communities excessive force has been used by the police to disperse protesting villagers or in other cases to sack entire villages.

However the combination of state repression and the distribution of federal largesse to the oil minorities ruling class factions have failed to resolve the minority question. From 1993 the oil minorities spread all over the oil producing states came together under the umbrella of a broad democratic coalition called the Southern Minorities Movement (SMM) whose primary goal is to change the existing inter ethnic 'national' power equation based on the right of self-determination of all ethnic groups, big and small, and a derivation-based redress in Nigeria's fiscal federalism.

According to the SMM:

> The Southern Minorities seek self-determination ... they want to rule themselves within the Nigerian Federation. Each ethnic group should therefore exercise control over all resources found on the surface, beneath the surface and in the airspace of each ethnic group.

The Southern Minorities Movement's desire is clearly linked to the issue of access to political power and oil rents, which they have historically been denied. They seek an equitable share of oil rents on the basis of the fact that over 90 percent of the nation's wealth is produced from under their lands and waters, which gives them a natural right to enjoy the oil wealth. Their quest also extends to key public offices which have hither to been the exclusive preserve of the "major tribes." What comes out of the current phase of oil and the minority question is the fusion of the struggle for equity and selfdetermination with the national-democratic question in Nigeria. This can only mean more democratic struggles, militancy, state suppression and subversion of the minority question. Thus the southern minorities have come out to play prominent roles in the national-democratic debates that followed the June 12 national crisis, debates over the future of the Nigerian nation-state, which continue to rage in spite of the return to democratic rule. Rather unfortunately, the victorious post-military government is yet to show concrete signs of the 'big three' making any real 'concessions'

During the Abacha Constitutional Conference, despite the heat generated by the quest for 'power shift' and a reversion to a derivation-based revenue allocation system, very little was achieved in terms of establishing an equitable relationship between the dominant ethnic, and oil minorities. Thus, the oil minorities had no option than to take their destiny into their own hands. This led to the widening of existing divisions within the oil minorities faction of the political elite. In a context where local authority in the Niger delta is being contested by an alternate emergent leadership made up of fierce nationalists: professionals, workers, student-activists, trade unionists and radical politicians, who seek self -determination, equity and democracy. The 'old guard' more desperate than ever can only rely on its 'old allies' to preserve existing national patrimonial networks and struggle for greater recognition and relevance within the context of the three registered political parties and the various levels of government in Nigeria. In this context we can only expect more violent struggles, amidst the widening of national and sub-national cleavages. The prospects for any real democracy which would open up the political space for popular forces to challenge the hegemonic bloc's monopoly of oil rent (and threaten the very basis of class rule in Nigeria) seen to be rather problematic in the short to medium term. So far, the changing forms of ethnic minority identity politics seek to take advantage of the democratic moment in Nigeria's political trajectory but it would need to deal with the formidable alliance of the dominant political class and global capital, whose basis of reproduction and rule is increasingly being integrated into, or tied to monopoly oil-based accumulation.

Conclusion

Nigeria today paradoxically exemplifies the fact that the fate of ethnic minorities and that of Nigeria as a nation-state are inextricably linked together, while the imperative of the political restructuring away from the currently highly centralised federal arrangement has become very urgent. Quite clearly, except that the ethnic minorities are made to have a sense of belonging to the 'new' national bargain, given equal access and rights to opportunities with a democratised socio-economic and political order, the nation-state project in Nigeria would remain in a state of crisis amid the grim possibility of a break-up. Just as the contradictions spawned by oil have widened inter and intra-ethnic cleavages largely as a result of historical and distributive inequities, oil can act as a cement of national unity and harmonious co-existence of the diverse ethnic pluralities, once its benefits are equitably shared in a commonly negotiated and agreed manner. A most critical point at this conjuncture is to meaningfully address the grievances of the oil minorities of the Niger delta, by granting them more control and access to oil resources, and greater protection of their ecosystem from the fallouts of oil production.

In seeking solutions to the current crisis, there is the need to deal critically with the minority question, especially the contending forces, and the linkages with global and domestic capitalism. This would underscore the importance of a democratic transformation of inter-and intra-ethnic relations in Nigeria, the change of the oil rentier nexus from its current monopoly and anti-development ethos. Thus, the resolution of the current crisis lies in a revolutionary transformation of state, society and economy in Nigeria in a manner that fundamentally addresses the developmental needs of majority of Nigerians.

References

Aina, Tade (1989), 'What is Political Economy?', The Nigerian Economic Society (NES) (ed), *The Nigerian Economy: A Political Approach.* London: Longman.

Ake, Claude (1994). 'A People Endangered by Oil', *The Guardian.* (Lagos) August 18.

Akinyele, R.T. (1992). 'Safeguarding Nigeria's Ethnic Minorities. The Relevance of the American Approach to Minority Problems', *Nigerian Journal of American Studies*, Vol. II, July.

Asiodu, P.C. (1980), 'Impact of Petroleum on the Nigerian Economy', Lecture delivered at the *Public Service Lecture*, Lagos, November 12.

Beblawi, Hazem (1987), 'The Rentier State in the Arab world', in Hazem Beblawi and Giacomo Luciani (eds), *The Rentier State.* London: Croom Helm.

Falola Toyin (1988), 'The Evolution and Changes in Nigerian Federalism', in Richard A. Olaniyan (eds), *Federalism in a Changing World.* Lagos: Office of the Minister for Special Duties, The Presidency.

Gbadamosi, Gbolahan (1992), 'Development Agency Set-up for Oil States: Citing the Federal Minister for Justice', in *The Guardian,* Lagos, July 11.

Ikime, Obaro (1986), 'Towards Understanding the National Question', Paper presented at the Seminar on the National Question in Nigeria. Its Historical Origins and Contemporary Dimensions, Abuja August 4-9.

Madunagu, Eddie (1982), *Problems of Socialism: The Nigerian Challenge.* London: Zed Books

Mustapha, Abdul Raufu (1987), 'The National Question and Radical Politics' in *Nigeria Review of African Political Economy*, No. 37, December.

Ngemutu Roberts F. O. (1994), 'Federalism, Minorities and Political Contestation in Nigeria: From Henry Willink to the MOSOP Phenomenon', paper presented at the 20th Annual Conference of the Nigerian Political Science Association at the Obafemi Awolowo University (OAU), Ile Ife, February 28- March 2.

Nnoli, Okwudiba (1978), *Ethnic Politics in Nigeria.* Enugu: Fourth Dimension.

Obi, Cyril (1994), 'Oil Minority Rights and Nation-Building in Nigeria: Prospects for Democratic Stability in Nigeria'. Paper presented at the NPSA 1993 Annual Conference, Ile Ife, February 28- March 2.

____ (1997) 'Globalisation and Local Resistance: The Case of the Ogoni Versus Shell', *New Political Economy*, Vol. 2 No. 1.

____ (1997b) Structural Adjustment, Oil and Popular Struggles: The Deepening Crisis of State Legitimacy in Nigeria. Dakar: *CODESRIA Monograph Series.*

____ (1998) 'The Impact of Oil in Nigeria's Revenue Allocation System: Problems and Prospects for National Reconstruction', in Kunle Amuwo et.al. (eds.) *Federalism and Political Restructuring in Nigeria.* Ibadan: Spectrum and IFRA.

____ (1998) 'Global, State and Local Intersections: A Study of Power, Authority and Conflict in the Niger Delta'. Paper presented at the Workshop on Local Governance and International Intervention, Florence, March 28-29.

____ (1999) 'Globalisation and Environmental Conflict in Africa', *African Journal of Political Science* (New Series), Vol. 4 No. 1.

Obi, Cyril and Kayode Soremekun (Forthcoming), 'Oil, the National Question and Crises in Nigeria: A Critical Review of Recent Developments', in R.T Akinyele and Jide Owoeye (eds), *The National Question.*

Okpu, Ugbona (1977), *Ethnic Minority Problems in Nigeria Politics.* Uppsala: Studia Historical Upsalrensa.

Olusanya G.O. (1980), 'Constitutional Developments In Nigeria 1861-1960', in Obaro Ikime (ed), *Groundwork in Nigeria History.* Ibadan: Heinemann.

Onah, J.K. (1983), *The Nigerian Oil Economy.* London: Croom Helm.

Osaghae, Eghosa (1986), 'Do Ethnic Minorities Still Exist in Nigeria?' *Journal of Commonwealth and Comparative Politics*, Vol. 24, No.2.

Osuntokun, Jide (1986), 'The Search for a Common Nationality in Nigeria'. Paper presented at the Seminar on the National Question in Nigeria: Its Historical Origins and Contemporary Dimensions, Abuja, August 4-9.

Philips, Adedotun (1992), 'Four Decades of Fiscal Federalism in Nigeria'. *Publius* Vol. 21,No. 4.

Saro-Wiwa, Ken (1992), *Genocide in Nigeria: The Ogoni Tragedy.* Port-harcourt: Saros.

____ (1995), *A Month and A Day: A Detention Diary.* London: Penguin Books.

Soremekun, Kayode and Cyril Obi (1993) 'Oil and the National Question', in F. Onah (ed), *The National Question and Economic Development in Nigeria.* Ibadan: Nigerian Economic Society.

Tamuno, Tekena N. (1970), 'Separatist Agitations in Nigeria Since 1914'. *Journal of Modern African Studies*, Vol. 8 No. 4.

Williams, Gavin. (1981) 'Nigeria: The Neo-Colonial Political Economy', in Dennis Cohen and John Daniels (eds), *The Political Economy of Africa.* London: Longman.

6 The Minority Question in Northern Nigeria

YIMA SEN

Introduction

The problem of pluralism, multi-culturalism or the national question or question of nationalities in the global society or in national boundaries, seems to be a major problem of the century. Even if social stratification along class lines supersedes the colour or ethnic line, in analytical terms, pluralism always intervenes for the purpose of dominating or emancipatory project.

This chapter argues that cultural differences have existed in human society for a very long time and in fact today, remain a fact of human existence. It goes further to submit that these differences can be interpreted and employed to foster social cohesion and human progress for the majority or to instigate social exclusion and promote development, skewed to favour a dominating class. In this sense, there is an interaction of cultural and class factors in society.

For this purpose, we begin this analysis of the question of minorities in northern Nigeria from a historical perspective. In other words, how did the various cultural groups or nationalities that inhabit northern Nigeria come to constitute the kind of community that we have today?

It is not the intention here to present a detailed history of northern Nigeria, what we will do is to provide a generalisation of the situation and how it has come to present a problem today. It is common knowledge that much of humankind is geographically located where it is today due to a series of migrations motivated by social, economic and political factors. These include the search for agricultural land, commerce, wars, missionisation, environmental factors, to mention a few. In northern Nigeria, disparate ethnic groups have come from the West, North, East and South, to occupy what was the northern protectorate front 1900-1914, northern Region front 1914-1967, and may arguably be referred to today as the northern states.

However, as observed by Kukah (1994), the Jihad of Usman dan Fodio in the 19th century has come to dominate historical analysis of northern Nigeria, very much to the chagrin of other Muslims and scholars, who cite the earlier practice of Islam among the people of the Bornu empire and how pagans and

Muslims coexisted symbiotically in the Middle Belt area long before the Jihad.

However, one of the most significant legacies of the Sokoto Jihad was the merging of large sections of northern Nigeria into what has come to be referred to as the Sokoto Caliphate and which some careless and uninformed analysts allege extended over all of northern Nigeria. It may, however, be the nature of British colonial intrusion into the north, its confrontation with, as well as its defeat and resuscitation of the political-secular authority of the Sokoto Caliphate and the application of the indirect rule model of colonial administration to consolidate what Kukah (1994) refers to as Anglo-Fulani hegemony, that properly establishes our analytical parameters. Essentially, what this means is that the question of ethnic minorities in Nigeria is rooted in a global problematic of pluralism and class factor, but with a particularity traceable beyond but inclusive of the Sokoto Jihad, British colonialism, and political struggles in the colonial and post-colonial periods.

Sociological Highlights

Northern Nigeria consists of different nationalities with clearly discernible ethnic - linguistic traits. Although anthropologists have tried so classify the people of northern Nigeria, as elsewhere, along such stocks, as Hamitic, or Bantu, it might, perhaps, be more useful to employ linguistic, occupational and religious indicators to study pluralism in northern Nigeria.

According to various census figures, the Hausa are the most numerous ethnic group in northern Nigeria, followed by the Fulani, the Kanuri, the Tiv and Nupe. However, it is not so much the number of ethnic groups in the North that matters, but how we can classify them to understand the minorities problematic. For this purpose, a four-category schema is being proposed as follows:

1. The Fulani aristocracy, whose social group is in reality a numerical minority when compared with the national majorities of Hausa, Yoruba and Igbo. However in northern Nigeria, because of the role they played in the Sokoto Jihad and their establishment of an Emirate system consisting mainly of Fulani rulers, they have come to occupy a unique dominating position within the political sociology of northern Nigeria. Their direct influence spreads over such states as Sokoto, Kebbi, Kastina, Kano, Jigawa, Kaduna (Zaria), Kwara (Ilorin), Bauchi and Adamawa. The Fulani aristocracy which gained ascendancy after the Sokoto Jihad, and employed their strong Islamic faith, must be distinguished from the pastoral Fulbe or cattle Fulani. It was through militant missionisation and politics that the more literate town Fulani in collaboration with the Fulbe and Hausa recruits were able to overthrow the Hausa rulers and replace them

with Fulani rulers.

2. The Hausa-Fulani-Kanuri community which is a broad alliance which emerged more visibly on the eve of independence, but which has been intistigated by the Fulani. As partly mentioned above, Hausa states were long established in northern Nigeria before the Fulani migrated into the area from the West. These Hausa states which were nominally Muslim consisted of essentially farmers and traders, that in fact also co - existed symbiotically with non-Hausa pagan groups. To the East there existed the Kanuri, who had developed a tradition of Islam and an empire of Kanem-Bornu, which was older than the Sokoto Caliphate, and consisted of a citizenry engaged in farming, trading and pastoral activities. However, it does seem that the nurturing of a Hausa-Fulani-Kanuri alliance was more a marriage of convenience, rather than a natural product of history. This is so because the basis of this alliance seemed to be religious and pragmatic, since Hausa - Fulani versus Kanuri rivalries have continued with the latter maintaining a strong sense of independence and sometimes opposition. It is however, the Hausa - Fulani that have developed a kinship and solidarity which was initially forged under the political leadership of the Fulani but now manifests itself in wide use of Hausa language by the Fulani and heavy inter-marriage. The Hausa themselves had developed a community from the original Hausa *Bakwai* or seven Hausa states viz: Biram, Daura, Gobir, Kano, Rano, Katsina and Zaria, and the "Banza Bakwai," or seven bastard states or those whose population had mixed and intermarried with foreign elements viz: Yoruba, Nupe, Gwari, Yauri, Bauchi, Zamfara and Kebbi (Omolewa, 1986). By this political formulation, Hausa has come to encompass. even non-ethnic but Hausa-speaking nationalities.

3. As noted above, some of the major northern minority nationalities such as the Kanuri and Nupe overlap into the Hausa Fulani cultural milieu. However, there are still social, economic and political traits which are peculiar to the major northern minorities such as the Kanuri, Tiv, Nupe, Birom, Gwari and northern Yoruba, to mention a few. These are essentially peasant communities and with the exception of the Kanuri and to some extent the Nupe, were initially largely pagan but have now adopted the Christian religion, mainly due to the work of Christian missionaries. Even in terms of traditional authority, the Nupe retained their own nationals as rulers, while in the case of the northern Yoruba in Ilorin, a Yoruba-speaking and socialised family is the ruling house. It is also interesting to note that when the main opposition against the Hausa - Fulani authority in northern Nigeria emerged, it was mainly from this category that it was articulated and enacted. The most notable leaders. of this opposition were from the strongly independent Birom, Tiv and the northern Yoruba.

4. The minor minority nationalities run into hundreds and although they bear different names and speak different languages and dialects, some of them actually come from the same larger ethnic- linguistic families. In the Benue valley, for example, there is a strong historical link between the Jukun, Idoma, Igala, Doma, Alago and other smaller ethnic groups which may have also facilitated the rise of the Kwararafa empire, and whose lingering culture may have only been disturbed, by the migration of the Tiv into their present abode. There is also anthropological evidence of a culture based on the Nok terra cotta, which stretches from southern Kaduna, eastwards to the Katsina-Ala area of present day Benue state. Elsewhere, in central northern Nigeria, is a collection of small Gwari ethnic groups that make up the major Gwari group referred to above. Even among the Hausa, are to be found smaller nationalities like the Maguzawa of Kano and Jigawa states. Other examples of groups that have close affinity include the Mbula and Bachama of Adamawa state. Anthropologists have also tended to cite the Tiv of Benue, Plateau and Taraba states as belonging to that same Bantu racial stock as the Mumuye of Taraba and the Bachama of Adamawa. The point being made here is to present a sketch of the kind of sociology that delineates the major from the minor nationalities in northern Nigeria. It is evident from this analysis that a case can be made for the existence of numerical and cultural minorities in northern Nigeria, and even if in their totality they outnumber the Hausa-Fulani cultural bloc, as independent socio-cultural units they are still minorities. In addition, the Northern minorities are largely non-Muslim and non-Hausa-speaking or both, but there are Hausa-speaking Christians like the Birom or those who speak their language but are Muslims like the Nupe, or the Tiv who do not speak Hausa and are not Muslims.

Elements of the Political Economy

The merchant, agricultural and pastoral pre-colonial economy of northern Nigeria was largely transformed with colonialism. Under colonialism, there began the construction of roads, rail lines, tin mining, hides and skins manufacture for export, and the promotion of cash crop agricultural products like ground-nuts, cotton and soya beans. Furthermore, with the establishment of a Northern regional government, it began a systematic implementation of a state-led model of development. According to Paden (1986) this model of development had the personal imprint of the first indigenous political leader of Northern Nigeria, Sir Ahmadu Bello, the Sardauna of Sokoto. Its emphasis was on the empowerment of indigenous northerners through a process called "northernisation", which initially involved human resources training and recruitment to assist the north "catch up" with the south, and some tokenism within the thirteen provinces. This policy involved generous scholarships, mass literacy schemes, expansion of teacher training schools, and the development of the Institute of Administration, Zaria, to train administrators and promote the ideology of northernisation. At the level of industrialisation and commerce, the Sardauna sought to establish industries to process locally available materials like textiles and ground-nut oil. This policy produced industries like Kaduna Textiles, Arewa Textiles, Norspin and others.

The main instruments for this industrial-commercial scheme were the Northern Regional Development Board (NRDB) and the Northern Nigeria Marketing Board (NNMB). Later the NRDB was to go through several name changes like Northern Regional Development Corporation (NRDC) Northern Nigeria Development Corporation (NNDC)and finally New Nigeria Development Company (NNDC) . Another thrust of this development programme was the development of infrastructural linkages like roads, rails and telephones. In the agricultural sector, model farms by government leaders were encouraged, cooperatives were organised for credit, irrigation schemes were developed and rural agricultural education encouraged.

In the early independence period, the Sardauna continued to aggressively implement his development policies as enunciated above, but he later set up the Ahmadu Bello University, incorporating the old Institute of Administration Zaria, and a whole network of other tertiary institutions in different parts of the north. In addition, he also set up the Broadcasting Corporation of Northern Nigeria (BCNN) and the *New Nigerian* newspaper, to mention a few of his developmental institutions.

The crucial issue about political and economic developments in the North from 1952 when the Macpherson constitution made the regional houses subordinate to the House of Representatives and by 1954 when the regional assemblies became fully independent, was that it gave the Northern People's Congress (NPC) full powers to run the government of the North (Okeke,1992).

The administrative style of the NPC and its leader the Sardauna had the following implications: government intervention in the economy became large-scale, and development policies, programmes and projects were skewed to favour strategic Hausa-Fulani or pro-north communities, and were usually administered by Sardauna confidants from the Hausa-Fulani bloc, or "contacts" from non-Hausa-Fulani-Kanuri Islamic communities. At any rate, most development projects and appointments always favoured the Hausa-Fulani core North. Recruitment and superficial pacification of the entire north seemed to be a device to use the northern bloc for control of power at the centre, or carry the minorities along (Okeke,1992).

The involvement of the state in the economy also meant that accumulation and appropriation favoured those who were in the good books of the leadership. Since the ownership and control of the means of production was determined by a state-capitalist government machinery and even the consciousness industry, education and mass media were state-controlled, it was easy for this emerging ruling class to perpetuate itself under the Sardauna, and to continue through the "Kaduna Mafia", upon his death in 1966 (Takaya and Tyoden,1987).

Struggle for Self-Determination

Much of the contemporary history of the north seems to be that of the struggle for self-determination by minority nationalities. In this regard, the Middle Belt movement is pre-eminent as the champion for this struggle for self-determination. Geo-culturally and politically, the Middle Belt area refers to the southern states of northern Nigeria consisting of Adamawa, Benue, Kaduna, Kogi, Kwara, Niger, Plateau, Taraba, parts of Bauchi, Borno and Yobe states, as well as the Federal Capital Territory, Abuja. Increasingly, the minorities of Sokoto and Kebbi states have come to identify with the Middle Belt. This area has less homogeneous characteristics when compared to the Hausa, Fulani and perhaps Kanuri to the north. Nevertheless they share many cultural, historical, economic and political characteristics. Their central location in the country places them between the predominantly Muslim north and the predominantly Christian South (Tyoden, 1993).

The Middle Belt movement epitomises the struggle for self determination in northern Nigeria. Due to the sociological peculiarities of this area which have been described above, especially its multi- linguistic nature, ethnic particularism and religious consciousness seemed to be the motivating micro–ideologies for the political struggle of the people of this area. Sklar (1983) has observed that the earliest non-parochial association of educated elements in this area was the Tiv Progressive Union (TPU), formed by the civil servants from the Tiv area, the largest ethnic nationality group of the lower north. The TPU became an ally of the National Council of Nigeria and the Cameroons (NCNC)in 1954.Motivated by a quest for their economic right vis-à-vis the activities of British miners, the Birom organised the Birom Progressive Union (BPU) in 1945, and it became the first organised group to espouse the cause of a Middle Belt state.

Although these groups were certainly not the only politically active ethnic associations, they seemed to be most prominent, perhaps because of their sizeable population (Sklar, 1983). A pan-Middle Belt movement may have actually started in 1949 when in the Northern House of Assembly, a private member moved that the northern regional government should curb the activities of the Christian missionaries in the north, and a small group of Christians responded by forming the northern Nigerian Non-Moslem League. The following year, the League changed its name to the Middle Zone League, to emphasise its political and secular agenda. When the Middle Zone League, with the BPU as its strongest tribal element, opted for cooperation with northern Nigeria's ruling party, the Northern Peoples Congress (NPC) in 1953, a splinter group led by Moses Nyam Rwang, a Birom, and Bello Ijumu, a Kabba Yoruba, and its dominant tribal element, the TPU, organised the Middle Belt People's Party as an affiliate of the NCNC. It was however in 1955 that both factions of the Middle Belt movement merged to form its best remembered political formation, the United Middle Belt Congress (UMBC) which after some initial flirtation with the NPC, formed an alliance with the Action Group (AG) in 1957 (Sklar, 1983). Sklar (1983) has also advanced two reasons why the Middle Belt movement gained in strength about a decade prior to 1960. These are its powerful ethnic constituents, especially the Birom and Tiv who were afraid of the cultural imperialism and political dominance of the numerically preponderant Hausas of the north, and secondly, the open and clandestine support of the movement by Christian missions.

Although Nnoli (1978) has suggested that the Middle Belt movement was essentially petit bourgeois and ethnic-based, there is evidence of a populism tending towards proletarian class interests. In its 1964 membership cards, the UMBC declared a socialist and Pan-Africanist stand in addition to its states creation agendum, and in the western part of the Middle Belt, for example, the intrusion of the Sokoto Caliphate in Ilorin and the absolutist rule of a Fulani emir created resentment among his Yoruba lower chiefs and subjects. The emergence of the Ilorin "Talaka Parapo" (Commoner's Party) may have been a part of this resentment. The alliance of the Middle Belt movement with the radical Borno Youth Movement (BYM), essentially the Kanuri variant of the Northern Elements Progressive Union (NEPU), the political formation of the Hausa Talakawa (common people) within the Northern Progressive Front (NPF), did indicate that there was more to the oppositional politics in the immediate pre and post-independence Northern Nigerian politics than ethnicity and religion. Both the BYM and the UMBC who received the support of minority nationalities, were as lower class in orientation as was NEPU with whom it sometimes collaborated. However, the ultimate objectives of both movements were for the creation of states in the North. A Bornu State in the case of the BYM, and a Middle Belt State in the case of the UMBC. Both movements were as a result, very disappointed with the report of the Commission of Inquiry into the Fears of Minorities in 1958, which confirmed the justifiability of fears of domination of minorities by the regional majority, but recommended against the creation of states.

Subsequently the struggle for self-determination took a very violent form, especially in the Tiv area, where a series of riots and revolts in the early 1960s showed the extreme frustration that had accumulated within the oppositional politics in the north. Later, a re-alignment of forces between the Middle Belt and Northern officers may have occurred because of the lack of sympathy of Major-General Aguiyi-Ironsi towards the project of a Middle Belt state after the 1966 coup d'etat (Nnoli,1978). Lt. Colonel Yakubu Gowon who replaced him in the same year, himself from the Middle Belt, may have gained popularity for identifying with this cause, releasing some political prisoners and eventually creating states in 1967.

If the creation of states was the main objective of the BYM and the UMBC, why has the struggle for self-determination continued in the Middle Belt area,for example? For even within these new states, as in the case of the former Benue - Plateau State, there have been severe cases of ethnic rivarly which led to the demands for more states (Sen, 1994). More than that, the intensity of the 1991 Bauchi and 1992 Zangon-Kataf ethno-religious social conflicts, attests to the deep-seated nature of the minority question in the North. The case of lingering social schism between the Tiv and Jukun, who co-exist on the land, share cultural features and have inter-married for years is also interesting. It might also be useful to look at the detailed cases of cultural imperialism, domestic colonialism and economic factors to further understand the problems of multiculturalism in northern Nigeria.

Minority Quest for Political Power

Nnoli (1978) has argued that the most ardent advocates of new states or regions have always been aspriants to high positions in the political, administrative, professional, and business fields who have failed to attain positions of pre-eminence at the national, regional, or state levels, and who hope to attain such heights in smaller constitutional entities, and rationalise their inordinate ambitions by pleading reasons of national unity. However, the fact of the existence of opportunism does not necessarily invalidate the persistence of injustice even after states creation. In the second republic, for example, Governors Solomon Lar and Aper Aku of Plateau and Benue states, respectively still pursued the cause of fighting for self-determination even within states that they politically controlled. Lar, for example, pursued with vigour and fanfare, his "emancipation" programme, with the national oppositional Nigeria Peoples Party (NPP) , while Aku led the minorities caucus to fight for minority rights within the nationally ruling National Party of Nigeria (NPN) (Sen, 1991). Tyoden (1993) has observed that this made the two Governors constitute the left factions within these two parties which were centrist (NPP) or rightist (NPN).

Perhaps the abortive Third Republic which was terminated in 1993 by General Sani Abacha, saw an attempt to formalise the Middle Belt movement, but also exposed some of its contradictions. As early as 1986, an initiative sponsored by Dr. Olusola Saraki, a Fulani-Yoruba from Kwara, brought together politicians, intellectuals and activists to Senator John Wash Pam's country home, near Jos. After a series of meetings, the concept of a Central Zone movement emerged. The group resolved to continue its activities at the emerging Constituent Assembly (CA) under the coordination of Col. Yohanna Madaki, from Kaduna state. Meanwhile, the movement's activities outside the CA were cowed by harassment from security agents, and the original intention to establish a Secretariat in Jos with Yima Sen as the resident Secretary, was abandoned. At the CA, the idea of a Central Zone movement reverted to that of the Middle Belt movement, guided by activists of the Christian Association of Nigeria (CAN) and the People's Solidarity Party (PSP). However, with the refusal to register nine short-listed political parties of the Third Republic by General Ibrahim Babangida, and his formation of the Social Democratic Party (SDP) and the National Republican Convention (NRC), the PSP and Saraki tendencies merged within the SDP, but not without also incorporating a small socialist tendency consisting of mainly younger elements from the labour and socialist movements and the academia. By 1991, Yima Sen, a member of this latter group emerged as Secretary of the now formalised Middle Belt Forum (MBF), with Secretariat in Jos.

It was these tendencies that dominated the third republic, and whose overt manifestations became clear over the support for Presidential aspirants within the SDP. As Tyoden (1993) has explained, while the Secretariat and its ideological formulation tried to pursue an independent line of a mass democratic organisation only aligned to the SDP and addressing the national question in its entirety and from a holistic and left-leaning perspective, the other tendencies were more interested in pursuing a Christian-minoritist-populist agendum, as in the case of the tendency that supported Professor Jerry Gana, but which was actually led by Lt. General T.Y. Danjuma, and the right-leaning Saraki group, which had the sympathy of the MBF Chairman, Dr. Selcan Miner. Senator Mahmud Waziri as a seemingly innocuous progressive businessman had no serious following within the MBF but his utterances and Presidential manifesto appealed to some of the younger elements.

The jockeying for political support for Presidential aspirants within the Forum was so intense that a communiqué which had been drafted by Haruna Dabin, the Political Adviser to the Governor of Plateau state, and was released by the MBF Secretary, correctly reporting the outcome of the' work of a joint committee of the Forum and the East, was deliberately or mistakenly portrayed in the press as the endorsment of Dr. Sola Saraki as the Presidential favourite of the MBF. This was followed by counter statements and even a court affidavit by the Secretariat explaining its stand. In fact an early attempt by that committee to get the MBF Secretary to sign its press release was refused.

In the final analysis what has happened to the Middle Belt movement is that it has been hijacked and divided by bourgeois and petit-bourgeois elements. Some members have actually pursued political projects in direct contradistinction to the positions of the Forum. Take the example of Chief Olu Falae's group in the MBF. Citing the need to retain country-wide alliances and led by Drs. Bala Takaya and Jonathan Zwingina, and with other supporters in Kaduna state, it worked against even the Middle Belt interests to support their candidate. Takaya had been financed by Falae in his bid to be Governor of Gongola and later Adamawa state, while Zwingina was Falae's Campaign Director. Takaya later organised to forcibly seize the MBF bus donated by Falae when the latter did not receive the Forum's endorsement for his Presidential aspiration. Another example of this form of unprincipled politics was the national seminar on the "Equity Question", held in Jos in 1994 to discuss the national question. Danjuma who funded and Takaya who organised the seminar did not inform or invite the MBF Secretariat, and later, the group tricked some members of the MBF to affiliate with the National Democratic Coalition [NADECO], without consultations with the broad membership of the MBF.

The Implication of the Minorities' Question

From the foregoing, it is clear that the problematic of the national question is real. ' British colonial activity created a multi-cultural Nigeria, and although multi-culturalism or multiethnicity is not unique to Nigeria, the Nigerian case has its own peculiarity. The indirect rule system of British colonialism in Nigeria produced a political system skewed to favour an Anglo-Fulani alliance and then a Hausa-Fulani oligarchy, which has also employed religion and various divide and rule tactics as indicated by various authors (Kukah, 1994; Okeke, 1992; Takaya and Tyoden, 1987). The problem of minorities exists all over Nigeria. It led to the creation of a Mid-West region shortly after independence as a response to agitations by minorities in the Old Western Region. In the East, the movement for the creation of the Calabar-Ogoja-Rivers State was also active and has continued in the more recent Ogoni and other Southern minorities struggles against economic exploitation and environmental degradation. While Tyoden [1993] has noted a tendency towards a proletarian and macro-nationalist orientation in the Middle Belt movement, this has not happened elsewhere. In fact even in the Middle Belt, right-wing elements have strongly resisted this tendency, as in the cases of Saraki and Danjuma. The phenomenon of bourgeois minoritism which has been indicated by Nnoli (1978) is clearly evident today, especially among the oil producing minority nationalities. The establishment and management of the oil Minerals Producing Areas Development Commission (OMPADEC), attests to this tendency, whereby elites of the minorities negotiate for and are gratified with accumulation-facilitating bureaucracies which do not actually address the fundamental problems of their people but only result in "settlement" of the elite. The fundamental problem is that throughout Nigeria's history, discourse and activism about the national question has been led and dominated by bourgeois or petit-bourgeois elements.

The subservience of a proletarian class focus on this issue has subjected it to parochial and provincial manipulations or sentiments of religion or biology. With a few exceptions. those who integrate a class with a national question analysis have been too theoretically and practically weak. Practical political work in the field reveals that sometimes domination of minorities by minorities can be as bad if not worse than majorities domination. There is therefore an imperative for the formulation of a nationality praxis to deal precisely with the problems of multiculturalism in Africa's post - colonial societies, and the prescription of an emancipatory paradigm that can promote social, economic and political justice as well as popular democracy and egalitarian development. In this regard, Therborn (1988: p.117) may be very useful when he suggests:

> Thus in all revolutions that have changed the character of the state, elements of class ideologies have been fused with other types of ideological mobilisation, religious or national, for example, and the revolutionary mobilisation has always taken a conjectural ideological form.

Conclusion

Throughout Nigeria's history, the Hausa-Fulani have remained the political ruling class, the Igbos were initially the leading bureaucratic and commercial class, until the Yorubas took over as both the bureaucratic and economic ruling class. The civil war was essentially a settling of scores between the Hausa-Fulani elite and the Igbo elite. The June 12, 1993 annulment of the Presidential election which started out as a national problem has degenerated to an ethnic contest between the Yoruba and the Hausa-Fulani, due largely to the mismanagement of the crisis by the elite of the two groups. These developments do not necessarily exonerate the elite of the minorities from their share of oppressive and exploitative attributes. What is needed, therefore, is for activists and social scientists who are pro-people to rescue the nationality theory, and discourse and activism on the national question from self-centred and opportunistic politicians and shallow scholars, and reformulate them to address the problems of underdevelopment as they affect workers, peasants, women, youth and the broad masses of ordinary people.

References

Kukah, M.H. (1994), *Religion, Politics and Power in Northern Nigeria*, Lagos: Spectrum.

Nnoli, O. (1978), *Ethnic Politics, in Nigeria* Enugu: Fourth Dimension.

Okeke, O. (1992), *Hausa-Fulani Hegemony* Enugu: Acena.

Omolewa, M. (1986), *Certificate History of Nigeria* Ikeja: Longman.

Paden, J. N. (1986), *Ahmadu Bello, Sardauna of Sokoto: Values and Leadership in Nigeria.* Zaria: Hudahuda.

Sen, Y. (1991), 'The Middle Belt in Nigerian Politics : A Futuristic Analysis', paper presented at Seminar for SDP Local Government Chairmen, Jos.

Sen, Y. (1994), 'Aku and Minority Politics in Nigeria : A Critical Analysis', Aper Aku Memorial Lecture, Benue State University, Makurdi.

Sklar, R.L. (1983), *Nigerian Political Parties*: Enugu: Nok.

Takaya, B.J. and Tyoden S.G. (eds), (1987), *The Kaduna Mafia* Jos: Jos University Press.

Therborn, G. (1988), *The Ideology of Power And The Power of Ideology*: London: Verso.

Tyoden, S.G. (1993), *The Middle Belt In Nigerian Politics*: Jos: AHA.

7 The National Question and the Politicisation of Ethnicity in Yobe State

IBRAHIM BABA GANA

Introduction

Recent political events in Nigeria have indicated that the national question has not been resolved as clearly seen by the persistent agitation and manipulation of ethnicity, by members of the ruling class. The Politicisation of ethnicity has taken a serious dimension in Nigeria because it has successfully permeated the political, social and economic institutions of the country, posing an obstacle towards the attainment of popular national consciousness and national unity (Jinadu, 1995; Tamuno, 1970). Despite thirty-nine years of independence, ethnic chauvinism and bigotry are the order of the day. It has reached the extent, whereby some members of the ruling class, are openly calling for the dismemberment and balkanisation of the country along ethnic autonomous states (Ilenre, 1994). Forgetting that Nigeria went through a civil war, to keep Nigeria one (Dudley, 1973). Empirical examples from different parts of the world have clearly shown that civil wars have been fought over the ethnic question, millions of people have been killed, due to the way and manner some individuals have pursued the ethnic question. According to Stavenhagen:

> The world has witnessed a number of often-murderous conflicts in which the Ethnic question has played a major role. The whole contemporary history of the Indian sub-continent (India, Pakistan, and Bangladesh) cannot be understood without it. The Biafran war in Nigeria had a major ethnic component. The conflict between the Hutu and Tutsi tribes in Rwanda and Burundi constitutes a particular poignant case in point (Stavenhagen, 1983: p.115).

Ethnic problems and conflicts exist at global and continental levels. From 1994 and 1999, Africa experienced ethnic crisis and conflict in Ghana, South Africa, and in Rwanda and Burundi. Empirically, no country has been able to make any meaningful political and economic progress, without addressing the ethnic question.

The fundamental objective of this chapter is to examine the material basis behind the persistence agitation and politicisation of ethnicity in contemporary Nigeria, with specific focus on Yobe State in Northern Nigeria. In order to achieve the above objective, the chapter is divided into five sections. In section one, key concepts are defined. In section two, a general outline of the historical basis of the national question is articulated. In section three, the historical origins and manifestation of ethnic politics is presented. In section four we intend to examine the nature of ethnic politics in Yobe State, with emphasis on Fika and Nongere Local Government areas. Finally, section five is an explanatory overview.

Towards a Conceptualisation

In order to put things in perspective, we would first of all define the key concepts, the national question and ethnicity. It is necessary to clarify what is precisely being said, so that we understand each. The national question, according to Ajayi, is like a code name for all the controversies that arise in a nation's search for stability, legitimacy and development. It is concerned with the composition of the nation, in terms of relationship, which exists between the nationalities in Nigeria, "with reference to the relationships at the level of language, culture, religion, territoriality, communal, ethnic and national identities" (Ade-Ajayi, 1992).

A nationality is defined as a group with a common ethnic origin and language; therefore, Nigeria is a Nation-State made up of Yoruba, Hausa, Igbo and many nationalities. These nationalities are referred to as ethnic groups. The national question is therefore *"nothing but the deliberate pursuance and persistence of separate, though not necessarily separatist, national identities and interests within the framework of a multinational policy"* (Usman: 1982: p. 28). The national question is therefore the processes whereby multinational systems, try to contain and manage the centrifugal and centripetal forces and tendencies of sub-nationalities within a given political entity. For our purpose therefore the national question in Nigeria, is concerned with the relationship that exists among the different nationalities or ethnic groups in the country. According to Eskor Toyo the national question, is expressed in a series of contradictions, manifested in the following tendencies:

> Nigeria versus imperialism, the contradiction between the majority nationalities, i.e., Hausa, Igbo and Yoruba; the North, south divide, between the major nationalities and smaller nationalities, inter-state rivalries, inter-ethnic rivalries in a mixed states, inter-sectional rivalries

within an ethnic group, or nationality, for example between the Egbas and Ijebus of the Yoruba Nationality, and finally interclan contradictions within a province or district (cited Mahadi and Mangvwat, 1986: pp. 4-5).

From the foregoing analysis, the National Question is expressed at national and local levels. On the other hand, ethnicity:

> Is a social phenomena associated with interactions among members of different ethnic groups. Ethnic groups are social formations distinguished by the communal character of their boundaries, the relevant communal fact may be language, culture or both (Cited in Mustapha, 1986: p.82).

Ethnicity is behavioural in character and conflictual in nature. This is because:

1. Ethnicity arises due to the relationship between different ethnic groups, within the same political entity.

2. Ethnicity is characterised by a common consciousness, whereby ethnic group A, considers itself different from ethnic group B.

3. Ethnicity is characterised by exclusiveness, a feeling of being distinct.

4. Finally, conflict is an important attribute of ethnicity.

According to Nnoli:

> This is inevitable under conditions of inter-ethnic competition for scarce valuable resources particularly in societies where inequality is accepted as natural and wealth is greatly esteemed (Nnoli, 1978: p.5).

Ethnicity is a set of subjective beliefs or perceptions about ones own or another's identity, which is acquired by being a member of a particular ethnic group or category. This subjective feeling of one's self has an impact on one's social behaviour and this has the tendency of influencing the existing social relationship and interaction in the social structure in a negative manner, because ethnicity breeds ethnocentrism leading to conflict. But it should be realised that ethnicity does not appear totally in its pure form, but it is associated with political, religious, juridical and other social views. In the case of Nigeria, ethnicity goes hand in hand with the manipulation of religion. Numerous ethnic conflicts have contributed to the destruction of social-political stability and economic progress in Nigeria. Ethnicity is therefore a reactionary and negative social phenomenon, which should be properly understood if it is to be transcended. In order to do that, we would situate our discussion of the national question in historical context.

The National Question and Its Historical Basis in Nigeria

Before we can meaningfully understand the ethnic problem, a discussion of the historical foundation of the national question in Nigeria is necessary. There is the general assumption, an erroneous one at that, within the political discourse of this country, that before the advent of colonial rule:

> Each tribe, ethnic group or nationality in this country, lived largely on its own, in its own sovereign kingdoms, city states, chiefdoms or village confederations under its natural rulers (Nnoli, 1978: p.5).

The historical evidence has shown that, before 1914, people living in this geographical region had political and economic connections for centuries. According to Y.B. Usman:

> The people of the Nigerian region had developed clans, tribes and nationalities, before the imposition of colonial rule. This meant that in many instances, the organising principles of society were not blood ties and linguistic affinity but such criteria like territoriality and occupation and the attendant processes of class differences and State formation (Usman, 1982: p.12).

The issue is that the sovereign kingdoms that the British conquered to establish the colony of Nigeria were not ethnic entities. Therefore in pre-colonial times, ethnic solidarity, had never been the basis for the formation and establishment of the political entities found in Nigeria, for instance, the Hausa States, Kanem Borno Empire, Oyo Empire, Benin Empire, etc. (cited in Mustapha, 1996). To further lend credence to this assertion, the nationalities in today's Nigeria, did not exist in their present size or form till the colonial period of our history. For instance, the term "Hausa" was not a political expression in the 17th and 18th centuries, but rather, the term:

> Represented a language spoken by many autonomous socio-political entities in and beyond the present geographical area. These socio-political entities whose language was Hausa did not see themselves as having a common interest (Usman, 1994: pp.35-52).

This was because they had diverse economic and political interests; they were always at war with each other. According to Abdullahi Madahi, the dominant historical development in pre-colonial northern Nigeria, from the 11th century to the 19th century was State formation.

> From the evidence so far it is clear that the process of state formations was a very complex one involving socio-economic and religious factors and processes which were both internal and external to the politics in the

formation. It is equally clear that racial and linguistic factors played no significant roles (Ikime, 1987: p.34).

For example, Hausaland meant the territory where Hausa language and custom prevailed. There was no development of a monolithic Hausa Kingdom. But there was in reality several state systems, which developed as states of *Kasar* Hausa. Furthermore, no mono-national state systems are known to have emerged or developed among the Tiv, Kanuri, Nupe, etc. A historical study of the Northern part of the country indicates that, there are more state systems, i.e., kingdoms, chiefdoms and chieflets than linguistic groups. In the former Plateau province, there are over 60 language groups or ethnic groups, and the province has about 400 chieftancies or polities, which underscores the point, that language and race, were not crucial factors in the development of the state systems in Nigeria. The crucial factors, behind the formation of states were the interplay of complex socio-economic and religious factors and processes, leading to the emergence of specific state systems as demonstrated in the case of Hausaland and Borno (Mahadi and Mangvwat, 1986: p.7). Similarly the term Yoruba did not come into existence until the 19th century and it did not apply to all Yoruba. The evidence shows that a common or similar language did not necessarily indicate common interest, as indicated by the Yoruba wars in the 19th century.

According to Falola, in pre-colonial times "Yorubaland was never a single socio-economic unit". Groups had their territories while citizenship was defined in relation to the membership of a state within a group. Land, an aspect of territorial sovereignty, was communal, and no pan-Yoruba authority ever emerged to control all land. Territorial sovereignty and citizenship were not defined in a Pan-Yoruba framework since there were different autonomous states (Mahadi and Mangvwat, 1986: pp.6-31). Those states did not evolve a loose political federation. The ruling class of the different states did not assume an overwhelming control over all others. Every Oba had sovereignty over his domain. In essence, therefore, there were several sovereign states within Yorubaland. Factors of intergroup relationship were trade, migrations, diplomacy and wars, which formed the basis of state formation. In the case of the Delta State, it should be realised:

> That those states did not see themselves as belonging to Ijo State or even commonwealth. Bonny, Kalabari, Okrika, later Opobo, each saw itself as a sovereign state and competition among them for available resources in their peculiar terrain was a recurrent feature of their history. What is true for the peoples here mentioned is true for other Nigerian peoples (Falola, 1986).

The reason why the discussion of Nigeria's historical past is important is to show that the process of State formation and political transformation, did not take an ethnic perspective, identification along ethnic lines, was nurtured within the context of the colonial and neo-colonial States. In order to understand the role of the state, it becomes necessary to trace the historical origins of ethnicity in Nigeria.

The Origins of Ethnic Politics in Nigeria

Ethnic politics in Nigeria has its roots in the imperialist conquest of Nigeria and the entrenchment of capitalist relations of production, which led to the establishment of colonial rule. Colonialism's principal objective was to exploit the socio-economic resources of the country. To facilitate this objective, a conducive administrative structure was imposed to effectively control the nation, and this was done by regionalising the country into East, West and North, all with the principal objective of siphoning economic resources to Britain. The issue is that ethnic politics can be traced squarely to colonialism, because it intensified ethnic particularalism due to the following reasons:

(a) The colonial system of education internalised attitudes of inferiority and superiority among the different communities or between regions by creating uneven development between them. Empirically, all across Africa there are ethnic groups, which claim they are superior over their neighbours on the basis of educational statistics. This has formed the basis of inter-ethnic conflict in, for instance, the civil service, the private sector, etc.

(b) Colonialism ensured the uneven development of the colonial territories; this forms a very important part of the colonial policy of divide and rule.

       The colonialists encourage ethnic sentiments among the Africans; it seized every available opportunity to spread the myth, that they are different. Emphasis was placed on their differences, nothing was revealed of the similaries served to divert attention away from colonial exploitation, oppression and domination. Instead Africans focussed on relations among themselves interpreting them to be inherently conflictual because of the assumed differences (Ikime, 1987: p.34).

This has created a platform for ethnic conflict and competition. For example, the policy of northernisation should be understood within this context. The regionalisation of socio-economic wealth has contributed to the politicisation of ethnicity in Nigeria. The colonialists decided who had access to these resources. Thus the character of politics took a regional and ethnic perspective during the colonial era. In this regard, the political elites who were created and nurtured by colonialism competed among themselves for control of state power. This competition during the colonial era, in terms of how socio-economic resources are to be allocated, took place between ethnically defined constituencies. Ethnicity was therefore socially created due to the specific historical situation. The Colonial State in Nigeria, regulated access to commercial opportunities, centralised in the State through the State monopoly marketing boards. This created a situation of scarcity of resources as clearly articulated by Nnoli:

> Therefore scarcity was pervasive of the colonial order. It was evident in the economic and political spheres of life. It effected employment, education, political participation and the provision of social services to the population. Under these circumstances the competition could be intense and destructive. Individuals had to rely on various useful devices to gain access to the scarce goods and services; one of these was individual communal groups, including the most inclusive of them, the ethnic group (Nnoli, 1987 : p.76).

Nigerian politicians at that period wanted to gain access and control of State resources, because the state was the primary source of accumulation for members of the petty-bourgeois class. By 1947, colonialism had started the process of planned decolonisation. Within this set up there was the gradual transfer of administrative and political offices, and thus control of revenue and resources to Nigerian politicians and bureaucrats. This petit–bourgeois class was created and nurtured by colonialism, the nature of politics, therefore was politically and economically competitive as clearly stated:

> Nigerian politicians and businessmen competed amongst themselves for the rents and profits to be derived from foreign business activities and foreign State Capital (Aid). They acted as agents for foreign firms and Foreign Governments, wishing to establish themselves commercially and politically in Nigeria (Nnoli, 1978: p.80).

Politics was shaped by the economy and it was characterised by intense competition among politicians. Instead of taking a national perspective, it took a regional and therefore ethnic perspective. From the foregoing the basis of ethnic conflict and antagonism is essentially material. In this case the colonialists acted as the arbiter in the constitutional conflict and electoral competition. In a situation like this, it was able to play off Nigerian politicians against each other by, for instance, either protecting the institutional base of Northern conservatism against the so-called progressive south. The politicisation of ethnic conflict was sharpened with the formation of political parties, which were strictly regionally based and they coincided with either a dominant ethnic group or minority ethnic group. For instance, in the North, the dominant political party was the NPC established to serve the interest of the so-called Hausa-Fulani, in the South, the NCNC, meant to serve the interest of the Ibo, while in the West, the AG. meant to serve the interest of the Yoruba. All the petty bourgeois politicians, who controlled the political parties, consolidated their hold over the regions by appealing to ethnic sentiments. During the Second Republic (1979-1983) the situation did not change fundamentally, while in the Third Republic the fallout of the June 12 election was given an ethnic and regional character. Within this context, the politicisation of ethnicity led to the emergence of what is referred to as the problem of ethnic minorities, who had started agitating for the creation of States, since the colonial era. This platform of struggle could be traced to the frustrations of the petty bourgeois factions of minority ethnic groups in their socio-economic and political competition with the factions of the dominant ethnic groups. The problems of ethnic minorities can be traced to the colonial era, when in 1957, the colonial Government set up the Willink Commission of enquiry to: "ascertain the facts about the fears of minorities in any part of Nigeria and to propose means of allaying these fears, whether well - or ill founded" (Williams, 1980).

At the end of the day, no State was created despite the high level of agitation. With independence in 1960, the expectation was that things would change for the better, but rather there was an intensification of ethnic conflict in Nigeria. The Politics of the First Republic was characterised by a high decree of inter-regional and inter-ethnic struggle between the major groups, and also between ethnic majority and ethnic minorities, for the spoils of office. Politics was a zero sum game, and no attempt was made on the part of the political leaders to foster a spirit of Popular National Consciousness. This is because ethnicity is a convenient ideological tool used by the different factions of the ruling class, to subordinate the masses and ensure their unfettered access to the neo-colonial state. Ethnicity is used to legitimise their control of the State by creating a situation of compliance among the masses. Thus by January, 1966, the politicians were overthrown through a bloody military coup, which served as the basis for the further exploitation of ethnic differences, this is because, the first coup was interpreted as an Ibo led coup against northerners. The backlash of this situation was the outbreak of ethnic violence in the country, leading to the killings of thousands of Ibos in the North. By July 1966, another coup took place, led by General Yakubu Gowon, culminating in a change of events, like Ojukwu announcing secession, resulting in a bloody thirty months civil war. The expectation is that, with the civil war over and twelve States created, the problem of ethnicity would be a thing of the past.

The reality of the situation is that, from the end of the civil war to date, the politicisation and manipulation of ethnicity by the different factions of the ruling class have persisted, as would be illustrated, using the case of the politics of State creation in Nigeria and the problem of ethnic minorities. Without mincing words the demand for the creation of States in Nigeria is a child of ethnic competition and a political strategy:

> Underlying the movement for the creation of States in Nigeria is the ethnic question. They arose out of the frustrations of the petty bourgeois factions of the minority ethnic groups in their socio-economic and political competition with the equivalent factions from the dominant ethnic group (Ekekwe, 1986: p.32).

The initial argument of the so-called ethnic minorities is that, they have been dominated by the majority ethnic nationalities, i.e., Hausa-Fulani, Ibo and Yoruba, by not being given access to the political and economic resources in the public and private sectors which is centrally controlled. The petty bourgeoisie of the minority ethnic groups justify their advocacy for state creation on the above premise. The expectation is that when there is creation of states, the ethnic tension would reduce.

> In each newly created state there were usually majority and minority ethnic groups with the dominant (formerly in the forefront of the minority agitation for separate state) proceeding to divert most resources to its own petty bourgeoisie (Nnoli, 1983: p.25).

The agitation for the creation of more states goes on *ad infinitum*. This is because the movement for the creation of states in Nigeria is ethnic in perspective. All over the place, ethnic champions are exploiting this problem by intensifying the agitation for more states along ethnic lines. In 1967, twelve states were created, in 1967, the number was increased to nineteen, while in 1992, there was a leap to thirty states and now to thirty-six states. In each of the recently created states, there is a high degree of ethnic animosity among the domicile ethnic groups. In Yobe it is the problem between the Bolewa and those from other parts of Yobe, in Kogi it is Igala *vs* Ebira, in Delta it is Urhobos *vs* Itsekiris, in Taraba, Jukun *vs* Tiv, etc. The root cause of the crisis is traceable to struggle for spoils of office within the state. The different factions of the ruling classes, within the state employ ethnicity to facilitate their economic objectives, as has been asserted:

> It is interesting to note in support of this assertion that ethnic prejudices and antagonism are mostly prevalent and most violently expressed in

situations where employment or business is involved. It is in circumstances involving employment in the civil service, in industry, in the Universities and in other places that one may become suddenly conscious of one's ethnic tag and ones difference from competitors depending on ones employment needs and interests are satisfied (Barongo, 1983).

The implication of the persistence of ethnic politics in the nation's body polity, despite the creation of thirty-six States in Nigeria, is that national unity and integration, is still a mirage. Illustrative of our case is the 1995 demonstrations, riots and mayhem in Jos, over the appointment of an Hausa man as the Sole Administrator of Jos Local Government Council, by the indigenous people. It is claimed in some circles, that the creation of nine more additional States by the Babangida and Abacha administrations was a response to political pressures for a more ethnically balanced Federation. (Olagunju, et.al 1995). The expectation is that, by now the agitation for the creation of more States should be a closed issue. But despite the crisis of the neo-colonial State, some members of the ruling class agitated for the creation of more States using the platform of the National Constitutional Conference. For instance, in the northern parts of the country, there is still a strong agitation for the creation of Gombe and Katagum States out of present Bauchi State, Savanna State out of present Borno State and Sardauna State out of present Adamawa State. The struggle for the creation of more States in 1994 is still anchored on ethnic lines. The agitation as pointed out is *ad-infinitum* as long as the reason behind the struggle is ethnic. On the other hand, it is expected that, when States are created, ethnic crisis and tension are supposed to decline. The reality on the ground is that the new states are characterised by a high degree of ethnic infighting and crisis, among the members of the major ethnic groups, for the spoils of office. Another fundamental dimension of the politicisation of ethnicity in Nigeria, is the issue of ethnic minorities. According to Osaghae, the origins of the minority problem can be traced to the regionalisation of the country under colonial rule.

> The regionalisation of Nigeria, process began in the 1940's under Governor Bouidillion and Richards institutionalised by the adoption of a Federal constitution in 1954, brought to light a clear cut numerical differentiation between the ethnic majorities and minorities in the regions (Osaghae, 1990).

Despite the fact that regions no longer exist, the issue of ethnic minorities is still a national reality as in the past. The dynamics of the majority *vs* minority relations is characterised by intense infighting between the majority ethnic groups, out to dominate the minority groups politically and economically. This has created the fertile ground for separatist agitation by the minorities from all the regions for the creation of states. Even though during the colonial era, a commission was established to look into the matter, but the matter as earlier pointed out, was not resolved. This issue bedevilled the stability of the First Republic, and was one of the crucial factors behind its collapse in 1966. After the collapse of the First Republic, successive military regimes have created new states to replace the regions. This is predicated on the belief that the fundamental barriers towards national integration in Nigeria was the "Federal Structure". Thus "the new structure of states will provide the basis for wielding together the heterogeneous communities of Nigeria into a nation. The internal structure of the new states will curb the excesses of any ethnic group and ensure peace and stability" (Osaghae, 1990: p.156). Osaghae is of the view that "the minorities have certainly come a long way in the Nigerian federation. From a position of dependence on the majorities to partake in the sharing of the national cake, they have, with the creation of separate states, become direct shareholders of the power in the federation (Osaghae, 1991: p.257). The general expectation is that with the thirty-five states structure, the issue of ethnic minorities, should be a thing of the past. But since the annulment of the June 12, 1993 presidential elections, there has been a strong agitation by ethnic minorities for the dismemberment and balkanisation of the country along independent autonomous ethnic entities.

The point would be illustrated by taking the case of southern minorities. Their argument is that since they are the producers of one of the nation's most important source of wealth, oil, they should benefit economically from it. Presently, they are experiencing nothing but deprivation of their resource and environmental degradation, due to the activities of transitional corporations such as Shell, Agip and Elf. This has contributed to their political marginalisation, because they have no control over their wealth. Abject poverty, misery and total neglect are the order of the day. The solution, they postulate, is that the Federal Government should be replaced by a confederation of autonomous ethnic political entities. Ken Saro Wiwa puts across this view very eloquently:

> In Nigeria (if the resulting State choose to keep the name), each ethnic group will have autonomy, i.e., rule itself politically, use its resources for its economic development, have adequate and direct representation as of right in all Nigerian national institutions, practise its religion, develop its culture and its environment and ecology from further degradation. But there are about 350 ethnic groups in Nigeria. Will there be 350 different autonomous and independent units? Yes, Why not? There are now 600

local governments. Has Nigeria collapsed? But 350 governors: Who said that the rulers of each group will be called governors, that they will all run identical paraphernalia of office (Saro-Wiwa, 1992: p.2).

In summary what is being advocated is the miniaturisation of Nigeria. An additional complementary position is the strong argument being postulated by some of the leaders of the ethnic minorities that political representation be based on "ethnic representation".

The National Question and Ethnic Politics in Yobe State

The Yobe State came into being on 27th August, 1991. It was carved out of the old Borno State. Yobe State covers an area of 47,153 Km, with a population of about 1.4 million. Yobe State is a multi-ethnic State. The notable ethnic groups in Yobe are Kanuri, Fulani, Karai-Karair, Bolewa, Bade, Hausa, and Ngam. There are thirteen local government areas in Yobe State (Yobe State Diary, 1995). The extent and dimension of how ethnicity has permeated, the political, economic and socio-cultural institutions of the nation can be illustrated by examining the politics behind the creation of Yobe State and the unfolding events in Nangore and Fika local government councils.

The agitation for the creation of Yobe State began with the presentation of the demand for the splitting of former Borno State into more states. According to the submission, the writers asked for an additional state, because they wanted the rapid development of the people, especially the rural dwellers. They therefore requested for the creation of:

(a)   Yobe State with Damaturu town as the suggested capital with an estimated population of 3.6 million people with a total of 12 local government areas.

(b)   Borno State, with Maiduguri as suggested capital, with estimated population 3.8 million people, with 12 local government areas. The request was signed by about 100 elites, representatives of all the communities and nationalities in former Borno State (Ciroma, private papers, n.d.).

The first request triggered a chain of reaction, whereby the people of Fika emirate wrote an addendum, addressed to the President of Nigeria. According to the memo, the under-signed claimed to have been forced to write in order to air their views "on the composition, criteria for selecting the capital and other related issues on the proposed Yobe State". The addendum was a response to the first write up, which included Biu and Shani (predominantly Bura local government areas) in the proposed Yobe State and suggested Damaturu as the capital of the State. The people of Fika Emirate objected to the inclusion of Biu in Yobe State on the grounds that the Emirs of Biu and Fika are in conflict with each other over the order of precedence in official matters among the two Emirs. This, according to the writers, led to open confrontation between the Emirs of Biu and Fika. Reference was made to the strained relationship between the Alaafin of Oyo and the Ooni of Ife. Based on the above reasons, the people of Fika suggested that Biu should not be part of Yobe State. Secondly they requested that the capital of Yobe State should be located in Potiskum, rather than Damaturu, because Potiskum being the second urban centre after Maiduguri in former Borno State, has all the necessary infrastructure and facilities necessary for the establishment of a State capital. The letter was signed by all the prominent elites of Fika Emirate (Ciroma, private papers, n.d).

The ethnicisation of the struggle for the creation of Yobe State was manifested in the struggle that went on between the ruling elites of Biu and Fika. On the part of the ruling elite of Fika, it was expedient for them to struggle for the non-inclusion of the people of Biu into Yobe State, because it would give them a dominant position in the civil service vis-à-vis the other ethnic groups in the state. On the other hand, it was the estimation of the ruling elite of Biu, that if they gained entry into Yobe State, it would give them a dominant position over all other groups in the civil service, because of their numerical strength in the former Borno civil service. Thus the agitation and struggle for the creation of Yobe State, just like in other parts of the country was pursued on an ethnic platform. When Yobe State was created Biu was effectively excluded and left in former Borno State. This immediately triggered a petition, by the ruling elites of Biu which was carried as an advertisers' announcement in the *Sunday Concord* of October 6, 1991 entitled "A call for the adjustment of Biu Emirate into Yobe State." In the said write-up signed by prominent elite of Biu, they questioned the validity of the arguments presented by the ruling elite of Fika, on the apparent conflict existing between the Emirs of Fika and Biu over the order of precedence. According to the write-up:

> Thus in some respects and to some degree the two communities (Biu and Fika) can be said to be even closer than either of them has ever been with the Kanuri's. Even more relevant to the fact that intermarriage between the two communities over the years has virtually become institutionalised to the extent that, today, a good number of the leaders of Fika emirate (the emir, some of his councillors the princes etc) are married to women from Biu emirate. Similarly but to a lesser extent, the same applies the other way. Given these facts therefore, it becomes difficult to understand the claim by the Bolewa's that we can not exist peacefully and harmoniously in the same State (Yobe) (*Sunday Concord,* October 6, 1991).

The overall conclusion that we can reach from the foregoing is that, the ethnic factor was dominant in the struggle for the creation of Yobe State, and this has facilitated the entrenchment of ethnicity in the body polity of the state. With the creation of Yobe State, the ethnic infighting was now internalised. The common front that emerged during the struggle for the creation of Yobe State, took a complete U- Turn. Within the civil service there is intense struggle for the spoils of office. The struggle is defined to be between the people of Fika and Nangere (i.e., Bolewa, Kara - Kara Ngizim and Ngamo) who are considered dominant and the majority, because of their high numbers in key positions in the civil service, and the others (i.e., Fulani, Bade, Hausa, Kanuri) whose representation in the civil service and key positions is small in number, thus they are considered as the minorities of Yobe State. This has defined the way and manner resources and appointments are allocated in the civil service. This struggle for spoils of office on an ethnic platform operates at the level of the State. The intensity of the ethnic struggle in Yobe State is better illustrated by the events that are taking place in Nangare and Fika local government council areas. To appreciate the intensity of the ethnic struggle going on in the area, a historical analysis is necessary. At independence in 1960, Fika and Nangare local government council areas, were administered as Fika emirate under the leadership of the Emir of Fika. This emirate, at independence, remained divided into two districts, but a third district Nangare was added. With the creation of additional states in 1968, no major administrative changes took place, until the mid 1970s, when local governments were created in Nigeria. This triggered the emergence of Fika local government area, covering 1700 square miles, organised around the three districts. In the 1980s Fika local government was divided into two local government areas - Nangare and Fika. The area in question consists of several Ethnic groups with a close affinity to one another. They are the Bolewa, Ngamo, Karai - Karal and Ngizim, with a mixture of Kanuri, Ngazar, Here, Abore and Fulani. In recent years large immigration of the Hausa in particular but also Yoruba, Igbo and others, has added to the cultural diversity of the emirate and also enriched the well being of its community as a whole. This multi ethnic area has a population of about half a million. It is the most heterogeneous and most populous territory in Yobe State. The Political relationship between the major ethnic groups especially after 1979 took an ethnic dimension (Waziri, 1989). This problem can be traced to the historical past of the community. The history and people of Fika and Nangare Local Government Areas emerged in the pre-colonial Kanem Borno empire. The combination of historico-linquistic, demographic and environmental evidence has shown strong indicators of common ancestry of the earlier settlers due to the processes of migratory movements and an established graduated occupation of the area by different peoples in historical times. In this regards, oral traditions and written evidence deduced from available historical texts on central Sudan indicate that the Ngizim, Bolewa, Karai - Karai and Ngamo people migrated from the shores or immediate vicinity of the Lake Chad Basin, even though oral traditions suggest eastern or Vemeni origins. The overwhelming evidence which gave credence to the fact of the common historical ancestry of the peoples of Fika is provided by linguistics. The linguistic evidence as presented by people like Greenbery, Benton and Locus groups all refer to the major groups as belonging to the Chadic sub-unit of the Afro-Asiatic branch of African languages. Furthermore, this common origin has led to a high degree of inter-group relationship at a political, economic and socio-cultural level amongst the people of the area in pre- colonial times. The Ngizim of Potiskum under Mai Potaskum Dangar were effectively in control of the Potiskum region, extending their dominance over the Karai - Karar. The Bolewa on the other hand, under the Mai of Fika held sway over Fika and its environs, extending their dominance over the Ngamo around Godiltills (Waziri and Gana, 1995).

The advent of British colonialism completely altered the geo-political situation of the people of the area. In the first place, they all lost their independence to colonialism, and furthermore by 1915, the leaders of especially the Karai-Karai and Ngizim were all disposed by the British, because of their involvement in one form of nationalist uprising after the other. They were then brought under the political control of the Emir of Fika. This was the first time that the Ngizim and Karai-Karai came under the authority of Moi of Fika. This control on them, according to Ibrahim, made the "Ngizim and Karai-Korai to feel suppressed by the over lordship of the Bolewa headed by the Emir of Fika (Waziri, 1989). The consequence was that it gave rise to ill feelings among the Ngizim and the Karai-Karai towards the Bolewa in general. To them the Emir of Fika and the Bolewa in general represented an even worse enemy than the British colonialist in whose behest and behalf the Emir of Fika became involved in the colonial administration of both Ngizim and Karai-Karai (Waziri, 1989). This formed the basis of antagonism and laid the foundation for the present agitation for ethnic autonomy and independence in the contemporary era. The nature of the ethnic animosity prevalent in this area is between the Bolewa/ Hausa-Fulani, who are considered as the dominant ruling class and thus oppressors versus the Ngamo, Ngizim and Kare-Kare (Waziri, 1989: p.40.). During the Second Republic, there was a political alliance among the members of the ruling elite of the three ethnic groups, which ensured that no Bolewa or Hausa Fulani candidate won elections into any elective office for local government, state or federal representation. The extent of the ethnic animosity between the Ngamu, Ngizim and Kare-Kare ruling elites, vis-à-vis their relationship with the Bolewa ruling elite has reached a pathetic stage, whereby open conflict is the order of the day. The argument of the "so-called oppressed ethnic groups", is that the Emir of Fika, who is Bolewa has been "enslaving" the Ngamo, Ngizim and Kare-Kare for so many years, civil rule, gives them the opportunity to correct this historically - created form of Patron/Slave relationship in favour of the oppressed ethnic groups. This has been the ideological basis of the ethnic agitation in Fika and Nangare Local Government Councils. It reached a point, during the Second Republic when large-scale political violence along ethnic lines erupted in Potiskum, leading to the killing of so many people. During the Third Republic the character of politics, in Fika and Nangare Local Government, was manipulated along ethnic lines. That formed the basis of the struggle for the creation of more Emirates in the former Fika Emirate, which consist of Nangare and Fika Local Government Councils. Before the creation of additional Emirates, the Emir of Fika, was the only traditional ruler, with supremacy over all the ethnic groups residing in the Emirate.

The State Government in 1993, under the Governorship of Alhaji Bukar Abba Ibrahim, who is the first Civilian Governor of Yobe State decided to create three additional Emirates from Fika Emirate, with the sole purpose of freeing the Ngizim, Kare-Kare and Ngamo, from the Yobe of Bolewa hegemony and oppression by giving to them their own Emirs with their own Administrative units carved out in a manner that gives them ethnic autonomy, within the area under study. The Emirates created are as follows:

(a)   Fika Emirate with Headquarters in Potiskum, Headed by the Emir of Fika, meant to serve the interest of the Bolewa and Hausa-Fulani.

(b)   Gudi Emirate with Headquarters at Gadaka headed by Mai Gudi, meant to serve the interest of the Ngamu.

(c)   Pataskum Emirate with headquarters, in Mamudo, headed by Mai Pataskumo meant to serve the interest of the Ngizim.

(d)   Tikau Emirate with Headquarters in Sobongarin Nangare, headed by Mai Tikau to serve the interest of the Kare-Kare.

The creation of these additional Emirates, has not in any way reduced ethnic tension, rather it has reinforced it, as clearly portrayed during the election of delegates for the Constitutional National Conference. What happened during the election is that the Ngamo, Ngizim and Kare-Kare elites mobilised their people along the above ethnic alliances (lines) and made sure that the person perceived to represent Bolewa interest was defeated. Ethnic conflict is also reinforced at another level. At present there is a strong agitation calling for abolishing of the Emirates, and this has elicited a response, from all the interested parties (*Sunday Democrat*, 5th ed. 12th February, 1995). The Emirates were created in a manner which reinforced the ethnic differences among the people to the extent that, two Mais were residing within Potiskum. It could be concluded that the raging battle for ethnic autonomy and independence among the dominant Ethnic groups, falls squarely within the context of the manipulation of ethnicity in Nigeria, which has at the end of the day contributed towards the under development of the people of these communities, as clearly seen by the low level of infrastructural development and the low standard of living of the majority of the people, irrespective of ethnic origin or place of abode. The present endemic agitation around ethnicity in Fika and Nangere Local Government areas is therefore a negation of the peoples pre-colonial history. The balkanisation of the people of the community in the form of multiple Emirates, built around ethnic cleavage not only negates the historical reality of the people but it fans the embers of ethnic disharmony. This is because historically no ethnic group or nationality within Nigeria was able to form a culturally distinct and homogenous sovereign nation or identity. The argument articulated by some elite, that an autochthonous nation existed among the peoples of Fika and Nangere lacks convincing historical evidence.

The basis of the creation of Emirates by the politicians during the Third Republic can be attributed to selfish reasons. So called "progressive politicians," pushed this agenda with the sole purpose of carving out for themselves a constituency for winning future elections, by giving "autonomy and independence" to groups that are considered marginalised. The backlash of this process is the fanning of ethnic conflict in the community to the advantage of some politicians, who use it as a basis of political mobilisation and the capturing of political power as clearly manifested in Fika and Nangere Local Government areas. In 1994, the government of Yobe State abolished all the Emirates that had been established by the civilian administration, and reverted to the pre 1993 status quo. At present there is some relative calmness in the community, but the animosity and ethnic hatred, was only been buried, to be reopened once the ban on political activity was lifted. The issue therefore from the foregoing is that ethnicity has been nurtured and sustained, within neo-colonial Nigeria, by different factions of the bourgeois class, and this has operated in their overall interest, for it has legitimised their dominance over the weak in society.

An Explanatory Overview

It is our contention that any agitation which puts the ethnic question in the forefront and as the most fundamental political problem within the framework of the marginalisation of certain majority or minority ethnic groups, is a tool used by the ruling class in order to institutionalise their hold over the neo-colonial state. We take off from the premise that any administrative or political arrangement, which is anchored on an ethnic platform, is likely to create unnecessary conflictual relationship between the peoples. Furthermore, there is no assurance, that if we redraw a territory along ethnic lines, break up a country into ethnic entities, there would be political stability. On the contrary, the chances are that Nigeria would be worse off with instability that cannot be contained. As rightly pointed out by Eskor Toyo:

> Those who imagine that Nigeria can be broken up into several independent states simply around a conference table are living in a fool's paradise. The conflagration that will ensue can make Lebanon, Somalia, Ethiopia and Yugoslavia look like a storm in a teacup (Toyo, 1994).

Conclusion

The persistence of the ethnic problem in Nigeria can be attributed to the absence of democracy in Nigeria, the total lack of democratic governance. In order to achieve that objective, the transcendency of the neo-colonial state and the establishment of an independent path of development geared towards self-reliance and the provision of basic needs and services to the people, anchored on a truly democratic and national ideology can help in solving the endemic crisis of ethnicity, that is facing this country. What is being advocated above is nothing short of a complete transformation of the present economic and political arrangement in Nigeria. This can be achieved by a revolutionary National Liberation Movement on an anti-imperialist and anti-capitalist platform. The National Liberation Movement should be an organ of the exploited classes in society, i.e., workers, peasants and other exploited sub-classes who would struggle for the transformation of the present neo-colonial set-up and its replacement with a more humanistic system which would cater for the interest of all nationalities, irrespective of where you come from. Any reform carried out within the present context is cosmetic and likely to be ineffective (e.g., quota system, Federal character, State creation), according to Fanon:

The function of a social structure is to set up institutions to serve man's needs. A society that drives its members to desperate solutions is a non-viable society, a society to be replaced (quoted in Wilmot, 1985: p. 40)

This should be the agenda of all democratic forces with respect to the future of Nigeria.

References

Ade-Ajayi,J.F (1992), 'The National Question in Historical Perspective', text being of the fifth *Guardian* Newspaper Lecture delivered at the N.I.I.A on Wednesday 4 November, 1992.

Barongo, Yolamu (1983), 'Alternative Approaches to African Politics', in Yolamu Barongo (ed), *Political Science in Africa: A Critical Review*, London: Zed Books.

Dudley, Billy J. (1973), *Instability and Political Order: Politics and Crisis in Nigeria*, Ibadan: Ibadan University Press.

Ewekwe, Eme (1986), *Class and State in Nigeria*, Zaria: Longman.

Falola, Toyin (1986), *'Pre-colonial Origins of the National Question in Nigeria: The case of Yorubaland'*, paper being presented at the National Seminar on *'The National Question in Nigeria. Its Historical Origins and Contemporary Dimensions'* held at Abuja, 3-4 August, 1986.

Ikime, Obaro (1987), 'Towards Understanding the National Question', *African Events*, April.

Ilenre, Alfred (1994), 'The Federal Structure', paper presented at ASUU Conference on State of the Nation, April 5-6.

Jinadu, L.A. (1985), 'Federalism, the Consociational State and Ethnic Conflict in Nigeria', *Publius*, Vol. 15, No. 2, spring.

Mahadi, Abdullahi and Mangvwat, Monday (1986), 'Some Remarks on the National Question in Pre-capitalist Formations: The case of Nigeria before 1900 A.D'. Paper being presented at the National Seminar on *The National Question in Nigeria: Its Historical Origin and Contemporary Dimensions*, held at Abuja 4-9 August, 1986.

McHenry, Dean (1986), 'Stability of the Federal System in Nigeria: Elite Attitudes at the Constituent Assembly Toward the Creation of States', *Journal of Federalism* , Vol. 16, No. 2, spring 1986.

Mustapha, A.R. (1986), 'The National Question and Radical Politics in Nigeria', *Review of African Political Economy*, No. 33.

Nnoli, Okudiba (1978), *'Ethnicity and the Creation of States'*, Roundtable meeting on Ethnicity in Nigeria: Implications for National Development, National Institute, Kuru, April 18-21.

Olagunju, Tunji, Adele Jinadu and Sam Oyovbaire (1995), *Transition to Democracy in Nigeria* (1985-1993), Spectrum Books.

Osaghae, Eghosa (1990), 'Do Ethnic Minorities still Exist in Nigeria?' *Journal of Commonwealth and Comparative Politics*, Vol. xxix No. 2, July.

Osaghae, Eghosa (1991), 'Ethnic Minorities and Federalism in Nigeria', *African Affairs*.

Saro-Wiwa, Ken (1995), 'The National Question: Confederation is the Answer', Citizen Magazine, Special Edition on the National Question in Nigeria and Fika Local Areas published in *The Democratic Weekly*, April 2 and 3.

Stavenhogen, Radoof (1983), 'The Ethnic Question and the Social Sciences', *The Journal of Culture and Ideas*, University of Ife.

Tamuno, Tekena (1970), 'Separatist Agitations In Nigeria Since 1914', *Journal of Modern African Studies*, No. 84.

Toyo, Eskor (1994), *Crisis and Democracy in Nigeria: Comment on the Transition Programme of the Babangida Regime*, Zaria: A.B.U Press.

Usman, Yusuf U. Bala (1982), 'The National Question Beyond Fairy Tales', Citizen Magazine, Special Edition on *The National Questions. What is the Answer?* Dec. 4.

Usman, Yusuf U. Bala (1994), *'The Formation of the Nigerian Economy and Polity'*, in Mahadi et.al (eds), *Nigeria: The State of the Nation and the Way Forward*, proceedings of the National workshop Organised by Arewa House, Kaduna, Centre for Historical Documentation and Research of the Ahmadu Bello University, Zaria. 2-3 February.

Waziri, Ibrahim and Ibrahim Baba Gana (1995), 'Towards Understanding the Ethnic Question in Nigeria and Fika Local Government Areas' published in the *Democrat Weekly*, April 2 and 9, 1985.

Waziri, Ibrahim Maina (1989), 'The Political Transformation of Fika (1903-1924)', paper presented at the Department of History Seminar, University of Maiduguri, held on January 23, 1989.

William, Gavin (1980), *State and Society in Nigeria*, Idanre: Afrografika.

Wilmot, Patrick (1985), *Sociology: A New Introduction*, London: Collins International Textbooks.

Magazine and Newspapers

Sunday Concord October 6, 1991.

Sunday Democrat February 5 and 12, 1995.

Vanguard, Monday November 7, 1994.

8 The Military and the National Question

SAID ADEJUMOBI

Introduction

In the current debate on the reform and restructuring of the Nigerian federation, a state institution that has come under the severest attack is the military. The Nigerian military, according to some, is at the heart of the current crisis of nationhood in Nigeria (Omoruyi, 1999). It is considered to be over–ethnicised and over-politicised, and rather than promote national integration, has enveloped the nation and itself in deep crises. The solutions put forward to ameliorate the problem vary quite widely. To some, Nigeria does not have an army in the proper sense of it. What exists is largely a coterie of praetorian soldiers who prey on each other and the nation.[1] As such, the military in its present form should be disbanded and the process of establishing a new national professional army put in place. To some others, the solution lies in regionalising the military. That is, for every geo-political zone of the country to have a regiment of its own made up mostly of people from that region. Better still, some argue, quite contrarily that what the nation needs is a thoroughly retrained and professional armed forces, which would balance the issue of the representativeness of the different ethnic groups and social cleavages in the country, with the search for merit, fairness and justice in its activities.

This attack on the Nigerian military tends to be a contradiction in terms. This is because the military, given its professional ethos and training, ought to be a vehicle for social and national integration. Enlistment in military service ought to afford a process of resocialisation and changed experience towards organic solidarity and a professional commitment and bond for those involved in it, even if they are from disparate ethnic and social cleavages. In other words, a military institutional order, which espouses nationalism and a professional ideology, ought to hold sway. At least, that is the orthodox conception of the character of a modern military organisation. Unfortunately, this seems not to be the case as evidenced by post-colonial developments in the military and the recent virulent attacks on the institution by virtually all segments of the Nigerian society. But how did the Nigerian military lose its integrative professional balance and ethos, become highly disfractured and assumed a platform for primordial and ethnic identities and politics? Is there a linkage between the state control of political power by the military (i.e. military rule) and the gradual disintegration of the military institution? To what extent has the military become an agency for ethnic identification and domination? And in what other ways do the military exacerbate the national question? The foregoing issues constitute the problematic of this chapter.

While a lucid conceptualisation of the notion of the "national question" has been done in chapter one, it is apposite for me to clarify my own perspective to it. There are two dimensions to the national question as viewed in this chapter. First is the perspective of inter-group relations often referred to as the nationality question. This deals with the tensions and contradictions that arise from this relationship dwelling on the issues of marginalisation, domination, inequality, fairness, and justice among ethnic groups. This may be real or imagined. The second dimension is the class dimension. That is, the exacerbation of class inequalities and antagonism in society between the rich and the poor, the affluent and the underclass or to put it in the Marxist parlance, the bourgeoisie and the masses. This often fuels and deepens ethnic tensions and contradictions, when it assumes alarming proportions. Our concern is to unravel the extent to which the military deepened those tendencies in its internal organisation and operation as an institution and also in the society. The latter relates to the effects of military rule on the national question in the society.

The chapter is divided into three parts. Part one provides a theoretical background on the nature of military organisation and traces the emergence and development of the Nigerian military explicating how ethnic identity and politics gradually crept into the institution. Further, it analyses the road to crisis in the Nigerian military, with the phenomenon of intra-officer factional struggles, cliques and ethnic intrigues, a development that virtually collapsed both the military and the nation. Chapter two focuses on how the logic of military rule accentuates the national question. This is done from three major perspectives. Part three is on retired soldiers and the national question. The issue addressed here is on how the "retired soldier" as a new elite of power, is increasingly entrenching the hegemony of the military constituency in the control of power and resources in the country and the implications of this for social and class contradictions in the Nigerian society.

The Nigerian Military: The Crisis From Within
Background Theoretical Issues

Early studies on the Nigerian military emphasise the fact that the Nigerian military, like other armies of the British colonial territories, was conceived in the classical British military tradition, both in organisational format and professional training (see, for example, Luckham, 1971: p.1). A military, which espouses the values of rationality, efficiency, managerialism, technical competence, professional discipline and integrity. Indeed, this was the premise on which the now discredited "modernising soldier" theory was constructed (Adekanye, 1978).

The reality of Nigerian and indeed, most African military formations, as Samuel Decalo (1986: pp.36-38) argues, is that they were simply "nominal or lineal descendants" of their colonial progenitors. The colonial powers expended little or no effort in the direction of either preparing indigenous leadership cadres (most colonial forces actually barred Africans from crossing the non commissioned officers rank until the 1950s) or building true cohesion in the colonial armies. The vaunted esprit de corp and strict discipline possessed by the colonial armies were less professionally rooted as reified by the early military historians. Such cohesion was due largely to the iron rule imposed on the institution and enforced by the expatriate colonial officers, rather than to any ingrained professional training. The course of events in the early post independence era was to later confirm this.

A major issue central to the internal cohesion and stability of any military organisation, and which has been a subject of theoretical discourse, is the nature of the internal composition and character of the military and how the organisation seeks to forge systemic integration within itself. In this regard three major issues come to the fore. First, is the recruitment pattern and how ethnic factor shape the internal organisation of the military. The questions that arise are; should recruitment be reflective of socio-cultural cleavages in the country, that is, obey the logic of ethnic balancing? Or should it be constituted purely on the professional basis of individual merit and ability devoid of communal and ethnic identity? Or should it be a combination of both? If the former option is taken (i.e. reflective of socio-cultural cleavages), further issues arise; are all communal and ethnic groups to be represented? If so, how is the representation to be effected? Should it be based on equal representation of all ethnic groups or proportional representation based on the population size of those groups? What are the likely impacts of ethnic representation on the cohesiveness of the military?

With regard to the aforementioned, some scholars have attempted to develop classificatory schemes of military organisations based on their recruitment patterns. For example, Bayo Adekanye (1979) identifies three types of military recruitment patterns. These are,

(a) Ethnic pluralising approach. This is a system in which ethnic cleavages form the basis of military recruitment.

(b)   The one-ethnic dominant approach. This is a situation in which an ethnic group holds sway in the military and recruitment is basically uni-ethnic. This approach is usually justified with a perverse "warrior tribe" ideology.

(c)   The individual nationalising approach. In this regard, recruitment is not based on ethnic identity, but purely on individual merit. The most heinous of those approaches in Adekanye's view, is the one ethnic-dominant approach, which has a tendency of perpetuating ethnic oppression through the military and may possibly envelop the state in crisis. This was vividly demonstrated in the crisis that engulfed Rwanda and Burundi (Adekanye, 1996).

Cynthia Enloe (1980a) in her very insightful work on ethnicity in the security forces of the military and the police identifies four major types of military organisations based on the nature of their internal composition. These are,

(a)   The assimilationist military type. In this case, all ethnic groups are proportionally represented throughout the hierarchy, and primary allegiance is to the organisation, without reference to non-military ties like class, clan, ethnicity, region or religion. This, in Enloe's view, is the ideal military type.

(b)   Pluralist-differentiated type. In this regard, various ethnic groups are represented beyond token levels, but the personnel of different ethnic groups play different roles in the military. In other words, there seem to be a form of ethnic functional specialisation of the armed forces, either in terms of tasks, departments or the various services.

(c)   The mono-ethnic military type. This is the same thing as Adekanye's one ethnic approach.

(d)   Pluralist-exclusivist type. In this case, although the military is multi-ethnic, but some ethnic groups are still left outside, unincorporated into the armed forces. Groups considered to be potentially threatening to the political formation are excluded from military service or recruited in very low or insignificant numbers and mostly apportioned civil functions in the military.

While the foregoing military classificatory schemes are useful, it is important to emphasise that military organisations may not be static in their types and recruitment patterns and the nature of the internal composition of a military organisation depends on many factors, some of which may be extra-military. Also, the internal cohesion and stability of the military may be mediated by other variables beside the nature of its internal composition.

The second issue germane to the internal cohesion and stability of the military is the purposive social integrative efforts or mechanisms evolved or foisted in the organisation. The questions that arise are; to what extent are military units fully integrated? Is there a frequent trans-community deployment of military personnel? Are promotion and career specialisation decisions based on perceived competence, rather than communal attachment? How does the military seek to inculcate national values and perspectives in training and professional military education for enlisted men (Dietz, Elkin and Roumani, 1991: pp.11-12). Furthermore what are the other cross cutting integrative social networks within the military like the level of solidarity and camaraderie among peers and course mates, inter generational interactions and perceptions and the conviviality of a boisterous officers' mess life? The third issue is the state/society-military nexus. This constitutes the environmental impact on the character and operation of the military. The questions that arise are; what is the level of boundary delimitation between the military, state and society? And what level of relative autonomy does the military enjoy in its relations with the state and society? To the extent that the military is basically an institution of the state and its strategic coercive arm, the military cannot be immune from state politics and ruling class interests, especially when such states are shred by ethnic cleavages or when the wielders of state power rely on ethnic mobilisation factors for power maintenance and consolidation.

In reality military professional autonomy tends to make less meaning in societies where state formation and consolidation is still very hazy and inchoate. In such societies, there is the strong possibility of the military degenerating into an "ethnic security outfit" in which the issues of recruitment, career advancement and deployment are subjected to ethnic arithmetic. Political leaders to use Cynthia Enloe's phrase often construct an "ethnic security map", where the army and security forces are dominated and controlled by officers from a particular ethnic group. Indeed, in most plural societies, with deep social and sectarian cleavages and where ethnic permutations form part of the political calculus, the vulnerability of the military to ethnic trappings is usually very high.

These three issues are quite complex, but essentially lie at the heart of the character, social composition and cohesiveness of any military organisation. The way these issues were played out in the Nigerian military before and shortly after independence, as I shall argue shortly, is central to the fissure and growing instability in the institution.

Road to Crisis

What is today known as the Nigerian military arose out of a coterie of disparate, but largely disorganised forces established to facilitate the process of colonial exploitation and domination. There are three major sources to this. These are the "Lagos Constabulary", the "Royal Niger Constabulary" and the "Niger Coast Constabulary" established 1863, 1886, and 1891 respectively. These forces were later to be merged with other local forces in the British West African colonial territories to form the West African Frontier Force (WAFF) at the dawn of colonial rule in 1898. However, in order to facilitate operational efficiency, national regiments were established under the control of a commandant. As the era of political independence approached, the WAFF was disbanded in 1957 with each country having its own force. Consequently, the Nigerian regiment was transformed into the Nigerian Armed Forces, although still superintended by the British Government through the British army council in London until April 1958. In 1960, the country assumed full responsibility for its armed forces, although the forces still bore the appalance "Royal Nigerian Army". This was dropped in 1963 when the country became a republic (see, NAECS, 1992; Achike, 1978). In terms of its numerical strength, the Nigerian military grew from a small force of 6,400 in 1956 to 7,480 in 1960, further to 7,816 in 1963, and 10,500 in 1965. By the immediate post civil war era in 1970, the Nigerian military was about 200,000.

The serious ethnocentric problems of political life were from inception reflected in the composition of the Nigerian armed forces (Wright 1991: p.185). The background to this was the colonial state policy of divide and rule instituted in the military, just as it was applied to the polity. The colonial regime constructed and manipulated a "martial ethnic group" ideology, in which certain ethnic groups were considered to be militarily more competent, as they allegedly display "physical strength", "courage" and "valour". Those groups constitute the prime target for military recruitment, especially at the subaltern level. The real, but undisclosed purpose of this strategy as Cynthia Enloe (1980b: p.35) argues is to recruit soldiers from ethnic groups that would least likely succumb to nationalist agitation and mobilisation so that they can be used as effective instruments to quell such agitation. In the Nigerian case, majority of the troops were recruited from the Northern part of the country, particularly from the northern ethnic minorities of the middle belt. On the other hand, in order to perpetuate its divide and rule policy, the colonial regime ensured that the few indigenous officers and cadets recruited (from 1945 when local recruitment into this cadre began) were largely drawn from an entirely different social strata and ethnic group. This policy as Samuel Decalo (1986: p.48) noted encouraged major ethnic/regional split, separating the officers' corp from the rank and file. This strategy was to prevent any form of vertical ethnic cohesion in the military, which may serve as a threat to the colonial regime.

In the Nigerian case, the officers were drawn mainly from the eastern part of the country. At independence, two thirds of the commissioned officers came from the eastern region and half of those in turn were Igbos (Miners, 1971: p.52). While, the subalterns as earlier noted were mainly from the north. This colonial strategy produced a military formation akin to what Cynthia Enloe described as pluralist-differentiated type, which we have earlier alluded to. While it is possible to argue that ethnic functional specialisation and differentiation in the military may promote some form of "ethnic balance of power" in the institution, however, it tends to provoke unnecessary tension and suspicion in the military. Also, as Stephen Wright (1991: pp.184-185) rightly noted the arrangement in Nigeria placed the military leadership out of balance with the political leadership at the level of the federal Government. According to him, while Igbo officers were quite apprehensive about their career prospects in a military under northern political leadership, they were at the same time resentful of domination of the federation by northern politicians and by the inability of non-northerners to make their voices heard. Apparently, the seed of ethnic discord was already sown in the Nigerian military with the colonial strategy in the composition of the institution.

The approach to independence by the politicians did little to enkindle stability and cohesion in the military. First, "military issue" became a purely political issue from which politicians sought to make cheap political gains. Embittered debate emerged among politicians, thrust essentially along ethnic lines, on what should be the recruitment and promotion policy in the Nigerian military. At the Ibadan General Conference of 1958, the political parties and the politicians were split into two ethnic camps on those issues. The northern politicians insisted that recruitment in the military should be based on geo-ethnic considerations. That is, the logic of proportional representation based on the population size of the ethnic groups should be adopted. This policy later earned the acronym of quota system. The west and the eastern politicians opted for merit based on individual performance and ability. The position of the northern delegates won the day, and from 1958, the quota system of recruitment was adopted in the Nigerian military. It was first applied to the non-commissioned ranks and later extended to the officers' corp from 1961. The quota recruitment formulae adopted was on the following basis: northern region-50%, eastern region-25%, and the western region-25%. When the mid-west was created in 1963, it was allotted 4%, while that of the western region was reduced to 21% (Oyediran, 1979: p. 24). In Bayo Adekanye's (1979) view, the policy had the inherent tendency of dragging the Nigerian military into the stormy terrain of political controversies and ethnic politics bedevilling the wider society. Billy Dudley was more definitive in his assessment of the decision. According to him, the policy marked a turning point in the politicisation of the military in Nigeria (Dudley, 1973: p.171). This policy was to foster political/ethnic consciousness, loyalty and identity in the Nigerian military. Since then, the "military issue" has become a recurring decimal in political discourse and negotiation in Nigeria.

At the 1964 general elections, the "military issue" resurfaced as an electoral matter. The major opposition alliance, The United Progressive Grand Alliance (UPGA), promised during its campaign that if voted into power at the federal level, it would upturn the existing recruitment policy into the armed forces. Also, at the September 1966 ad hoc constitutional conference the "military issue" was raised. The western and Lagos delegates to the conference proposed that in order to have a true federation, the then existing four regions should be split into eighteen states and the control of the armed forces should be by those states (see, Osaghae, 1998: p.62). Recently, the option of a regional control of the armed forces has been strongly articulated by some members of the political class and civil society, especially from the southern part of the country.

Admittedly, while the military should not be treated like "Caesar's wife", not to be discussed by the wider society, the point is that military issue should not assume a political game. Perhaps, a plausible way to go about it is to involve all stakeholders in the defence sector, like politicians, military officers, academics and civil society actors, with a bent for military issues to engage in a national dialogue through which an acceptable national Defence and Security policy can be drawn up for the country. It is this policy document that would specify the immediate, short, and long-term defence and security needs and goals of the country, the nature and composition of the armed forces and the professional prerequisites and needs of the armed forces. This approach is more likely to promote cohesion and stability in the armed forces, than a periodic and unsystematic ad-hoc political arrangement, in which the military continue to be a pawn in the chessboard of politicians (see, Adejumobi, 2000a,b).

The second approach to independence, which further attenuated the internal stability and cohesion of the armed forces, was the process of the nigeriansation of the military, after the exit of expatriate military officers. The process, which was largely accompanied in haste, encouraged many politically inspired and extra-ordinary promotions. This created what William Gutridge (1975) referred to as "professional disorientation" in the military. Given this policy, there was little difference in age and experience between officers at the upper and lower levels of the hierarchy, a phenomenon that undermined normal relations of command and control and distorted career mobility (see, Luckham, 1971: pp.3-

4; Decalo, 1986: p.49). In the context of politically accelerated promotions in the military, military officers had to jostle for political "godfathers" in order to secure such promotions. This development had negative effects on the corporate solidarity, identity, and professionalism of the armed forces.

Undoubtedly with the above fragile base, the stage appeared to have been set for an implosion in the military. The bubble was to burst with the military involvement in politics in 1966. The January 1966 coup led by what came to be known as the "five majors" [2] had mostly northern political leaders as victims. This was easily interpreted by northern military officers, the political class and the traditional oligarchy in the north as an ethnic conspiracy against them that must be avenged. The incident provoked intense ethnic hostilities within and outside the armed forces. In addition, every step that was taken by Aguyi-Ironsi, the military Head of State, was interpreted by his northern colleagues, in ethnic terms. These include, the alleged accelerated promotion of eighteen officers from the eastern region out of a total number of twenty-one officers promoted. This promotion it is further stated was not approved by the Supreme Military Council, the highest ruling organ under the military regime (see, Mohammed and Haruna, 1979: p.28). Also, Ironsi was accused of posting easterners to strategic military positions, and reluctant to punish the January 1966 coupist because they were mostly his kinsfolk, from the eastern region. The consequence was the counter coup of July 1966 led by young northern military officers. These include, Murtala Mohammed, Yakubu Danjuma, Mohammadu Buhari, Ibrahim Bako, Shehu Musa Yar'dua, Musa Usman and Joseph Garba. Essentially, the coup was ethnic inspired, meant to atone the "loses" suffered by the north in the January 1966 coup and recapture political power for the north (see, Adejumobi, 1996). Indeed, it is averred that in the conception of the plot, there was broad consultations and consensus among the northern elite, which comprised of top northern military officers, traditional rulers and politicians (see, Osuntokun, 1987; Madiebo, 1986; Oluleye, 1985). In more specific terms, Jide Osuntokun in his biography of Sir Kashim Ibrahim noted that Kashim Ibrahim was in constant touch with Major Usman Katsina after the coup and impressed it on him that the coupists must not hand over political power to a non-northern military officer (Osuntokun, 1987: p.112).

Gowon's ascendance to power through an ethnic motivated military coup only deepened the ethnic animosity and tension in the Nigerian military. Issues of seniority, order and procedure were completely ignored in Gowon's appointment. For example, there were five officers senior to Gowon, who were from the western and eastern regions but sidelined (*see*, Ademoyega, 1981: p.130). While it may be naive to expect coup plotters to respect order and procedure as the logic of a coup is predicated on political and institutional disorganisation, however, this trend points to the apparent breakdown of professional norms and ethos in the Nigerian military. Gowon's ethnic platform to power through a military coup was soon to engender a backlash in the military with dare consequences for both the military and the nation. Ethnic and personality distrust and rivalry between northern and eastern officers deepened tremendously. A struggle that was personalised in the conflict between Ojukwu and Gowon. Ojukwu refused to recognise Gowon as military Head of State, claiming that Gowon's ascendance to power violated military culture and procedure and that Gowon could not guarantee the security of the eastern people. The result of this struggle was a 30-month civil war. After the civil war in 1970, the policy of reconciliation was enuciated in the military and society. In the military, specific policies were embarked upon to promote reconciliation and social integration in the armed forces. These include, the regular changing of unit commanders on a two year basis, ensuring that no unit is mono-ethnic, the establishment of military base in towns that previously lacked a military presence, the mounting of education programmes especially for the officers' corp and ensuring that selection for training was based on non-ethnic criteria. Despite all those, it appeared that the ranks remained loyal to their ethnocentric linkages through culture, religion, language and political manipulation (Wright, 1991: pp.194-196).

Since after the civil war the perception of northern ethnic domination in the military has remained very high. Northern officers are seen to control strategic positions in the military and have enjoyed better career advancement than officers from other parts of the country. For example, virtually all the Chief of Army staff appointed since independence has been predominantly northerners.[3] Successive regimes, both military and civil, are alleged to have perpetuated a "northernisation" policy in the armed forces. For example, during the Shagari civilian administration (1979-1983) it was observed that the Federal Government displayed open bias in the promotion of northern officers by hastening such, while demoting or removing from office a number of officers from other ethnic groups largely the Yorubas, who were perceived to be potential threat to his Government (Wright, 1991: pp.186, 194). General Alani Akinrinade, a Yoruba man was speedily removed from the position of Chief of Army staff and posted to a sinecure position of Chief of General/Defence staff. Akinrinade had served for only one year as army chief when Shagari removed him. He was replaced by General M.I Wushishi, as Chief of Army Staff. The military suffered greater fissures and polarisation under the Babangida and Abacha regimes, especially as the *dramatis personae* in those regimes, Generals Babangida and Abacha sought to perpetuate themselves in power through dubious political transition programmes and the obvious manipulations of their primary constituency - the military. By the time they were both forcibly removed from power, the military had become a shadow of itself. Ethnicised, polarised, and dangerously riddled with corruption and sharp contradictions and internal divisions. We shall in the subsequent sections of the chapter detail the processes through which those regimes decimated and completely discredited the Nigerian military.

On a summary note for this section, what is obvious is that ethnic considerations as Henry Dietz (1991: p.215) rightly noted has been a core and resilient variable in the structuring and operation of the Nigerian armed forces. This promoted ethnic divisions and virtually shattered the professional basis and values of the institution.

Military Rule And The National Question: Triple Dimensions

In this section, I seek to unravel the three major dimensions by which military rule exacerbated the national question in Nigeria. These are, first, how military rule undermined and disfractured the military itself by reinforcing primordial identities, generating tension and setting it on the path of disintegration. Secondly, is how the nature and logic of military rule deepens social contradictions and exacerbates ethnic differences and divisions in the society. Thirdly is on how the military through its economic policies accentuate poverty and the marginalisation of the people from the economic arena. This provokes mass disillusionment and frustrations that often seek expression in inter-group conflicts and crisis.

It is regrettable, yet true that the military is usually the worst victim of military rule (Adejumobi, 2000a; Hutchful and Bathily, 1998). The professional autonomy and institutional integrity of the military is usually undermined by military regimes. There are two reasons for this. First, is the politics of regime survival and second is the imperative of accumulation. These two factors in coalescence often promote or exacerbate primordial tendencies in the military. With regard to regime survival, most military regimes, especially the personalist military type, as experienced under the Babangida and Abacha regimes usually foist a personal security network and build a cult of loyalists within the military, which is to serve as their power base and security safety net. This group is usually drawn largely from the ethnic base of the ruler. They are often favoured with appointments and promotions with little regard for rules, norms and procedure in the military. For example, in the case of the Babangida regime, a group of young, but brilliant military officers popularly known as the "Babangida boys" [4] were assembled, they ruthlessly sought to protect the interest of the regime. This group witnessed rapid career mobility and were favoured with choice political appointments under the regime. They displayed little respect for senior colleagues, were unabashedly arrogant, and virtually became a law unto themselves. The practice of the Abacha regime was more debilitating for the military. Very junior military officers close to the dictator like majors were feared and respected by their senior colleagues. Many of the latter had no access to the ruler, not even those who occupied high political and military command positions under the regime, except at the behest of these junior officers. Junior officers gave orders to and kept their senior colleagues under close surveillance. The height of this perfidy and institutional decay was when top military officers began to prostrate themselves for very junior ones like majors.[5] During this period, there was complete disorderliness and a total breakdown of professional norms in the Nigerian military. General Salisu Ibrahim (retired), a former Chief of Army Staff graphically depicts this decay:

> We became an army of "anything is possible". It became the norm for subordinate officers to sit and not only to discuss their superiors, but to pass judgement on them, of course in absentia. We became an army where subordinate officers would not only be contemptuous of their superiors, but would exhibit total disregard to legitimate instructions from such superiors (*See Tell*, December 20, 1993).

The disorderliness that rocked the military also assumed largely an ethnic dimension. Officers from the southern part of the country seem to have been at the receiving end. As Omo Omoruyi (1999: p.14) noted, while officers from the north could meet freely, and discuss in the northern lingua franca-*Hausa*, in the barracks, on the other hand, southern officers were expected to be "careful" and "well behaved". In addition, there was the unwritten rule that southern officers were expected to "spy" on one another in order to please the powers that be.

Group hegemonic politics under military rule also relates to who controls what position in the military? The top hierarchy of the military and major command positions, as Kunle Amuwo observed were dominated by northern officers, as political power was controlled by the same group of people (Amuwo,1999: p.93). In particular, there was the penchant to give expression to micro-ethnic relations, such as clan and village or local group ties in the military, by those in power.

For instance, the rise of the Babangida regime was associated with the popularity of a group called the "Lantang mafia", who were senior military officers from the middle belt (the geo-political zone of General Babangida) and occupied strategic positions under the regime. However, the dialectics of power contradictions gradually led to the displacement and sometimes "humiliation" of some of those officers under the Babangida regime.[6] In the case of Sanni

Abacha, real political and military power under his regime lies with a small "kitchen cabinet", which revolves around him. The members of this kitchen cabinet include, Brigadier General Bashir Magashi, commander of the Brigade of Guards, General Jeremiah Useni and Brigadier General Sarki Muktar, Head of the Directorate of Military Intelligence (see, Africa Confidential, November 4, 1994, Vol.35, No.2: p.6). They were later joined by officers like Major General Isa Bamaiyi and Brigadier-General Ibrahim Sabo, who later assumed the post of Director of Military Intelligence. Most members of this "kitchen cabinet" were mainly of northern ethnic extraction. Officers from other geo-political zones who occupied top political positions under the Abacha regime did so only to fulfil the convention of the federal character principle, and wielded little or no power either in the regime or in the military.[7] They were later to be hauled into detention with the fabrication of a coup story in 1997.[8] Indeed, the popular perception in the society at least from the Southwestern part of the country, was that the purpose of the 1997-fathom coup story was one of "ethnic cleansing" of a particular ethnic group from the top hierarchy of the military.[9] While ethnic consideration may have been part of it, the truth is that it was a project of power maintenance and consolidation by General Sanni Abacha.

The second dimension to the rupture of the military under military rule as we earlier noted, is the imperative of accumulation. Although access to political power has often been a staircase to wealth, not only in Nigeria, but also in most underdeveloped countries, however, the issue took a completely new dimension from the inception of the Babangida regime in August 1985, in Nigeria. Corruption was institutionalised and became somewhat one of the "directive principles of state policy. As Segun Osoba (1996: p.373) observed, Babangida elevated corruption to new heights, from "petty thievery" of the previous regimes, to "army robbery". The public treasury assumed the primary vehicle for reckless private primitive accumulation. What are the implications of this for the military? First, as the regime openly aided and abetted theft of public funds, most military officers preferred political postings to military appointments. Through this process, they hoped they would secure a share of the "pie". As General Alani Akinrinade observed, most young military officers aspired to be political Generals who would fill political posts rather than being professional army Generals, in the barracks.[10] As such, the young officers deployed all available tactics in order to clinch political posts. These included, intense lobbying through traditional rulers, retired soldiers and top military officers, blackmail, intrigues, and dirty politicking.

Also, as political power conferred easy wealth and privileges on some young military officers, social and class differences became highly skewed in the military, a phenomenon which provoked deep anger and tension in the institution.

The situation was more appalling as the new *noveau riche* young military officers settled for ostentatious lifestyle and owned properties and estates in selected high brow areas of major metropolitan cities like Lagos, Kaduna and Abuja. This development engineered two kinds of social and class contradictions in the military. On the one hand, there was a lot of tension between the professional soldiers, who were largely cut off from the accumulation process and the young political officers, who were having a field day with the national treasury. On the other hand, there was also tension between the political officers and the large band of the subalterns or non-commissioned officers, whose standard of living continued to deteriorate under harsh economic conditions [11](see, Adejumobi 1999, 2000a). In addition, the clientelist and selective policies of the Babangida regime in the military like the issue of promotion and social benefits (e.g. car gifts) only reinforced those social and class contradictions.[12] The result was a deep internal crisis in the military, which was clearly demonstrated through the abortive April 1990 coup (see, Ihonvbere,1990). The maiden national broadcast of the coupists clearly confirmed the deep internal divisions and crisis in the military and also showed the extent to which such crisis had assumed ethnic dimension/interpretation. With regard to the latter, the coup plotters sought to excise five states from the Federal Republic of Nigeria, areas that they considered had produced most of the political and military personnel who have been the bane of Nigeria's political and economic progress.

The second perspective to the issue of military rule and the national question is on how the former exacerbated the latter within the context of the larger society. Generally, the attempt to concentrate or increase political power, whether under civil or military rule often provokes ethnic tensions (see, Adejumobi, 2000b; Smith, 1981; Enloe 1980a). In particular, military regimes usually exhibit a strong centralising character which curtail political and social space to the people and deny them opportunity to fully realise themselves. In addition, highly centralising regimes, which lack a mobilisation ideology or democratic basis usually, rely on traditional and primordial identities and values to elicit support for their regimes. This reality was palpably demonstrated under the Babangida and Abacha regimes. Primordial differences, loyalties and divisions of ethnic, clan, religious, class, and professional identities were fully exerted, and dubiously exploited and manipulated by those regimes through their public policies. For example, the issues of which states and local governments to be created and which should not, where should the capitals and headquarters of those states and local governments to be sited, and which religion should be given leverage over the other, were issues through which the regimes sought to secure group loyalties and support. In the process, groups were played against each other, with the result of inter-group crisis in the country.

A classic example of a divisive state policy was the issue of Nigeria's full membership of the O.I.C. (Organisation of Islamic Conference) in November 1985. Hitherto, Nigeria had maintained an observer status in the O.I.C for seventeen years. Shortly after the assumption of power by the Babangida regime in October 1985, the regime negotiated full membership of the organisation for the country in November 1985. A series of religious conflicts followed thereafter. Religious conflicts occurred in Ilorin in 1986, Kanfanchan, Kaduna, Katsina, Funtua, Kano and Zaria in 1987, and Bauchi and Kano in 1991. Similarly, inter-ethnic inferno rocked the country like a wild fire. These include, the Zangon Kataf crisis of 1992, the Tiv-Jukun conflict and a series of inter-communal conflicts in the oil producing areas of Rivers, Cross Rivers and Delta States. In most of those conflicts, the complicity of the state was evident either directly or otherwise. The press, human rights and pro-democracy groups have seriously alleged the role of the state in inter-communal conflicts in the Niger Delta, especially between the Ogoni and Andoni communities. This growing ethnic, communal and religious feuds, deepen inter-group distrust and disunity in Nigeria, a problem which partly accounts for the current clamour for the holding of a Sovereign National Conference (SNC) that would discuss and resolve the nationality question in Nigeria.

The third dimension by which military rule accentuates the national question is through their economic policies. Between the decade and a half of 1985-1999, the economic policies of military regimes and the nature of their management, wrecked incalculable damage on the lives of the people. While harsh economic policies were imposed on the people, the government and its officials relished in financial profligacy and reckless public spending. For the Babangida and Abacha regimes, both the Central Bank of Nigeria (CBN) and the Nigerian National Petroleum Corporation (NNPC) were placed under the control of the presidency in order to afford personal control of those institutions. The Babangida regime had a notorious reputation for extra-budgetary spending and the misappropriation of the nation's oil export earnings through various unofficial processes. For example, the report of the Okigbo Panel on the activities of the CBN confirmed that between 1988 and 1994, some $12.5 billion were unaccounted for in the nation's oil earnings. Under the Abacha regime, Nigeria's oil sector became a private property, which the General parcelled out to himself and his foreign business associates mostly from Asia, the Middle East and Europe. Thus, very obscure names in international oil industry like Changouri and Ferrostall, the latter a German construction company, both with no record of oil exploration or trading business became main actors in Nigeria's oil lifting business (see, *Africa Confidential*, Vol.35, No. 4, February, 1994: p.3). Illegal financial transfers by the ruling clique under the Abacha regime through the oil industry were estimated at around $3-4 Billion in 1997 (see, Africa Confidential, Vol.38, No.21, November 1997: p.3). The ingenious means adopted to effect this included, unaccounted transfers, charging of unofficial commissions, awarding of dubious and unnecessary contracts, upstream fees, inspection services and the importation of fuel. Indeed, the oil network of importation, distribution and sale of oil, became the most lucrative business, which the military cadres from the military ruler, to his aides, the officers' corp and the subalterns were all hooked up to. The net result was the virtual collapse of the oil sector.

While all this was going on, the majority of the people were subjected to excruciating structural adjustment measures, which devalued their lives drastically. The contraction of public expenditure and declining real wages that were the hallmark of the adjustment measures had deleterious effects on social livelihood and welfare. All variables of human welfare plummeted during this period. For example, Nigeria's GNP per head dropped from $1,160 in 1980 to $240 in 1997, placing Nigeria amongst the 20 poorest nations of the World (see, *Africa Confidential*, Vol. 38, No. 14, July, 1997). The deteriorating quality of life of the average Nigerian under structural adjustment has been well documented (Adejumobi, 1995; Olukoshi, 1991, 1993, Mustapha, 1992). The deepening material poverty of the people had negative effects on inter-group relations by reinforcing existing contradictions and divisions in society, which generate conflicts of various dimensions-ethnic, communal, religious, industrial, and class. Extant studies have confirmed that the pressures of economic crisis, debt and structural adjustment in most African countries, which exacerbate the marginalisation and impoverishment of the people fuels ethnic tensions in those countries (see, Adekanye, 1995: pp.355-374, 1997; Adejumobi, 1996).

The situation in Nigeria was not different. Indeed, the clamour for a Sovereign National Conference (SNC) meant to address the nationality question started as an economic agenda. It emanated from the attempts by some civil society groups who wanted to hold a national conference on "alternative to Structural Adjustment in Nigeria", with the aim of challenging the SAP policy of the Babangida regime and setting an alternative economic agenda for the country. This conference was brutally foiled by the Babangida regime as the conference venue was cordoned off by farce looking policemen. However, as the contradictions in the society deepened, the issues of concern for those civil society groups expanded, and their demands, revised. They therefore insisted that what Nigeria needs is no longer just a new economic blueprint, but the convenance of SNC, in order to address the nation's multi-dimensional problems.

Those groups sought to create a linkage between Nigeria's economic and political processes. They argue that Nigeria's economic morass would not have been possible without the nature and structure of political power, the defective structure of Nigeria's federal system and the poor quality of leadership. The solution, according to them, is that a SNC must be convened before harmonious inter-group relations, political stability and economic progress could be achieved in Nigeria.

To summarise this section of the chapter, military rule has impacted negatively on the national question, both from the internal dimension of the military itself and that of the wider society. Indeed, by the time the military finally exited from political power in 1999, the call for a sovereign national conference in order to address the issues germane to the national question had become a popular cliché for most civil society groups in Nigeria.

The Retired Soldiers and the National Crisis

The Nigerian state seems to have the highest number of conventional retired soldiers in Sub-Saharan Africa. This category excludes demobilised militias and armed wings of liberation struggles, who are mostly disarmed and demilitarised after a local war or in a post-liberation era. The large band of military retirees in Nigeria reflects the high level of personnel turnover and the apparent level of disguised instability in the institution. Indeed, the military is one of the unstable state institutions in Nigeria, although it portends an external picture of cohesion, stability and tranquillity.

The factors involved in the large spectre of military retirees range from pure professional and labour regulatory factors like attainment of retirement age, disability and professional incompetence, to political factors. The political factors are however much more profound. This includes the high level of political attrition resulting from coups, counter coups, political blackmail, suspicion, and intrigues among military officers. For example, any military coup, successful or abortive is usually accompanied by large-scale retirement of military officers. When a military coup is successful, members of the ousted regime and their supporters in the military are often retired, if not detained. On the other hand, when a coup is abortive, the culprits are regarded to have committed treason, and thereby not only dismissed from the military, but also mostly executed. Also, when a military regime is disengaging from power, such process usually involves the retirement of top military officers, especially those who have served the regime in important political positions (Adejumobi, 2000a: p.37).

Apart from the Nigerian civil war (1967-1970) which led to the retirement and demobilisation of ex-Biafran soldiers, who were mostly before the war, part of the federal armed forces, political attrition especially under the Babangida and Abacha regimes was quite key to the dramatic increase in the population of the military retirees between 1985 and 1998. During this period, four reported cases of actual or potential coups were made public. Two of them attracted summary execution of the alleged culprits, in 1985 and 1990 (both under the Babangida regime), while in all of them there was a score of military officers retired, either as participants in the alleged coup, being accessory to the facts of the coup or sympathisers or mere close friends to the coup plotters.[13] In addition, it is also widely believed that many other politically motivated retirements were secretly carried out in the military without being reported, during this period. For example, General Sanni Abacha's aversion for officers who were sympathetic to the cause of the democratic forces or made comments in favour of democratic rule was quite open. Such officers are quietly sent packing, if not arrested.

The consequence of the foregoing is that Nigeria has a large number of young military retirees, whose adaptation and social mobility in a post-military life continue to stir conflict and tension in the society. The point is that most of these ex-officers especially of the middle and higher ranks like retired colonels and above, and the Generals, often exploit their proximity to the state under military rule to negotiate their way to fame, wealth and power. In other words, as Bayo Adekanye (1993) observed, the machinery of the state is usually put behind them to achieve this goal. They are favoured in contract awards by the state, political appointment as ministers, commissioners, members of board of parastatals and government agencies, in land acquisition and also in credit facilities by the banks because of their political influence. In addition, they also became the "beautiful bride" for the private sector especially the subsidiaries of multinational corporations who are in search of "political cover" and easy access to the state and its contracts. In some cases, the retired soldiers make recourse to the wealth they illegally appropriated while in power, and seek to consolidate it through the leverage over the political process that they have, under military rule.

Although the issue of the rehabilitation, resocialisation and resettlement of retired military officers to civil life has been part of the official state policy from the 1970s, however, such was left to the military institution to handle. The Ministry of Defence (MOD) has a resettlement package which includes programme of retraining for vocational skills, prompt payment of pensions and other entitlements and assisting the ex-officers to get placement in both the private and public sectors of the economy. This in reality applied only to the subalterns of the military. The bulk of the retired officers' corp, especially from Colonels and above often use their political connections and academic training which they acquired while in service to eke out a living. It was not until the inception of the Babangida regime that the full might of the state was mobilised to support a process of accumulation for senior retired military officers. Various steps were taken by the regime in this regard. In July 1986, the regime issued a circular through the office of the Chief of Army Staff (COAS), directing seven Federal Ministries as well as State Governors under the regime to give consideration to retired military officers in the award of contracts so that "they could earn a living in a respectable manner" (See, Adekanye 1999; p.169). The seven ministries approached are, internal affairs, communications, information, youth, sports and culture, transport and aviation, labour and productivity and trade. Also, retired officers were encouraged to take up farming with incentive for easy land acquisition, support for farm materials and inputs through the Directorate of Foods, Roads and Rural Infrastructure (DFFRI), a state agency manned by a retired Air Force Officer, Air Vice Marshall Larry Koinyan, and assistance to secure loans through the specialised agricultural banks and the conventional banks in which the state either owned or had majority equity interest.

In addition, there was large-scale appointment of retired officers to virtually all sectors of the public service. This ranged from the state parastatals to the boards of banks and also to the diplomatic service as ambassadors to foreign countries. The most important of all these was the role of the state in the support for retired military officers in the de-regulation and privatisation programme of the state under the structural adjustment programme of the Babangida regime. In the deregulation of the financial sector, retired soldiers became prominent actors mostly favoured with the issuance of banking licence. It became the norm that for any group of businessmen to apply for and acquire a banking licence, at least one retired soldier must be part of them. As I noted elsewhere, a new crop of "retired Officers-Gentlemen Bankers" arose, marching from the "barracks to the banking halls"(Adejumobi, 1999: p.418). Virtually all the new banks that were licensed at this period had retired soldiers on their boards. In 1993, no less than 17 new banks established in the post adjustment era had former military officers listed on their boards. Lewis and Stein (1997; p.7) also observed that a survey of some financial institutions in 1993 revealed that no less than 61 retired military officers were involved in sixty-five firms. In most cases, such involvement is usually in an interlocking manner. Rules and procedure counted for little in the bank licensing process as it was directly controlled from the presidency and used as a form of political gratification for "old friends" and professional colleagues in the military. Given the nature of the ownership of those banks, the regulatory mechanisms for their operations from the banking regulatory agencies, namely the Central Bank of Nigeria

(CBN) and the National Deposit Insurance Corporation (NDIC), were ineffective or completely broke down. Political connections and power by retired military officers in the banking arena took precedence over order and procedure to regulate those banks, in which they were involved. The inevitable result was a banking scam in which several banks collapsed in 1993, with fear and loss of credibility gripping the Nigerian banking and financial sector.

Apart from the financial sector, various state parastatals and state owned commercial ventures that were privatised were sold off to retired military generals or to conglomerates linked to them (See, Fayemi 1999: p.5). In some other cases, serving officers in power who seek to participate in the state divestment process used their retired colleagues as fronts in doing so, since they were officially precluded from doing so. The implication of this analysis is that the retired soldiers have emerged as a new elite of power, "an ultra elite" with enormous wealth, power, and position in the society. Their business interests span the broad spectrum of the Nigerian economy ranging from banking, insurance, agriculture, transport, aviation and shipping, import and export, media, consultancies and even non-governmental organisations (NGOS) engaged in various activities. They seem to be reconstituting the ruling class structure with expansive connections in the economy, society and politics. The latter, that is, politics constitutes their latest area of "conquest", where they dominate the political arena and seek to entrench and institutionalise their hegemony and control over the state in Nigeria.

Although retired soldiers have been participating in politics in Nigeria since 1979 during the second republic, but their number was very limited and their role and influence in party politics negligible. From the Babangida Political Transition Programme they tend to have crowded out to the political terrain, a development that reached an unprecedented level under the Abubakar Political Transition Project (1998-1999). Currently, they (i.e military officers) are the most powerful political force in Nigeria. They largely control the ruling party at the federal level, the Peoples Democratic Party (PDP). It is estimated that there are no less than one hundred and thirty rich and influential retired military officers in the party. Amongst them, at least thirty are of the rank of Major General and above. Thus, the PDP has been aptly described as a party of "army arrangement" (see, Adejumobi, 2000a: p.37).

While it is true that retired military officers are Nigerians and enjoy full citizenship rights which enable them to freely participate in politics and the economy of the country, the issue in contention is the extent to which the state has served as a vehicle of social and class mobility for them and the implications of this for the society. The implications are twofold. First, as Julius Ihonvbere rightly noted, the undue privileges and access to the state that they enjoy have generated extensive alienation among non-military factions of the bourgeois class and the populace at large (Ihonvbere, 998: p.513). Secondly, the issue about citizenship is being raised. The question is; are soldiers and their retired counterparts better citizens than the civil populace? There seems to be a trend of social differentiation and feeling of unequal citizenship between the retired officers and civil elite. This has continued to generate tension in the society. Indeed, this was the major controversial issue in the political campaign for the presidential election in 1999, when General Olusegun Obasanjo contested as the presidential candidate of the PDP.[14]

Conclusion

The military, as I have argued in this chapter, has been central to the process of its own systematic collapse and the gradual disintegration of the Nigerian state. The military has been fraught with sharp divisions and contradictons along political, class, regional, ethnic, and religious lines. This polarization as Kunle Amuwo (1999: p.92) rightly noted, has assumed both vertical and horizontal dimensions. Regrettably, the military institution has become an agency for ethnic expression, identity and domination. The decline in professional values and the rise of ethnic politics in the military is a function of both the historiograghy of the military and its involvement in the political arena. Furthermore, the control and management of political power by the military has in various ways exacerbated tensions and contradictions in the society, with the level of inter-group relations deterioriating remarkably in Nigeria. Indeed, it is believed that the current religious and ethnic conflicts being experienced under the new civilian regime of Olusegun Obasanjo is a direct consequence of the actions and policies of the erstwhile military regimes.[15] However, the fact that the military has been succesfully disengaged from political power,[16] offers some hopes and possibilities for the reconstruction and rehabilitation of the military. The depth of institutional decay of the Nigerian military may be despicable, but not irredeemable. As a retired military General commented, the Nigerian military is one of those few national forces in Africa that has never witnessed a mutiny, despite the fact that it has been riddled with conflicts and crises.[17] This gives a ray of hope for its rehabilitation.

The Obasanjo civilian administration has initiated some policies aimed at re-professionalising the military and reclaiming its institutional integrity and credibility. These include, gradual down-sizing and demobilisation in the military, instituting regular local training programmes for officers, and securing technical and financial support of the major foreign powers and the international community in the reorganisation, re-education and re-retraining of the nation's armed forces. The objective of those policies as the Minister of Defence in the Obasanjo administration, General Theopilus Danjuma (rtd) noted, is to "cleanse the military and militarise it". Those policies may soon begin to have some pay-offs.

However, there are other two major policy issues the regime will still have to tackle on the military. The first is the issue of exclusion and marginalisation of some ethnic groups in the military, and the second is the issue of evolving a national defence and security policy for the country. The latter if properly fashioned may resolve, or at least, attenuate and have some salutary effects on the former issue.

Notes

1.   See, the comments of Colonel Emokpae, in an interview with the Tell magazine, *Tell*, No.15, April, 12,1999. pp. 20-28.

2.   The five majors who were the leaders of the 1966 military coup are; C.Nzeogwu, E. Ifeajuna, D.Okafor, C.I Anuforo and A. Ademoyega. Most of them are from the eastern part of the country.

3.   All the Chief of Army Staff Nigeria has had from 1970 after the civil war (till 2000) have been from the north except two, David Ejoor (1970 - July, 1975) and Alani Akinrinade (October 1979-1980).

4.   The rank of the "Babangida boys" include, Colonels Abubakar Umar, Lawan Gwadabe, Alilu Akilu and Brigadiers Chris Garuba, Raji Rasaki, and Tunji Olurin (See, *Africa Confidential*, Vol. 33, February 1992, No.4, p.3).

5.   Under the Abacha regime, junior military officers who were close to the dictator were very powerful and kept close survillance on the senior ones. Indeed, during the trial of the 1997 coup suspects, part of the scene was that senior military officers like Generals were reported to have prostrated for some junior officers. Although the junior officers were not part of the interrogation team, but they constantly harassed and intimidated those suspects. One of the junior officers who was alleged to have been central to all these was Major Al-Mustapha. See, *Tell*, No.51, December, 20,1990; *Tell*, No.2, January 11, 1999; *Tell*, No, 5, February 1999.

6.   For example, General Domkat Bali was relieved of his post as Chief of Defence Staff without being formally notified by General Babangida. General Babangida during his reign had a perchant for "humiliating" those who served him, especially when he wanted to relieve them of their posts.

7.   Many of the senior military officers who held political posts under the Abacha regime (especially those from the non-northern areas) like General Oladipo Diya, the Chief of General Staff later narrated their experiences under the Abacha regime claiming that although they were in "government, but not in power". Which means that they were marginalised in the decision-making process and wielded little or no power at all, despite the high political posts they held. The post of Chief of General Staff is the equivalent of a Vice-president position.

8.   Those who were alleged to be the leaders of the fanthom 1997 coup plot were the most senior military officers from the southwestern part of the country. These were, Generals Oladipo Diya, Tajudeen Olarewaju, and Abdukarim Adisa.

9.   The alarm raised from the southwestern part of the country was that the 1997 coup story was meant to wipe out the senior officers from the region, who were all implicated in the coup charade.

10.   See, Interview by General Alani Akinrinade (rtd) with the Tell Magazine. *Tell*, No. 5, February 1999, pp.28-34.

11.   Although there were few salary increases for the military under the Babangida regime, these could not keep pace with the rate of inflation and cost of living in the country. Majority of the subalterns in the military lived in abject poverty and squalor under the Babangida regime.

12. General Babangida often doled out "gifts" to his military constituency in order to elicit their support for his rule. This included the "gift" of cars to the officers' corp. However, those "gifts" are usually in short supply, and are therefore rationed on the basis of perceived loyalty to the regime. In most cases, this tends to lead to rancour and in fighting among the officers.

13. Many military officers were arrested on spurious charges which were dubbed coup related offences. These include, being "accessory" to the facts of a coup, a "close" friend or "girlfriend" to a coup plotter, etc. Indeed, those reasons are not only ridiculous, but also laughable.

14. The issue of power not being handed over to a retired soldier became a very serious issue in the presidential elections of 1999. The opposition coalition made up of two parties- The Alliance for Democracy (AD) and the All Peoples Party (APP), with Olu Falae as their joint presidential candidate canvassed the position that handing over power to a retired soldier means continuing military rule by other means, which the electorate must resist.

15. See, Saxone Akhaine, "Shekari Blames Military for Crisis". *Guardian*, March 4, 2000.

16. The military was disengaged from power on May 29, 1999.

17. This is the observation of a retired military General, in a private interview I had with him in the course of my field-work for this study.

References

Achike O. (1978), *Ground Work on Military Law and Military Rule in Nigeria*. Enugu, Fourth Dimension Publishers.

Adejumobi, S. (1995), 'Structural Reform and Its Impact on The Economy and Society', in S. Adejumobi and A. Momoh (eds), *The Political Economy of Nigeria Under Military Rule: 1984-1993*. Harare: SAPES.

—— (1996), 'The Structural Adjustment Programme and Democratic Transition in Africa'. *Verfassung Und Recht In Ubersee. Law and Poltics in Africa, Asia and Latin America*. Vol. 29, No.4.

—— (1996), 'Yakubu Gowon and the Outbreak of the Nigerian Civil War'. *Afrika Zamani*. No.4.

—— (1999), 'The Military as Economic Manager: The Babangida Regime and The Structural Adjustment Programme'. Ph.D Thesis. Department of Political Science, University of Ibadan.

—— With Abubakar Momoh (1999), *The Nigerian Military and the Crisis of Democratic Transition: A Study in the Monoploy of Power*. Lagos, Civil Liberties Organisation.

—— (2000a) 'Demilitarisation and Democatic Reorientation in Nigeria: issues, Problems and Prospects', *Verfassung Und Recht In Ubersee.Law and Poltics in Africa, Asia and Latin America*. April. Vol. 33, No.1.

—— (2000b), 'The Nigerian Crisis and Alternative Political Framework'. Paper Presented to an International Conference on 'The 1999 Constitution and The National Question in Nigeria', organised by the Centre for Demilitarisation and Constitutionalism, Lagos, January.

Adekanye, B. (1978), 'On the Theory of the Modernising Soldier: A Critique'.*Current Research on Peace and Violence*. Vol .8, No.1.

—— (1979), 'Military Organisations in Multi-Ethnically Segmented Societies'. *Research in Race and Ethnic Relations*. Edited by C. Marret and C. Leggon. Greenwich CT: JAI Press Inc. Vol. 1.

—— (1993), 'Military Occupation and Social Stratification'. *Inaugural Lecture*, University of Ibadan.

—— (1995), 'Structural Adjustment, Democratisation and Rising Ethnic Tension in Africa'. *Development and Change*. Vol. 26. No.2.

—— (1996), 'Rwanda/ Burundi: Uni-Ethnic Dominance and The Cycle of Armed Ethnic Formations'. *Social Identities*. Vol. 2, No.1.

—— (1997), 'Dynamics of Ethnic Conflicts in Africa', in Volden, Ketin, Smith and Smith (eds), *Causes of Conflicts in the Third World*. Oslo, Idegruppen/PRIO.

—— (1999), *The Retired Military as Emergent Power Factor in Nigeria*. Ibadan, Heinemann.

Ademoyega A. (1981), *Why We Struck*. Ibadan: Evans Publishers.

Amuwo K. (1999), 'Waiting for Godot: Will There Be a Fourth Republic?', *L'Afrique Politique*.

Butts K.H. and S. Metz (1996), 'Armies and Democracy in New Africa: Lessons from Nigeria and South Africa'. *Strategic Studies Institute Monograph Series*, United States Army War College.

Decalo S. (1986), 'Military Rule in Africa: Etiology and Morphology' in Simon Bayham (ed), *Military Power and Politics in Black Africa*. London and Sidney: Croom Helm.

Dietz H. (1991), 'Conclusion' in H. Dietz, J. Elkin and M Roumani (eds), *Ethnicity, Integration and the Military*. IUS Special Edition on Armed Forces and Society. Westview: Colorado.

Dietz, H, Elkin J.and M Roumani (eds), (1991), *Ethnicity, Integration and the Military*. IUS Special edition on Armed Forces and Society. Colorado: Westview.

Dudley B. (1973), *Instability and Political Order:Politics and Crises in Nigeria*. Ibadan: Ibadan University Press.

Enloe C. (1980a), *Police, Military and Ethnicity: Foundations of State Power*. New Brunswick: NJ: Transaction Press.

—— (1980b), *Ethnic Soldiers*. Athens G.A: University of Georgia Press.

Fayemi K. (1999), 'Entrenched Military Interests and the Future of Democracy in Nigeria'. *Democracy and Development*. Vol. 2, January–June.

Hutchful E. and A. Bathily (1998), (eds), *The Military and Militarism in Africa*. Dakar, CODESRIA.

Ihonvbere J. (1998), The Military and Nigerian Society: The Abacha Coup and the Crisis of Democratisation in Nigeria in E. Hutchful and A. Bathily (eds) (1998). *The Military and Militarism in Africa*. Dakar, CODESRIA.

—— (1991), 'A Critical Evaluation of the Failed 1990 Coup in Nigeria'. *Journal of Modern African Studies*. Vol.29, No.4.

Lewis P. and H. Stein (1997), 'Shifting Fortunes: The Political Economy of Financial Liberalisation in Nigeria'. *World Development*. Vol. 25, No.1.

Luckham R. (1971), *The Nigerian Military: A Sociological Analysis of Authority and Revolt: 1960-1967*. London: Cambridge University Press.

Madiebo A. (1980), *The Nigerian Revolution and the Biafran War*. Enugu: Fourth Dimension Publishers.

Miners N. (1971), *The Nigerian Military: 1956-1966*. London, Methuen.

Mohammed T. and M. Haruna (1979), 'The Civil War', in O. Oyediran (ed), *Nigerian Government and Politics Under Military Rule: 1966-1979*. London: Macmillan.

Mustapha R. (1992), 'Structural Adjustment and Multiple Modes of livelihood', in Gibbon P. Bangura Y. and A. Ofstad (eds), *Authoritarianism, Democracy and Adjustment: The Politics of Economic Reform in Africa*. Uppsala: Scadanavian Institute of African Studies.

Nigerian Army Education Corps (NAECS) (1992), *A History of the Nigerian Army*. Lagos: Gabumo Press.

Olukoshi A. (1991), *Crisis and Adjustment in the Nigerian Economy*. Lagos: JAD Publishers.

—— (1993), *The Politics of Structural Adjustment in Nigeria*. London: James Currey.

Oluleye J. (1985), *Military Leadership in Nigeria: 1966-1979*. Ibadan: Ibadan University Press.

Omoruyi O. (1999), 'Representative Military in Plural Societies and Democratic Transition in Africa'. *Paper Presented to the Conference on 'New Directions in Federalism in Africa'*, Organised by the African Centre for Democratic Governance (AFRIGOV), Abuja, March.

Osaghae E. (1998), *Nigeria: The Crippled Giant*. London: Hurst.

Osoba S. (1996), 'Corruption in Nigeria: Historical Perspective', *Review of African Political Economy*. No.69.

Osuntokun, A. (1987), *Power Broker: A Biography of Sir Kashim Ibrahim*. Ibadan: Spectrum Books.

Oyediran O. (1979), (ed), *Nigerian Government and Politics Under Military Rule: 1966-1979*. London, Macmillan.

Smith A. (1981), *Ethnic Revival*. New York: Cambridge University Press.

Wright S. (1991), 'State Consolidation and Social Integration in Nigeria: The Military's Search for the Elusive' in H. Dietz, J. Elkin and M. Roumani (eds), *Ethnicity, Integration and the Military*. IUS Special Edition on Armed Forces and Society. Colorado: Westview.

Magazines and Newspapers

Africa Confidential, Vol. 33, February, 1992.

—— Vol.35, No.4, 1994.

—— Vol. 38, No. 14, July 1997.

Guardian (Lagos) March 4, 2000.

Tell, (Lagos), No.2, January 11, 1999.

—— No. 5, February, 1999.

—— No.15, April 12, 1999.

—— December 20,1993.

9 Language and the National Question

UNYIERIE ANGELA IDEM

Introduction

The national question is concerned with 'how to order relations between the different ethnic, linguistic and cultural groups' living in Nigeria 'so that they have the same rights and privileges, access to power and equitable share of national resources' (Ajayi, 1992 cited in Fashina, 1998: p.87). It seeks an effective formula for integrating these diverse affiliations, with a view to creating a sense of cohesion and nationhood. It presupposes an underlying problem manifested in unequal distribution of resources, injustice and discrimination in many domains of national life among the groups. There is a general tendency to see the national question in socio-economic, political, ethnic, cultural or religious terms. The issue of language is often avoided or simply glossed over, taken for granted, or dismissed as irrelevant to the national question. The aim of this chapter is to show that there exists a strong relationship between language and the national question. Not only does language constitute the most natural and crucial basis for the organisation of groupings in Nigeria, it plays an important role in the continued unification or fragmentation of the country. Experience around the world shows that language matters when handled carefully can bring peace to the society, but when handled insensitively can become explosive, causing intergroup conflicts and even wars.

The resulting conflicts, instability and stagnation of national development have plagued the country for years. The national question therefore involves the search for an effective formula for integrating diverse units of a highly heterogeneous society, with a view to creating a sense of belonging and cohesion, borne out of equity in the inter-relationships of such affiliations in all facets of national life.

The national question has been discussed from many perspectives: socio-economic, political, ethnic, cultural and religious. It is also the case that the language matter closely intertwines with socio-economic, political, ethnic and religious issues. Many conflicts that stem from these other factors often have language undertones.

Some Perspectives On The National Question

Before examining the relationship between language and the national question we shall briefly consider some conceptualisations of the national question. For some scholars the national question is predominantly a socio-economic-political problem (Fashina, 1998). That is, a class problem manifesting itself in the exploitation and impoverisation of the Nigerian masses by the ruling class in collaboration with imperialist forces. Marxists argue that with the elimination of poverty and class distinctions the clamour for political autonomy, secession and self determination would disappear or reduce considerably. They de-emphasise the role of ethnicity and religion in the national question, viewing these as deliberate and manipulative ploys by the ruling class to protect its interest. They argue that membership of the ruling class transcends all ethnic groups, and that each ethnic wing oppresses fellow co-ethnics alike (workers, peasants and the marginalised (Fashina, 1998: p.91). Yet for others ethnicity and religion are foundational to the national question, and cut across class divisions. Shawulu (1998: p.78) points out that 'the only reason why most people from the dominated group do not get certain national benefits to the same level as other groups is basically because of their ethnicity and religion. Members of these communities, whether the elite or the masses suffer certain inherent disadvantages.' The point is that the psychological and political reality of ethnicity and religion cannot be denied or swept under the carpet of class struggles. As Akinyanju (1998: p.130) notes, 'the nation is convinced that it is composed of different peoples and the need to forge cohesion among the peoples has been the underlying question of all constitution-making efforts.' While recognising manipulation as a veritable tool in the hands of the leadership, he asserts that such manipulation eventually becomes a sort of reality for the manipulated, and the facts become the essence of political contest (Akinyanju, 1998: pp.131, 132). Jibrin (cited in Akinyanju, 1998:132) puts it aptly 'If people have been marginalised from power because they are some specific group, then the consciousness of ethnic marginalisation becomes an objective part of their reality and they cannot but fight within the context of that particular marginalisation'.

Nigeria has had a long history of ethnic and religious conflicts, climaxing in the Nigeria-Biafra War (1967-1970), the crisis of the 1980's and 1990's in the North, and the more recent clashes in the Niger-Delta and the West (see Egwu,1998a, 1998b; Plang, 1998; and Sako, 1998); there is no denying that in many cases conflicts accentuate during a major economic crisis (e.g. the Structural Adjustment Programme), but they may also relate to land/territorial matters, chieftaincy matters, arbitrary change in political headquarters, individual and media propaganda, domestic matters, political power sharing, and so on.

Other people see the national question as a geo-political problem, that of 'internal colonialism' evident in the centralisation and concentration of political and economic power by a discernible geo-political group - the Hausa Fulani of the North - and the subjugation of other sections of the country to this northern hegemony (Okoye, 1998). The group which maintains its dominant position through the control of the Armed Forces is seen as 'colonialists', and the others as the 'colonised.' It is argued that the 'colonialists' do not operate alone, but in collaboration (albeit on unequal power basis) with some favoured segments of the 'colonised' who also assist in the subjugation of their own people (Akinyanju, 1998). Critics of this view reject the analogy with colonialism, and maintain that the so-called 'internal colonialism' only reflects uneven distribution of power within the ruling class (Fashina, 1998). They deny all ethnic/religious connections with the problem. In fact, it is stated that the dominant wing of the ruling class is of northern extraction, and mainly of a particular religion, is explained as purely coincidental. They also argue that the control of power by this 'small click' in no way benefits their co-ethnic masses. They cite as evidence the abject poverty of the majority of northerners. While this may be the case, it does not obviate the fact that (a) power has circulated generally in one geographical area for a long time, (b) 'power consciousness' has permeated the psyche of the entire group (including the masses), which believes it has a divine right to rule, and (c) other sections of the country, especially the minorities, feel left out of the country's affairs. Perhaps the term 'internal colonialism' does not correctly describe the situation, however the facts still remain as such. To what extent the situation will change with the newly installed democratic government is as yet a matter of conjecture.

A major lacuna in many debates on the national question is the absence of matters related to language. Language issues are dismissed as irrelevant to the national question, or taken for granted and subsumed under the umbrella of ethnicity without being explicitly discussed, or are deliberately avoided because of the highly volatile controversies they often generate. Those who deny the relevance of language to the national question claim that it does not form the core of ethno-nationalist demands for secession or self determination (Fashina, 1998). Two cases in point are that the Ogoni demand for autonomy did not anchor on language (though this was included in their Bill of Rights), but on the socio-economic and political well-being of their people, and that the Yoruba demand for secession hinged not on language, but on the breach of democratic processes that saw the annulment of the June 12, 1993 presidential elections won by M.K.O. Abiola (a Yoruba ethnic). Even the Nigeria-Biafra

War that saw the killing of 2 million Igbos is explained in the same light. The argument is that there are no purely language-based antagonisms. Yet, the stage was set for such conflicts in the 1988/1989 Constituent Assembly when during the debates on language members representing 'minority' ethnic groups walked out in protest against the imposition of the three 'majority' languages - Hausa, Igbo and Yoruba, in addition to English - as the official languages of business in the National Assembly in the anticipated Third Republic (Egwu, 1998a). In fact language based antagonisms underlie the unsuccessful implementation, or non-implementation of the national language policy in many parts of the country. Minority groups have continued to fight the imposition of these languages in all facets of national life.

The notion of ethnicity goes together with language such that ethnic matters are, indirectly, language matters. The weakness of many debates on ethnicity is the failure to emphasise this fact. 'Ogoni', 'Yoruba', 'Igbo', 'Ijo', 'Hausa', 'Ibibio are not vacuous abstract terms but describe specific groups of people with specific identificational traits, language being the strongest. Other traits are culture, mode of dressing, manner of telling jokes, religious practices, etc (Egwu, 1998a), but no other factor 'is as powerful as language in maintaining by itself the genuine and lasting distinctiveness of an ethnic group' (Giles and Saint-Jacques, 1979: p.ix; see also Crystal, 1987; Fishman, 1997; and Mare, 1993). Fishman (1997) points out that the link between language and ethnicity is obvious because the major symbolic system of human species must be associated with the perceived dimensions of human aggregation. 'If people group themselves into different speaking collectivities ... then their languages become both symbolic of as well as a basis for that grouping' (Fishman, 1997: p. 330). Language sets up boundaries and identifies ethnic group A as being different from ethnic group B. However, Crystal (1987: p.34) states that language is a significant index of ethnic or nationalistic movements because it is a widespread and evident feature of community life, has clear links with the past (a shared ancestry, history), and has the tendency to act as a natural barrier between cultural groups, promoting conflict rather than co-operation.

Ethnicity and language are inseparable though it is possible for one to exist independently of the other in certain contexts. This chapter is not concerned with those contexts, but Fishman (1997), Giles and Saint-Jacques (1979) and Tabouret-Keller (1997) have reasoned discussions of fluidity and variability in the perception of ethnic and language identities. The link between ethnicity and language is particularly salient in the Nigerian context. The number of ethnic groups (about 400) in the country equates the number of languages spoken. It follows therefore, that discrimination on the basis of ethnicity equals discrimination against the language that identifies an ethnic group. The exploitation of the Ogoni people is the exploitation of people identified by the use of a 'code' called 'Ogoni'. The killing of Igbos in the 1960s pogrom was the killing of people identified by the use of the code 'Igbo'. Masterminders of discrimination and injustices are also identified by the code they use. There is no over-emphasising of the language dimension of these conflicts.

It is the recognition of the relevance of language to the national question that has informed the promulgation of the National Policy on Education (1977, revised edition 1981) which embodies the national language policy, and government legislation on what languages should be used at National and State Assemblies (the 1979 Constitution). The underlying assumption is that language is crucial for national integration, and therefore some deliberate intervention by way of legislation and policy making is required to bring about such national integration. The question is how far such language planning has succeeded in fostering the much desired cohesion and understanding among the different ethnic groups. For instance, to what extent does converging the multilingual repertoire of Nigerian citizens towards the so-called majority languages guarantee greater national unity? Or is it the case that the development of a sense of nationhood is more difficult for multilingual than monolingual states? (Fasold, 1984). These are the issues that this chapter seeks to address. In the following sections we shall review the current language situation in Nigeria, discuss the different policy pronouncements on language and how they relate to the national question, and suggest ways in which language can play more beneficial roles in national integration.

The Language Situation In Nigeria

As stated earlier, Nigeria has approximately 400 indigenous languages or precisely 394 according to Essien (1993) - spoken by about 100 million people, and spread across three broad language families - Niger Kordofonian, Afro-Asiatic and Nilo-Saharan. About 70% of the languages derive from the Niger-Kordofonian stock, a majority of which are concentrated in the south and some parts of north eastern Nigeria. The remaining 30% derive from the other two families and are found in the northern parts of the country. The languages are further subdivided into three groups - national, regional and local - depending on a number of factors which include the demographic and geographic spread of their users, range of functions, the extent and use in formal education and the degree of official recognition (Akinaso, 1991: p.32). Often a broad distinction is made between 'majority' and 'minority' languages, but this classification does not always give a complete picture of their status and functions. For example, minority languages include both regional and local languages, and the majority ones also serve as regional languages.

The national or major languages are Hausa, Igbo and Yoruba according to the Constitution of the Federal Republic of Nigeria (1979, Section 51) which recognises them, in addition to English, as 'official' languages of the National Assembly. It must be noted that these languages have acquired their majority/ national' status solely on the demographic strength of their speakers, and not because of any inherent qualities they possess that the other languages lack. Speakers of the national languages constitute about 70% of the population. The rest are spoken by about 30% of the population. Hausa has approximately 30 million speakers, and is spoken in the northern states, and some parts of Kwara. The dialect of Kano serves as its standard. Before and immediately after independence Hausa was the official language of the northern region (Mann, 1990). Yoruba is spoken by about 19.9 million people in the western states, and some parts of Kwara and Kogi States. The Oyo dialect serves as its standard. Igbo speakers number about 16.4 million and occupy the eastern states and some parts of Delta and Rivers States. The Owerri dialect is the standard.

Regional languages include Fulfulde, Kanuri, Nupe (in the north), Idoma, Igala, Tiv, Igbirra (in the middle belt), Edo, Efik/Ibibio, Ijo, Itsekiri (in the south). As indicated above, there is some overlap between national and regional languages such as Hausa, Yoruba and Igbo which also perform regional functions. Hausa, for example, is a second language to many other northern ethnic groups (Fulani, Kanuri, Nupe, Tiv, Tuareg, etc.). Yoruba serves as a second language to some ethnic groups living close by - Ijos, Edos, Igbirras, etc., (Mann, 1990). Pockets of Igbo speakers are found in border areas of neighbouring states, e.g., Akwa Ibom, but the language may not be regarded as a regional *lingua franca in* the same way as Hausa and Yoruba. Igbo is the least widely distributed among the three. 'Local' languages constitute over 80% of the estimated languages, but are spoken by a small fraction of the population. More than two thirds are found in the north, and the remaining one third cluster around Akwa Ibom, Bayelsa, Cross River, Delta, Edo and Rivers States in the south.

Superimposed on these Nigerian languages is English, of which no more than 20% of the population can understand and use adequately (Emenanjo, 1997). English serves a variety of functions which include official language of government and administration, the judiciary, dominant language of the media (newspapers, radio and television), main language of internal communication (the national *lingua franca* in the absence of an indigenous one) and of external communication, and language of education from upper primary to tertiary levels. Anglo-Nigerian Pidgin is not officially recognised, but serves as a convenient neutral language of inter- and intra-ethnic communication especially in the south (Mann, 1993). Until a couple of years ago French was classified as a foreign language, whose use was restricted to the academia and diplomatic circles. But the government of the time pronounced it Nigeria's second official language, it was a ridiculous and unrealistic move given the sheer difficulty of implementing such a policy. While it is desirable that Nigerians learn to speak French in order to enhance communication with neighbouring Francophone countries, giving the language an official status is not the solution. It is therefore not surprising that the policy has died a natural death. Arabic plays a restricted role in that it is used mainly for Islamic religious purposes, and predominantly in northern Nigeria.

Language Policies and the National Question

Language Planning and Policies In Nigeria

Language planning is the organised pursuit of solutions to language problems that arise in a country. It involves two kinds of activities: corpus planning activities which affect the structure of a language variety, e.g., spelling reforms, orthography design/reforms, grammar, vocabulary; and status planning activities which concern the roles and functions of languages in the society, as in which language(s) should be official, national, local, language(s) of education, the media, judiciary etc. However, the distinction is not always clearcut as there is some overlap between the two types of planning activities. On the one hand, the choice of a national language may depend on how much corpus 'work' has been done on it already. On the other, a language may be accorded national status for extra-linguistic reasons, and corpus planning follows in order to ensure that it functions adequately in its new role.

The outcome of language planning is the promulgation of language policies. Different ideologies motivate actual decision making regarding such policies. Nigeria practises linguistic pluralism which recognises the coexistence of different languages. Under normal circumstances the formulation of policies should follow robust and detailed sociolinguistic surveys involving data collection, establishment of goals and means, decision-making and feedback (Fasold, 1984). The problem with the language policies of many African countries is that they are formulated prior to any surveys. A proper survey of peoples' attitude to the use of certain languages, for example, would not only guide planning agents as to 'how to' but also 'whether to' promulgate particular policies. Consequently, many conflicts that often threaten to tear the country apart would be avoided, or at best minimised.

According to Crystal (1987: p.366) 'one of the most important ways in which a country's language policy manifests itself is in the kind of provision it makes for the linguistic education of children'. The first of such pronouncements in pre independent Nigeria was the 1882 Education Ordinance enacted by the colonial administration to promote the sole use of English in teaching. Prior to this, language matters were left in the hands of missionaries whose main interest was the propagation of Christianity. This was carried out mainly in the native languages, and marked the genesis of language development in Nigeria as the missionaries set out to codify the languages. It also marked the beginning of modern education in the teaching of basic literacy skills. The schools set up by the missionaries initially trained catechists, mass servers and preachers in the native languages, but this changed with the 1882 Ordinance as the colonial government became interested in their activities, and de-emphasised mother tongue education. Not only did the schools produce 'English literate' local clergy, they also became 'clerk making' machines providing, the colonial administration and trading companies with lower cadre staff. Conditions for obtaining government grants rested on the pupils' success in English.

A change in policy was effected when in 1922 the Phelps-Stokes Commission recommended the use of Nigerian languages for lower primary education, while retaining English for upper primary education and beyond (Akinnaso, 1991). Other official enactments and decisions soon followed. For example, the European Language Examination Scheme required all Europeans to become familiar with one or more local languages (Mann, 1990) In 1926 the International Institute of African Languages and Cultures was established. In 1927 the Conference of Colonial Officers re-emphasised mother-tongue based primary education, while 1931 saw the introduction of papers in African languages in the London Matriculation Examinations (Mann, 1990).

The colonial policy on language education continued after independence, but Nigeria was faced with other language problems such as whether to retain English as the language of administration, or promote and develop national languages. It must be noted that by independence certain regional languages (e.g. Hausa, Igbo, Yoruba, Efik, Nupe, Igala) had already emerged having undergone various stages of standardisation. However, immediate pragmatic concerns influenced the new government's decision to retain English as the language of administration and all officialdom. With regard to education, some changes took place. For instance, while mother tongue for lower primary education continued in the south, the north opted for 'a straight for English' approach in the entire primary system. The advantage of maintaining mother tongue education was that it encouraged experimentation with and development of indigenous languages. For example, the Rivers Readers Project headed by

Professor Kay Williamson surveyed and produced textbooks in Rivers languages. The Ife Six-Year Primary Project proved that the entire primary education could be successfully conducted in the mother tongue.

The most concrete post-independence pronouncement on language is the 1977 National Policy on Education (NPE, revised edition 1981) which, in addition to re-echoing the 1922 recommendations, requires that every secondary school student learns the mother tongue and at least one national language in the first three years. If she/he already speaks a national language, she/he is obliged to select from the remaining two. It also recommends the study of one national language in the last three years for the Senior Secondary School Certificate Examination (SSCE). From the political perspective, the 1979 Constitution gave legal backing to Hausa, Igbo and Yoruba (in addition to English) as official languages of the National Assembly, when adequate arrangements have been made. For the State Houses of Assembly, the Constitution recommended, in addition to English, the use of Nigerian languages native to each state. Decisions regarding choice are left to the state legislature.

Implementing the NPE has been a major problem. Obstacles against implementation include (a) lack of personnel, materials and financial resources to support the teaching of the major languages; (b) unwillingness by state governments, due to financial constraints, to sponsor the teaching of any Nigerian language not native to their states, (c) absence of a federal machinery to monitor the implementation of the policy, (d) lack of motivation on the part of learners, (e) low rating of the languages, (f) lack of public interest and investment, and (g) lack of incentives for those who would want to invest in materials production for Nigerian languages (Banjo, 1989; Emenyonu, 1989; and Emenanjo cited by Aja, 1999). Perhaps, the greatest obstacle is the prestige that English continues to enjoy. This is not surprising given its status as a world language, but moreso because it acts as a compromise candidate in a delicate multilingual set up bedevilled by ethnic nationalism (Odumuh, 1989: p.15).

Language and the Question of National Unity

The national question is concerned with how the different peoples of Nigeria can coexist, and have the same rights and privileges, and equal access to power and the nation's resources. It is about fostering unity, understanding, fairness and justice. The idea of national unity runs through the Constitution, and underlies the federal character principle. The same idea underlies the NPE whose objectives are to build a just and egalitarian society, inculcate national consciousness and national unity, and correct imbalances in inter-state and intra-state development (Section 1, pp.7-8). The government recognises the unifying potential of language and therefore 'considers it to be in the interest of national unity that each child should be encouraged to learn one of the three major languages other than his own mother-tongue' (Section 1, p.9). As already indicated, these languages are Hausa, Igbo and Yoruba which all have national status.

The assumption is that learning a national language should engender national consciousness, unity, loyalties, and empathy towards speakers of the national language. There should be a sense of belonging through acquiring a national language. Our identity as citizens of a nation should derive from speaking that national language. There are problems with this assumption. The first problem concerns the 'object' of our national identity itself. The choice of 3 languages out of almost 400 as symbols of national identity is a gross misrepresentation and misconception of what constitutes Nigeria's identity. Are we to believe that our 'Nigerianness' is determined by three ethno-linguistic groups who happen to occupy certain colonially-demarcated regions of the country? Why must the identity of over 390 other ethno-linguistic groups be subsumed under these three? Some Nigerians are usually embarrassed when asked whether they are Hausa, Igbo or Yoruba. While, there is nothing wrong with being Hausa, Igbo or Yoruba, the point is that these groups do not represent all of our national identity.

The second problem relates to the first, and concerns the conceptualisation of national unity. It is fallacious to presume that the mere fact of learning another language suffices to foster national consciousness, unity, or empathy towards its speakers. Fasold (1984: p.4) points out that a person can be bilingual and have good control of a second language and still feel unified with speakers of his first language and separated from speakers of his second language.' That one speaks Hausa/Igbo/Yoruba in addition to Urhobo, Ibibio or Ejagham does not, by itself, make one nationally conscious or loyal. Converging the multilingual repertoire of Nigerians towards the major languages is not enough, to guarantee greater national unity and understanding (Mann, 1990). *In other words, it is simply not a matter of learning another language.* After all, prior to the writing of the Constitution or NPE many Nigerians had always learned one another's languages for functional purposes, and still do so. Multilingualism has been the norm, but one which has not resulted from any kind of legislation.

That language can serve as a unifying force is not disputed. But, its potential to unify is relative depending, among other things, on what that language is, and whether it has the unifying potential accorded it. In largely monolingual nations the question of language-derived unity is not an issue. In multilingual nations, however, the unifying potential of a language often relates to its perceived neutrality vis-à-vis other languages. In a few cases though, this potential has been enforced by political ideology. For instance, in the former USSR the Russification of non-Russian speaking Soviet Republics was enforced by communist assimilation ideology. The same ideology also informed the classification of mutually unintelligible Chinese varieties as dialects of Chinese, rather than as separate languages labelled differently.

A language is perceived to be neutral if its use in a multilingual setting does not bestow special privileges/prestige on members of some ethnic groups over others. A language may acquire neutrality from being (a) a widely distributed endogenous *lingua franca,* (b) a trade language, or (c) an exogenous (foreign) language, i.e., not native to the environment where it is used. In Tanzania and Kenya, Swahili, a widely distributed endogenous *lingua franca,* is the symbol of national unity. In Indonesia it is Bahasa Indonesia, a local variety once widely used as a trade language. In Nigeria it is English, an exogenous language. English is neutral with respect to the indigenous languages, which is why it has become the compromise candidate in a volatile multi-ethnic society. Another language which shares in this neutrality is the Anglo-Nigerian Pidgin, though it is not officially recognised. Nationally, Hausa, Igbo and Yoruba do not have neutrality, and therefore cannot be *potentially unifying* at that level no matter what the Constitution or NPE states. No doubt they are symbols of unity within their local contexts, as are other languages. Regionally though, Hausa has some neutrality for speakers of minority northern languages who often use it as a *lingua franca.*

The notion of perceived neutrality is based on that of 'perceived', not 'imposed' symbolism of a language. The status of national languages was 'imposed' on Hausa, Igbo and Yoruba by political legislation. The question is whether many Nigerians see them as such or as something else. A language elevated to national status gains in prestige in relation to those not elevated, and so do the native speakers who in turn view other languages and their speakers as 'subordinates'. Such prestige relates to other things as power (political and economic), dominance, influence, and special privileges. Thus, the choice of Hausa, Igbo and Yoruba places these languages and their speakers in a position of power, influence, and dominance over others. This is particularly poignant if the three groups were already 'seen' in these capacities prior to legislation. Legislation has only served to consolidate their hold over others.

Speakers of minority languages resent the imposition of these languages. They see the NPE and Constitution as disadvantageous documents that do not guarantee equal and fair treatment of their languages, and therefore their ethnic groups. They argue that such policies deny them equal right to participation in national development, and deliberately stagnate their languages. They resent the subordination of these languages, and their treatment as second class citizens. Moreso, they see the imposition as not only of languages, but also of the customs and traditions that go with them. It is Chief Anthony Enahoro who once remarked that 'As one who comes from a minority tribe, I deplore the continuing evidence in this country that people wish to impose their customs, their languages, and even more their way of life upon smaller tribes' (cited in Mann, 1990: p.93).

In essence, the so-called national languages are anything but national, if they do not have the capacity to unite Nigerians. Their imposition has been a source of conflict rather than unity. Minority groups have protested against their use in many domains. It will be recalled that representatives of minority ethnic groups walked out of Constituent Assembly deliberations on language in 1988/89 (Egwu, 1998). Minorities also protested the use of majority languages on NTA network news sign-offs. In many states the implementation of the NPE has failed not solely for financial reasons or lack of teachers/ materials, but also because the NPE does not represent their interest. Minority language speakers even resent the use of the term 'minority languages' because of its negative connotation. Consequently, some linguists have suggested 'non major languages' as an alternative. It is not quite clear where the semantic difference lies between the two. The point is that changing tags neither alters the policy nor attenuates people's resentment of what they perceive to be linguistic suicide against their languages.

However, the controversy does not revolve round the 'majority-minority' dichotomy alone. There is so much internal rivalry among speakers of majority languages, especially regarding which one would eventually replace English as the nation's *lingua franca*. An eminent professor of Linguistics and native speaker of a major language remarked, at a recent conference, that he would never accept the other two as Nigeria's *lingua franca*. It was not clear from his speech what would be his reaction if the choice fell on his own language. Members of majority groups are highly suspicious of one another, and resent any attempt to prioritise one language over another. This is particularly so, as there appears to be subtle indirect moves towards a particular choice, something that would lend credence to the 'internal colonialism' thesis, and generate more antagonism. Furthermore, many majority language speakers are unwilling to learn other major languages. Apart from internal and ethnic rivalries, they see no reason for learning, because they feel that they already could speak a major language. They think that learning a major language is for only the minorities. In other words, the recommendations of the policy apply to others not them. This is a flagrant misinterpretation of the NPE which states that *each child*, not *the minority child*, should learn one major language in addition to his/her` mother tongue, even if the mother tongue is a major language.

Language matters are highly sensitoire and volatile. They are often avoided, or couched in vague phrases that sometimes indicate fear of commitment in order not to cause conflicts. Even the NPE is guilty of evasion. It is interesting that while government recommends learning national languages in the interest of national unity, this is 'subject to availability of teachers', and such teachers are never available. The 1979 Constitution states that business at the National Assembly is to be conducted in Hausa, Igbo and Yoruba 'when adequate arrangements have been made therefore. The 1995 Draft Constitution (Abacha's Constitution, now moribund) mentions no specific names, but simply states that 'Nigerian languages shall become additional languages ... as the National Assembly shall by law prescribe' (Section 58, p.49). That the government, in spite of its pronouncements, has not 'forced' the implementation of the NPE by monitoring or imposing legal and other sanctions on defaulting federal, state or local governments and their agencies as Emenanjo (1997) recommends, indicates that language matters must be treated with caution.

Prospects

How do we resolve the national question as far as language matters are concerned? Over the years several proposals have emerged. Some of these offer no new suggestions, and are mere extensions of existing official policies. Mann (1990) discusses some of the options which include Wazobia, Esperanto/ Guosa, Swahili, Hausa, Anglo-Nigerian Pidgin and English.

The *Wazobia* option follows directly from the National Policy itself, and was promoted intensively in the 1980s. The word *wazobia* is a combination of words for *come* in Yoruba, Hausa and Igbo, in that order. It reflects one of the first words learnt in any language. The assumption is that Nigerian children would acquire basic communication skills in each of the three major languages to enable them to function in them. Mann (1990: p.98) points out that this option 'is a symbolic compromise solution, which appeases the major tribes, but ignores the minor ones.' In reality, it compounds rather than solves Nigerian language problems, and is practically unworkable. A variant of the *wazobia* option proposes a quadrilingual repertoire for each Nigerian child to include knowledge of the mother tongue, one major language, English and French -

official quadrilingualism (Mann, 1990). This is a broader approach which incorporates Nigerian languages and languages of wider communication. It is not really different from the NPE in the sense that by the time a child completes secondary education s/he has come in contact with these languages. It does not ensure mastery of any of the languages. Like *wazobia* it offers no solution to our language problems.

In a bid to evolve ethnically neutral and unaligned languages for the country, Esperanto and Guosa - artificial languages - have been proposed. Guosa, the brainchild of Peter Igbinokwe, involves the construction of an indigenous language by combining elements and structures from Nigerian languages (major and minor). There are problems with this option. The shear task of evolving such a language is enormous and impracticable in our context. The criteria for structural combinations, and for weighting the languages are not clear. Moreover, it is impossible to borrow from all minor languages, so what criterion informs the selection? Esperanto, proposed by Farukoye in 1983 is a European artificial language based on Indo-European languages. Both Guosa and Esperanto are unsuitable because they possess a socio-historico-cultural void that cannot be filled.

The choice of Swahili, a hybrid *lingua franca* of East and Central Africa, has been advocated by people with pan-africanist inclinations such as Wole Soyinka. They see this choice as taking the unifying potential of language beyond Nigeria's borders while dispensing with former colonial languages. Swahili as a neutral language would minimise linguistic antagonisms, but Nigeria does not need a foreign language for her national purposes. Some other people have suggested Hausa because of its numerical strength, and its wider distribution in the north and across the West African sahel belt. We already know that existing ethnic tensions make this choice an impossible one. The alternative for many people would be Anglo-Nigerian Pidgin which though officially unrecognised, is probably the language of widest inter -ethnic communication in the country (Mann, 1990). Its neutrality gives it a higher unifying potential than main indigenous languages. The problem is that it has very low rating, especially among the educated elite. This problem is further compounded by the fact that many northerners find it a threat to Hausa, and have vehemently opposed any suggestion for its consideration as a national language.

We are then left with English which many people want retained at all cost, not only because of the many advantages of using it (nationally and internationally), but also because of its neutrality and its capacity to hold together a shaky confederation of ethnic groups. The major problem with making English a permanent *lingua franca* of Nigeria is that it discourages the development of

Nigerian languages. For this reason many have called for a review of its status, and for priority to be given to indigenous languages. The best we can do for the present is to develop Nigerian languages alongside English.

The language policy as it stands is not satisfactory, and needs further revision. There are different ways in which this can be achieved. The policy may be reviewed in favour of minority languages to allow for their teaching, alongside majority languages, up to SSCE level. This will assuage the fears of minority groups and still protect the interest of majority groups. The main problem with this option lies with selecting from the myriad of minority languages. The criterion for selection should be that they already serve major regional state functions. Another option would be to make the study of major languages optional rather than compulsory. Non speakers would feel better motivated to study the languages if they were not 'imposed' on them. Major languages have functional uses for non speakers. Anyone travelling in the north, for example, would appreciate the need for some knowledge of Hausa in order to get by. But people must not be coerced into learning Hausa (or any other major language) under the false impression that they are doing so for national unity. Legislative compulsion does not solve the problem. National unity does not derive from *merely* learning a language.

Another option would entail conferring national status on all 394 languages, thus placing them on the same pedestal. Minority groups would favour this option, but majority groups may see it as a threat to the so-called supremacy of their languages. The advantages of this option are that it would reduce linguistic prejudices, minimise inter-ethnic conflicts and ensure equal treatment of languages. Critics, however, argue that it would defeat the purpose of normal sociolinguistic practice which is to carve out roles for languages, and that it is impossible to have 394 languages all serving the same function in a country. They claim that it would increase competition and rivalry among the languages. The languages do not need to serve 'national' functions in the same capacity. Obviously, some would do it better than others, or in more domains than others. But, they would still be serving national purposes. We believe that the essence in declaring them national languages is to show that they have a place in national life, and are co-participants in national development.

An alternative (albeit an extreme one) to the last option would entail non legislation on national languages. In other words, not making official pronouncements that recognise specific languages as national. This does not preclude having an official language policy which retains English. The languages would then be left to sort themselves out with time. The rules of competition will decide the functional relevance of the languages. The most relevant for our national aspirations will eventually emerge. It may not depend on the numerical strength of speakers, or level of standardisation of the languages. Major deciding factors would be saliency in national matters, and neutrality.

Conclusion

In this chapter we have examined the relevance of language to the national question which is concerned with how members of a heterogeneous society can coexist as one nation. Language plays an important role in the nation's affairs: it not only constitutes the strongest organisational basis for ethnic affiliations, but also serves as a potential instrument for the unification or destruction of these affiliations. The significance of language is such that necessitates careful planning to enable it to function positively in society. Yet the language policies promulgated by government have been a source of conflict rather than unity. The ideology of unification underlying linguistic convergence towards the major ethnic languages at the national level is highly deceptive. Moreso, when there is continued discrimination on ethno-linguistic basis with respect to rights, privileges, access to power and the nation's resources. The consequences are mutual hostilities which manifest at two levels: between minority-majority language groups, and within majority groups. The inculcation of national unity and consciousness does not depend on mere acquisition of *other* languages, but on equity, justice and fair treatment in all domains. While planning for a nationally accepted language remains a political issue, it is pertinent that such planning has a theoretically adequate and socially acceptable basis. This calls for constant re-evaluation and adjustments of policies to reflect the realities on ground.

References

Aja, U. (1999), 'The Problem with Our University System', *The Source,* June 14: 29-30.

Akinnaso, F. N. (1991), 'Toward the Development of a Multilingual Language Policy in Nigeria', *Applied Linguistics,* Vol. 12.

Akinyanju, P. (1998), 'Ken Saro-Wiwa and the Nationality Question', In Olorode, O., Raji, W., Ogunye, J. and Oladunjoye (eds), *Ken Saro-Wiwa and the Crises of the Nigerian State,* Lagos: CDHR.

Banjo. A. (1989), 'The Status and Roles of English as a Second Language', in Jibril, M., Macaulay, J. I., Ikegulu, B. O. Adelola, B. A. and Ukwuegbu, E. (eds), *Handbook for Junior Secondary School English Language Teachers* (1-4), Lagos: NERDC.

Crystal, D. (1987), *The Cambridge Encyclopedia of Language,* Cambridge: Cambridge University Press.

Egwu, S. G. (1998a), *Democracy at Bay: Ethnicity and Nigeria's Democratic Eclipse; 1986-1995,* Jos: African Centre for Democratic Governance.

Egwu, S. G. (1998b), 'The Political Economy of Ethnic and Religious Conflicts'. In Okoye, F. (ed.), *Ethnic and Religious Rights in Nigeria,* Kaduna: Human Rights Monitor.

Emenanjo, N. (1997), 'Language and Development'. Paper presented at the Seminar of the Department of Linguistics and Nigerian Languages, University of Uyo ll April, 1997.

Emenyonu, E. N. (1989), 'National Language Policy in Nigeria: Implications for English Teaching', in Kennedy, C. (ed), *Language Planning and English Language Teaching,* London: Prentice Hall.

Essien, O. E. (1993), 'On enhancing the Status of Nigerian Languages', *Nigerian Language Studies,* No.1.

Fashina, O. (1998), 'Reflections on the National Question'. In Olorode, O., Raji, 'W., Ogunye, J. and Oladunjoye, T. (eds), *Ken Saro-Wiwa and the Crises of the Nigerian State.* (Lagos: Committee for the Defence of Human Rights)

Fasold, R. (1984), *The Sociolinguistics of Society,* Oxford: Basil Blackwell.

Federal Republic of Nigeria (1979), *The Constitution of the Federal Republic of Nigeria,* Lagos: Federal Ministry of Information.

Federal Republic of Nigeria (1981), *National Policy on Education,* Lagos: Federal Ministry of Education.

Fishman, J. A. (1997), 'Language and Ethnicity: The View from within' in Coulmas, E. (ed), *The Handbook of Sociolinguistics,* Oxford: Blackwell Publishers.

Giles, H. And Saint-Jacques, B. (eds), (1979), *Language and Ethnic Relations,* Oxford: Pergamon Press.

Mann, C. C. (1990), 'Choosing an Indigenous Official Language for Nigeria', *British Studies in Applied Linguistics,* Vol. 6.

Mann, C. C. (1993), 'The Sociolinguistic Status of Anglo-Nigerian Pidgin: An Overview', *International Journal of the Sociology of Language,* Vol. 100/101.

Mare, G. (1993), *Ethnicity and Politics in South Africa,* London: Zed Books.

Odumuh, A. E. (1989), 'Nigerian English: A Sociolinguistic Study of Variation in English Usage', *Savanna,* Vol. 1. No.1.

Okoye, F. U. (1998), 'Power Shift: The Debate, the Controversies and the Future of democracy in Nigeria', *The Witness,* Vol. 1. No.8.

Plang, D. (1998), 'Constitutional Protection of Ethnic and Religious Rights', in Okoye, F. (ed).

Sako, R. (1998), 'The Crisis of Ethnicity in Kaduna State', in Okoye, F. (ed).

Shawulu, R. (1998), 'The Politics of Ethnic and Religious Conflicts in Taraba State', in Okoye, F. (ed).

Tabouret-Keller, A. (1997), 'Language and Identity', in Coulmas, F. (ed).

10 The Nigerian Press and the National Question

WALE ADEBANWI

Introduction

Following the authoritarianism and subordination wrought by successive military regimes in the face of want, neglect and exploitation, many nationalities urged for a re-think of the bais of continued association.

While the Buhari - Idiagbon duo, under the pretext of instilling discipline and providing national direction, outlawed discussions on the democratic future of Nigeria using terror as a major instrument, (Soyinka 1996) the charismatic General Ibrahim Babangida reversed the trend at the initial stage, using "subversive generosity" as his own instrument of state policy.

The fallouts of all these brought to the fore, with a force denied it before then, the glaring imbalances in the Nigerian union, with a new coalition of forces insisting on a sovereign National Conference to discuss the National Question - under which several fundamental issues are subsumed. The annulment of the June 12, 1993 presidential election won by a Southerner, Chief Moshood Abiola, and generally believed to have been annulled through a conspiratorial Northern elite for many, was indicative of the fact that Nigeria could no longer avoid a talk-shop, since, like Manent's (1999) description of the European project, the Nigerian project had become "an imperious, - indefinite and opaque movement (which though an) initially happy ambiguity has now become paralysing and threatens soon to become fatal".

General Sani Abacha's was to concede to the need for a talk-shop but turned-round to subvert this by instituting a constitutional confab which was an absurd parody of what was proposed. Abacha's attempt to *end Nigeria's history* if only to achieve his ambition of perpetual rule again threatened the unity and continued coexistence of Nigeria's multiple ethnic nationalities.

In all these, and in fact before the 1980s, the Nigeria press was placed at the vortex of power and opposition to power in its many manifestations. The Nigerian press has defined and continues to define the parametres of this battle over resources (material, human and *psychological*) becoming in fact, one of the major sites for these contestations. The press constantly reflects the tensions inherent in the plural nature of the Nigerian society (Kayode, Oyejide and Soyode, 1994). Even though this press is the liveliest and the most irreverent in Africa, it is able to act largely outside the purview of the state at the cost of being captive to special, geopolitical interests (Agbaje, 1992).

Against this backdrop, this chapter examines the role of the fourth estate of the realm and in fact, the lead institution in the Nigerian civil society, the press, in the construction and deconstruction of the National Question. What are the parametres through which the press frames the emotive and volatile issues embedded in the National Question? What are the issues embedded in the National Question? Is the press an important definer of these?

We proceed by briefly providing the theoretical context for the main arguments, then we explore the history of the Nigerian press as it relates to the national question. Thereafter, we examine the coverage of the national question by the press in recent years.

Conceptualising the National Question

One of the major huddles in the way of the *progress* of post-colonial states is the problem of defining the terms under which the various ethnic groups and nationalities forced to live together within post-colonial polities (Casmir, 1991: p.x; Richmond, 1984; p.5). Doornbos (1990) advances that critical issues of state power and state capacity vis-a-vis national identity and unity have largely defined the debate about the nature and role of the post-colonial state; they are also central to understanding the present dilemmas and future hopes of troubled polities (Casmir, 1991).

The national question has become the buzzword that seeks to capture the various dimensions of the foregoing dilemmas. In the tradition of the French revolution, the national question is the question of whether relations among peoples conscious of their separate identities shall be based on liberty, equality and fraternity' (Toyo, 1993: p.4).

Against this backdrop, Eskor Toyo casts the national question, as arising out of a drive by a culturally-integrated and self-conscious whole seeking advantage over similarly constituted whole or seeking self-determination . He states further that,

> It concerns the constitution of different peoples into a nation or the self-determination or integrity of a group identified as a nation. The question is engendered by contradictions and signifies the difficulties and struggles that arise in efforts to induce or coerce self-conscious cultural-linguistic groups of states into larger organic formations or keep them in those larger moulds (Toyo, 1993 p.4).

For Anyanwu (1993: p.28) general issues of the composition of the nation or the fundamental basis of the political existence of same are implicated in the nation question. Being concerned with the political union, or the unity, integrity, autonomy or viability of states as composed of ethnic groups or nations, Toyo (1993: p.2), applying the historical materialist method, relates the national question as a social phenomenon, to the totality of the socioeconomic formation on which it is based. Consequently, he draws five points from this. Three of these are relevant here:

(a) Man has a need to be his own master but the rise of economic surplus in history encourages some to permanently dominate others. The conflict arising from this move and opposition to it leads to the national question.

(b) Leaders of ethnic (or racial) groups which have advantage strengthen their domination in the socio-economic realm while those who are disadvantaged struggled to terminate or reverse the hierarchy.

(c) Exploitation, antagonistic competition, uneven development, and domination throw up and deepen the national question (Toyo, 1993 p.3).

There are other conceptual frameworks apart from the Marxian perspective. We can tease out from the above the fact that there are many factors inherent in the national question. That is, the national question has many dimensions: economic, social, religious, racial, ethnic, etc. Again, it is clear that conflict-whether open or convert-is integral to the construction of the national question wherever it appears.

Explaining the National Question - The Nigerian Experience

Perhaps the most eloquent explanation of the national question in Nigeria was given by J. F. Ade Ajayi while delivering a public lecture in 1992. He describes it as:

> The perennial debate as to how to order the relations between the different ethnic, linguistic, and cultural groupings so that they have the same rights and privileges, access to power and an equitable share of national resources; debate as to whether or not we are on the right path to nationhood, or whether the goal itself is mistaken and whether we should seek other political arrangements to facilitate our search for legitimacy and development (Ajayi, 1992: p.14).

This more or less captures the essential political and socio-economic aspects of the national question in Nigeria. These debates and discussions date back to 1914 when the British amalgamated the southern and northern protectorates to form one country. Since this amalgamation the country has not sailed smoothly. Three nationalist leaders and torch-bearers of the interests (and grievances) of their sections of the country aptly demonstrated the tensions of the Nigerian Union. While Chief Obafemi Awolowo (who later became the first premier of the Western Region) states that his task was "to unite the various clans and tribes in Yorubaland and generally to create and actively foster the idea of a single nationalism throughout Yorubaland, (and) to accelerate the emergence of a virile, modernized and efficient Yoruba State" (emphasis added); Dr. Nnamdi Azikwe, former Premier of Eastern Region, averred that "the God of Africa has specifically created the *Ibo nation* to lead the children of Africa from the bondage of ages. The martial prowess of the Ibo nation *at all stages of human history* has enabled them not only to conquer others but also to adapt themselves to the impact of pressure. The *Ibo nation* cannot shark its responsibility" (emphasis added). Their northern counterpart, who was to become the Prime minister, Abubakar Tafawa Balewa, stated that "many Nigerians deceive themselves by thinking that Nigeria is *one*. This is *wrong*. I am sorry to say that this presence of unity is *artificial...*" (emphasis added) (Unongo, 1968).

Contemporary echo of this somewhat separatist, divisive and intrinsically hegemonic sentiments was the statement credited to Alhaji Maitama Sule. Nigeria's former permanent representative to the United Nations. He stated that the Hausa-Fulani is ordained for leadership, the Yoruba for diplomacy and the Igbos for commerce. This infamous statement kick-started a fierce national debate, becoming a spark of thunder in an already raging inferno.

The national question in Nigeria has two aspects: external and internal. The internal is the more important one here, since it has to do principally with harmony among Nigeria's ethnic groups (Mustapha, 1986; Toyo, 1993 p.16). However, it goes beyond the strictly political spanning wealth distribution, power concentration, equity in resource allocation, balanced development, accountability, effective government, free and fair elections, political and religious tolerance, competitive party politics, a competent and incorruptible bench and bar, a pluralistic and inquisitive press, democratic legitimacy and so on, which manifest in public discourse (Onah, 1993: p.v). The control of oil, being the major export commodity in Nigeria, is the ultimate central lever. Oil is therefore inextricably linked to the national question (Soremekun and Obi, 1993). Against this backdrop, Kayode (1993) argues for de-emphasising the ethno-cultural aspects of the national question and focus on uneven access to resources which, he avers, is basic to the national question.

Even though many of the writers on the National Question in Nigeria mention 'democratic legitimacy, and accountability' assure of its crucial elements, they often fail to pin-point military rule, which has more than any other factor, brought the important issues surrounding the National Question to the fore. This, however, is not the trend among activists who talk about the national question. Ekeh (1997) also holds the military responsible for most of the problems revolving round the national question. The military is crucial to the national question for two important reasons. One, the military has ruled the country for more years than the civilians, and, two, the military is dominated by northern officers who consequently emerge as *booty-sharers* in Nigeria.

A 'Questioning' Press

Since its inception in 1859, the Nigerian Press has played crucial roles in both the conflictual and cooperative (overlapping) relationships among social, economic and political forces in Nigeria. It has been pivotal in constructing, expanding and sometimes contriving the socio-political space in the colonial and the post-colonial eras. The formation of this important institution predates the formation of the Nigerian State. This, as we shall see, has implications for the character of the press in the colonial and postcolonial periods. The first newspaper was started in Abeokuta by a missionary, Rev. Henry Townsend. It was called *Iwe Iroyin fun awon ara Egba ati Yoruba.* "Newspaper for the Egba and the Yoruba", which was geared towards getting "the people to read... to beget the habit of seeking information by reading" (Omu, 1982; Coker, 1968). The newspaper was published in Yoruba language until March 8, 1960 when it became bilingual with English language section. Several other newspapers were to be established in the western belt (particularly Lagos) of the yet-to-be-amalgamated country. Townsend's *Iwe Iroyin* was, for him, the principal weapon in his "ambitious political propaganda and shrewd manoeuvring for power in England" (Omu, 1982; Coker, 1968). This indicates that from inception, the press in Nigeria has been located at the vortex of power. By December, 1862, Governor Freeman had to lodge a complaint against *Iwe Iroyin* at the colonial office in London. Apart from its general involvement with power relations, the press was specifically in the Vanguard of the struggle for independence. As early as the 1880s, the *Lagos Times* had started raising issues on independence (Omu, 1982: p.43; Coleman, 1986: p.184).

Also, the battle between pro-establishment and anti-establishment press was noticeable in this period. The *Nigerian Pioneer* which hit the streets in 1914, the year of amalgamation, was dismissed as a quisling-medium of the colonial government. The *Lagos Weekly Record* denounced it as "a thorough-going like-spittle journal sworn to the blind defence of government policy" (Omu, 1982; Coleman, 1986). Ajasa, the *Pioneer* publisher, defended himself by stating that he was averse to "bridled personal vilification or (deliberate) hostile effusions against authority".

While there was a steady growth of the press in the south, it was not until the 1930s that newspapers were set-up in the north. Even then, unlike the trend in the south, the colonial government established the newspapers. The first government-owned print medium in Nigeria was *Jaridar Nigeria TaArewa* (Northern Nigerian News) which was joined on January 1, 1939 by yet another government-owned medium, *Gaskiya Ta Fi Kwabo* (truth is worth more than a penny). The private press owned by southerners intervened in this process later. The Zik Group of Newspapers (its flagship been the *West African Pilot*-started the *Comet* in Kano in 1949 and *Northern Advocate* in Jos, the same year. The Tribune Group owned by Chief Obafemi Awolowo also established the *Middle-Belt Herald* in Jos and *Northern Star* in Kano.

Thus was set a divide in the Nigerian press, this divide was to be accentuated by ethno-religious and political fragmentation occasioned in the late colonial and particularly post-colonial period. As Agbaje (1992) notes, "the press (in this context) became so enmeshed in the struggle for political power that it found it virtually an uphill task to rise above the personal, political and ethnic acrimonies" of the period.

From the period of the march towards political independence, the burning issues which were to become the national question polarised the press often times along spatial, geopolitical lines. While most southern newspapers were supportive of early independence (along the lines of southern politicians who also owned many of the newspapers); northern newspapers, supporting the lines of leading northern politicians, opposed it, suspecting that, unless barricades were put in their path, southerners would over-run the north in the event of early independence. Owing to the limited number of newspapers (and newspapers readers too) in the north, southern voices drowned northern voices in this debate, which even degenerated into personal vilification of northern leaders. Essentially, the outcome of the matter was differing perspectives on the national question. From this period up to the present, the press has had to set the tone and tenor of the debate, moreso since ownership of these media is predominantly in the areas which have been schemed out of political power through a combination of factors including the politics of resource allocation.

As Peter Gouing argues, the Nigerian press was "born through" anti-colonial protest, baptised in the flood of nationalist propaganda and nurtured in party politics. It is a press that is often times a captive, as Agbaje (1992) advances, of spatial geo-ethnic and religious blocs; yet, it is able to sometimes shed these cloaks for egalitarian functions'. However, many writers on the *Press in Nigeria* use the term *Nigerian Press* as if it is unproblematic. What constitutes the Nigerian press - particularly in the context of the dominant issues (national question) of the Nigeria Union? Is it constituted by the "Arewa Press" (which leading voice is the *New Nigerian* – wholly owned by the Federal Government but solely defensive of northern interests, – and the defunct *Hotline, Citizen, Trust and Today,* among others)? Is the *Nkenga Press* (whose present touch-bearer is *the Champion and the defunct Newswave and The Post Express,* among others) constitutive of that Nigerian *press?* What about the dominant *Ngbati* press? However, the *Ngbati* press is conceptually mixed up with *"Tiwan-Tiwa"* press'. While *Tiwan Tiwa* press can easily be said to be led (until recent times when it began to waver) by the *Nigerian Tribune* and can be said to include the *Punch, Sketch* and magazines like *The News and Tempo, the Ngbati* Press denotes the *Lagos-Ibadan Press axis,* which is often erroneously seen as the Yoruba Press.

As I noted elsewhere:

> Although this press is located on Yoruba soil, nurtured by their (the Yoruba's) relative educational, cosmopolitan advantage and their 'competitive, ambitious ethos (added to) their dynamic impulse to self-aggrandizement (this) press is not a Yoruba press. It is a press sustained by the intra-and inter-class competitions that is sometimes reflected in the impatience and the dissatisfaction of the middle-class journalists who-dominate the press (Adebanwi, 1995: p.141).

In fact, the ownership of the major media of the *Ngbati* Press is vested in the minorities. One could say in a sense that the fourth realm is the "Minority (if you like, old *Bendel*) Press" including *The Guardian, This Day and Vanguard.* The foregoing argument is, of course, without prejudice to the pressures exerted by the readership which is centred around Lagos, on these media. The reading public which the press often panders to is dominantly Yoruba. But this *pandering* can be understood in the context of the fact that the middle-class journalists who are products of the libertarian and egalitarian culture of Lagos are protective of this culture, which in the larger arena of Nigerian politics is associated with the Yoruba. As literary and political essayist and journalist, Odia Ofeimun conceptualises it, the *Ngbati* press is:

> A press that is voluble if not cantankerous, a press that is buoyed by a no-holds-barred approach to matters of national interest, and with a capacity for advocacy and adversarial haggling against those it considers

guilty of malfeasance objective, this could be just a description of the Nigerian Press (Ofeimun, 1994: p.15).

While Ofeimun's description is apt and useful, it fails to include in the generalization (of Nigerian Press) the pro-establishment, *illiberal* section of the press. To say that the *Ngbati* press is the Nigerian press will be incorrect. Without doubt, the *Ngbati* press is the dominant section of the press in Nigeria. In fact, it is theoretically seen as the Nigerian press, but empirical evidence point to the fact that the *Arewa* press which is not "bouyed by a no-holds-barred approach to matters of national interest" and has little capacity for "advocacy and advesarial haggling against those it considers guilty of malfeasance objective" (at least in the context in which Ofeimun uses it) is an essential part of the Nigerian press. The Nigerian press is constitutive of all these "sectional" *presses* and those which are not often implicated in these divisions such as *Newswatch, Daily Times, etc.* are however, on their part, implicated in the anti-establishment/pro-establishment divide. The Nigerian press is a complex press whose neutrality on rational discourse cannot be readily established. There are various tendencies in the Nigerian press, with differing interests, motivations, and agendas.

However, whether it is considered from the ethno-religious perspective or agenda - *Ikenga* press, *Arewa* press, *Tiwan-Tiwa* press, Minority press; or from the socio-political complex/agenda - Advocacy press, pro-establishment press or contractor press, the Nigerian press has defined the parametres of the debates on the national question, constructing and deconstructing words, issues, personalities and geo-ethnic blocs in ways that are fundamental to the crises of Nigeria's federalism. One dominant pattern inherent in the various faces of the Nigerian press is that it is a critical press that often raises important questions on pertinent national issues. The extent to which the press allows for an inclusive process of discourse on issues raised and provides a platform for the articulation of tentative answers by a broad spectrum of the Nigerian people to those questions it raises, may be questionable. In other words the Nigerian press may not necessarily provide a voice to all Nigerians.

The Press and the Crises of the Nigerian State

Nigeria is a polity of several nationalities and these nationalities in their narratives clash and contend within the context of the attempt to create a Nigerian nation. As Anderson (1991) argues, the formation of Western European nation-states was linked to a number of factors, including print-capitalism. The emergence of daily, newspaper reading, Anderson observes, was an example of a case in which a nation is constituted as imagined community through printcapitalism. Newspapers and the press in general, play a key role in the way the nation is understood in terms of time and space (Brookes, 1998). Consequently, identities are constantly reconstituted through strategies of exclusion and inclusion owing to perceived threats from within or without ((Brookes, 1998: p.249 Schlesinger, 1991: p. 299-300).

The major issues around which the national question revolve in Nigeria include access to political power/monopoly of political power, resource allocation/distribution, good governance, democracy, the minority question, uneven development, educational imbalance, and the secularity of the Nigerian State. In many ways, the press has constructed the above (and other issues related to the national question) as being predicated on access/monopoly of political power.

Although a frank discussion of these issues - taken as settled by the ruling elite is fanatically opposed by those who benefit from the present state of affairs. The late 1980s and 1990s witnessed a loud and sustained effort at re-thinking the basis of the continued relationship of Nigeria's disparate ethnic nationalities. *Newswatch* captured it thus:

> For some time now, the national question has remained a barely audible whisper. Any effort to discuss it in the open has always been seen as an attempt to stir the hornets' nest because it was considered a volatile issue. And like a seething volcano, it has, since independence, sat precariously on the national psyche. But the underground whisper of yesterday has become the whirlwind of today, as Nigerians seem more eager than ever before to discuss the issue (July 9, 1990).

The crisis resulting from the annulment of the June 12, 1993 Presidential Election won by a Southerner was to make the need for a national talkshop almost uncontestable. This crisis carried within it the major contending issues of the national question. For the *Ngbati* (Advocacy) press, June 12 and how it was to be resolved would determine future of the Nigerian federation.

In October 1993 in the wake of the June 12 annulment crisis, *Tell* Magazine noted:

> ... It seems to suggest that, put bluntly, Nigeria's days as a single nation are numbered, especially if the hard issues of contention are not quickly addressed by way of a national conference (quoted in Adebanwi, 1995 p.214).

As the year 1993, which Kaye Whiteman described as Nigeria's "*annus incredibilis*", passed without any thing concrete happening to the June 12 mandate beyond another group of coupists capturing power, the *Ngbati* press, began projecting into the possible break-up of Nigeria . *The News* in a cover story entitled "If Nigeria breaks... the shape of what will come" *The News* asked:

> If at the end of the proposed constitutional conference, delegates voted that the nation pull apart for now, what would be the consequences of such a decision? Is a (Czech-Slovak velvet divorce possible in Nigeria? (*The News*, 21/2/94)

The press also addressed the lopsided nature of the Nigerian federation in other subtle ways. For instance, in a cartoon which appeared in *The News* in October, 1994, Nigeria's Coat of Arms was captured as "Nigeria's Coat of Harms". Also, instead of the normal eagle atop the national symbol, the cartoon's eagle had the long Kanuri tribal marks with dark spectacles (General Sani-Abacha's trademark). "Unity and Faith", the usual words below the Coat of Arms were changed to "Unity and Caliphate" suggesting that the Nigerian union was under the suzereignty of a hegemonic (Sokoto) Caliphate.

Two broad categories of interviews are usually published by the advocacy press in relation to the national question. The first are those generally from the south which raise fundamental questions on the issue of political power. The other are interviews with "northern irredentists" who speak in defence of northern monopoly of power. Why the latter are occasionally given a voice is mainly to raise the stakes to show how unrepentant and resolved those providing sectional (feudal) answers to the national question are.

Examples of the two categories are as follows:

> (i) The Hausas have been ruling us for the past 33 years. The first time that a southerner won an election they do no want to relinquish power.

> (ii) Always, northerners will lead. Because we know you (southerners) are born to work. You understand. You can't lead. Quote me anywhere.

The *New Nigerian,* flag-ship of the *Arewa* Press, unlike the *Ngbati* Press, did not see the resolution of the June 12 crisis in favour of the unofficial winner as a solution. In fact, in a significant return to its establishment cum ethno-regional position, *The New Nigeria* that had earlier stated that the declaration of the winner of the election would be a "historic moment in our march towards enduring democratic polity" now argued in a frontpage editorial entitled, "Our Nation, our Destiny" against the validity of the same election because of;

Some happenings that in their essence might have serious consequences for the democratic process... key among them and which are widely reported, are the general apathy, low voter turn out, the court verdict and the more insidious foreign interferences... the situation was more serious in the northern states where majority of the voters are peasant farmers who cannot help but attend to their farm...

While the June 12 debacle lasted, the *Arewa* Press pummeled those "ethnic champions" and "tribalists" who wanted the House of Lugard rebuilt, while the *Ngbati* Press reflected that the House should either be rebuilt or "the question (would be) no longer whether the country would break up but how". *The Ikenga or Okoro* press was ambivalent, focussing more on the place of the Igbo in the ensuing crisis (Adebanwi, 1995a: p.243), in spite of Sina Odugbemi's claim that 'the middle ground has vanished forever. On its part, the Minority Press reflected the sentiments of the larger *Ngbati* Press, given the fact that its fundamental interest - resource allocation/distribution was centrally implicated in the crisis.

Good governance and democracy are often linked with military rule and domination in the coverage of the national question. There is constant claims that the "incompetence" of northern rulers who have ruled for a very long time in the post-independence years, is responsible for the current state of affairs in Nigeria. Implicated in this is the military who except for the two instances of civil rule (Tafawa Balewa and Shehu Shagari) have been in the saddle of power. This is connected to the national question not only because military rule is inimical to good governance and democracy, but because the military is seen as dominated by the north which uses the instrument of power to its own advantage. As *Tell's* lengthy interview with social crusader, Gani Fawehinmi, indicates, the dictatorship of the military could "break up Nigeria".

The Nigerian military that comes out of this exercise is a factionalised, corrupt, inept, incompetent, sectional and selfish institution in which competitive thievery is the order of the day as symbolised by the "vagabond in power" or "thieving vampire" as *Tell* 31 and Pini Jason, respectively, described General Sani Abacha. Several stories in the press on particularly Generals Babangida's and Abacha's years bear this out.

The issue of education has also resulted in controversy. While the south has educational advantage, the north lags behind. However, given its political leverage, the disadvantaged section make educational policy for rest of the country. Consequently, the press runs its searchlight on the federal educational institutions whose headship are monopolised by the north such as Joint Admission and Matriculation Board, (JAMB) (yet to be headed by a Southerner since inception), National University Commission, (NUC), National Board for

Primary Education, (NBPE) and the Ministry of Education. The pattern of coverage of the *Nigbati* press is to point out the "glaring" ways in which the north "holds" down the south while in a subtle way mocking the north for its failure to catch up with the south. The *Arewa* Press publishes statistics and facts, to show the "obvious" and "unacceptable" imbalance in the number of schools, higher institutions, teachers, etc. which Alhaji Dauda Birmah, a northerner who was Education Minister, was to phrase as the south's "mad rush" for education. Editorials regularly appeared in impassioned language on this issue particularly in three newspapers *The Guardian, Nigerian Tribune* and *New Nigerian.* For instance, when the Oyo State University (now Ladoke Akintola University of Technology) Ogbomosho was to be started, the *Tribune* wrote an editorial showing statistics of qualified Oyo State indigenes *denied* admission to Federal Universities because of "quota system" which allowed students with lower scores from "educationally disadvantaged" areas to take their places.

Expectedly, the "quota system" and "federal character" are glorified and defended by the *Arewa* press while the *Ngbati* press deconstructs them as systems that encourage incompetence and indolence.

The *Ngbati* Press constantly seeks to show that the constitution which provides for appointments at the federal level "ensuring that there shall be no predominance of persons from a few states or from a few ethnic or other sectional groups in the (Federal) Government or in any of its agencies (Section 14 (3), 1979 Constitution) is often ignored in practice. For instance, *The News* (8 April, 1996) published a story on the "Arewa Agenda" in which it listed a preponderance of major federal offices filled by northerners.

The role of religion, as an instrument of domination in Nigeria has received a lot of scholarly attention. The divide in the press is also along the usual lines since religion is linked with ethno-polities in Nigeria. While the *Arewa* press, given the nature of its society, has sympathy for religion (Islam) and supports its agencies and programmes like Sharia Courts, etc, the *Ngbati* Press is at best supportive of the secularity of the Nigerian State. The latter therefore covers religious crises in the north within the discourse of traditional versus modern society. The north is constructed as a traditional society trapped in religious (Islamic) fundamentalism or zealotry which impedes, not just peace, but also development in a secular context. However, even within the so-called Ngbati Press, Northern voices intervene in this discourse and contest its validity. Yakubu Mohammed, one of the *Newswatch* editors, for instance, argues that religious riots in the north are instigated by "invisible and mindless manipulators" (read, southerners) whose mission is to fight "feudalism" and liberate the society from the grip of the so-called Hausa-Fulani oligarchy".

Mohammed consequently warned northerners, implicitly, of the consequences of the loss of political power. This bears out our earlier argument that the religious component of the national question, like others, is linked to the political question.On the whole, the Nigerian Press, in its various faces, is implicated in the construction and deconstruction of what constitutes the national question and how the problems are to be solved.

Conclusion

The Nigerian Press - in its various cultural agendas - encourages common-sense identification (Brookes, 1999) with the ethno regional bloc as the dominant form of identity in politics. This is done most times through the evocation of images and representations of explicit or even implicit ethnicity, constructing ethnic blocs through the schemes and advances of *others*. Although, Schlesinger (1991, 1993) has shown scepticism on the effectiveness of the media acting alone in constructing such collective identities as the above. However, following Brookes (1999) we have argued that the Nigerian press is effective in this task because it is reporting socio-economic and ethno-religious events and issues which are over-determined by the lopsided nature of the polity and by the different cultures of peoples forced to live together within a largely irresponsive and irresponsible political geography.

This chapter points to the relevance of "discursive strategies" (Fowler, 1991: p.164-9) for the identification of press hysteria coverage of political crises, the national question debate in Nigeria being an unbroken chain of crises. These include: vocabularies emphasising negative emotions (fear and confusion), risk and danger, melodramatic and metaphoric language, and the rhetoric of qualification.

References

Abubakar, Atiku, (1994), 'If We have a Conference...', *The Sunday Magazine (TSM)*, February 27.

Adebanwi, Adewale N. (1995), 'Construction and Deconstruction of Political Reality: The Nigerian Press and the June 12 Crisis', M.Sc. Thesis, Department of Political Science, University of Ibadan, Ibadan.

Adejumobi, Said and Abubakar Momoh (1995), (eds), *The Political Economy of Nigeria Under Military Rule: 1984-1993*, Harare: Sapes Books.

Agbaje, Adigun, (1992), *The Nigerian Press, Hegemony and the Social Construction of Legitimacy, 1960-1983*, Lewinston: The Edwin Press.

Ajayi, Ade (1992), 'The National Question in Historical Perspective', *The Guardian*, Nov. 5.

Anderson, B. (1991), *Language in the News*, London: Routledge.

Anyanwu, John (1993), 'Conceptual Framework for the Analysis of the National Question: A Critique and the Nigerian Perspective', *The-National Question and Economic Development in Nigeria*, Ibadan: The Nigerian Economic Society.

Anyimadu, Amos (1997), 'Overdrawing the Nation: The National Question in the Political Theories of Ghananian Constitutions', in Nzongola - Ntalaja and Margaret C.Lee (eds), *The State and Democracy in Africa*, Harare: *AAPS Books.*

Baber, Karin (1981), 'Documenting Social and Ideological Change Through Yoruba Oriki: A Stylistic Analysis', *Journal of the Historical Society of Nigeria.*

Brookes, Rod, (1999), 'Newspapers and National Identity: The BSE/CJD Crisis and the British Press', *Media, Culture and Society*, Vol. 21, No.2 March.

Casmir, Fred L. (1991), (ed), *Communication in Development*, Nooword, N. J. Ablex.

Coker, Increase (1968), *Landmarks of the Nigerian Press*, Lagos.

Dare, Olatunji (1994), 'The Academy and the Press', Post Graduate School Inter-disciplinary Discourse Forum Lecture, University of Ibadan: Ibadan.

Doornbos, Martin (1990), 'The African State in Academic Debate: Retrospect and Prospect', *The Journal of Modern African Studies*, Vol. 28, No.2.

Ezechukwu, Uche (1997), *Abacha: The Myth, The Man* Abuja: Sputnik.

Hendricks, Cheryl (1997), 'The National Question, Ethnicity, and the State: Some Insights on South Africa', in Nzongola-Ntalaja and Margaret C. Lee (eds), *The State and Democracy in Africa*, Harare: AAPS Books.

Kayode, M. O. (1993), 'The National Question and Revenue Allocation: An Articulation of Some of the Problems and Issues', *The National Question and Economic Development in Nigeria*, Ibadan: The Nigerian Economic Society.

Kayode, Femi, Ademola Oyejide and Afolabi Soyode, (1994), (eds), *Governance and Polity in Nigeria: Some Leading Issues*, Ibadan: FEE.

Kirk-Greene, A.H.M., (1983), 'Ethnic Engineering and the 'Federal Character' of Nigeria: Bone of Contentment or Bone of Contention?', *Ethnic and Racial Studies*, Vol. 6, No.4, October.

Ofeimun, Odia (1994), 'The *Ngbati* Press', *The News*, February, 14.

Omu, Fred (1982), *Press and Politics in Nigeria: 1880-1973*, London: Longman.

Onah, F. E. (1993) 'Introduction', *The National Question and Economic Development in Nigeria*, Ibadan: The Nigerian Economic Society.

Osaghae, Eghosa E. (1990), 'The Crisis of National Identity in Africa: Clearing the Conceptual Underbush', *Plural Societies*, Vol. xix, No.2 & 3, March.

Osaghae, Eghosa E, (1995), 'The Minorities Question,', paper presented at a Conference on Nigerian Democratisation Programme, Niagara Falls, Canada.

Osaghae, Eghosa E. (1998), 'Managing Multiple Minority Problems in a Divided Society: The Nigerian Experience', *The Journal of Modern African Studies*, Vol. 36, No.1.

Schlesinger, P. (1991), 'Media, The Political Order and National Identity', *Media, Culture and Society*, Vol. 13, No.3.

Schlesinger, P. (1993), 'Wishful Thinking: Cultural Politics, Media, and Collective Identities in Europe', *Journal of Communication*, Vol. 43, No.2.

Soremekun, Kayode and Cyril L. Obi (1993), 'Oil and National Question', *The National Question and Economic Development in Nigeria*, Ibadan: The Nigerian Economic Society.

Soyinka, Wole (1996), *Open ore of a Continent: A Personal Narrative of the Nigerian Crisis*, Oxford: Oxford University Press.

Toyo, Eskor, (1993), 'Conceptual Issues in the National Question', *The National Question and Economic Development in Nigeria*, Ibadan: The Nigerian Economic Society.

Uche, Luke, Uka (1989), *Mass Media, People and Politics in Nigeria*, New Delhi: Concept Publishing.

Uchida, Ryuzo, (1999), 'Memory and the Transformation of Social Experience in Modern Japan: Rethinking the Song Home', *Media, Culture and Society*, Vol. 2 1, No.2, March.

Unongo, Paul L. (1968), *The Case for Nigeria*, Lagos: Town and Gown Press.

Magazine and Newspapers

African Guardian
Daily Champion
Hotline
New Nigerian
Newswatch
Nigerian Tribune
Omega Weekly
Tell
The Guardian
The News
The Sunday Magazine
Trust
West Africa

11 The Federal Solution and the National Question in Nigeria

EGHOSA E. OSAGHAE

Introduction

Is federalism a solution to the national question? References to it as a "cure for micronationalism" (Sawer, 1969: p.57), a framework for accommodation of diversity which is considered necessary for the stability and survival of multiethnic polities (Rabushka and Shepsle, 1972; Embree, 1973), and a solution to minority problems (Wheare, 1967; Friedrich, 1968), would suggest that it is, or at least that it provides a framework within which the question can be addressed. Indeed, a direct linkage between the federal solution and the national question is found in Friedrich's (1964: pp.34-5) assertion that federalism provides the only voluntary approach to the task of accommodating the forces engendered by the demands by nationalities for self-maintenance and self-determination. It does so because of the opportunity it offers for self-expression and autonomy and, we may add, negotiations for equity and justice. This assertion is representative of the views of several leading students of federalism. Even Lenin who, unlike earlier Marxists, favoured an accommodationist approach to the national question in the old USSR, agreed that a federal system was the most suitable form of political organisation for a multi-ethnic state (Szporluk, 1973).[1]

It is precisely because of the presumed suitability of federalism for multi-ethnic states troubled by fissiparous tendencies that it is a popular constitutional option in such states. The fact that the federal solution has not always worked (the disintegration of the former Soviet and Yugoslav federations are cases in point, notwithstanding the so-called non-federal features of these socialist federations), or at any rate, has not eliminated or resolved the national question in those countries where it has worked (Canada is a very good example here), has done little to reduce its appeal as a magic wand. Neither has the argument of those who oppose federalism on the grounds that it encourages and perpetuates division and uneven development among different parts of a country (it was on this ground that the African National Congress (ANC) rejected the federal option in post-apartheid South Africa).

In spite of these, federalism as we have said, retains its allurement for divided polities. This is no less so in Africa where the post-colonial state has struggled to survive the protracted crises and conflicts that shake its very foundations (cf Nzongola-Ntalaja, 1987; Olukoshi and Laasko, 1996). The urgent need to save the state from disintegration has brought federalism back into national question discourse in countries such as Sudan, Uganda, Kenya, Cameroon, South Africa, Tanzania, and Congo Democratic Republic. Even unlikely candidates such as Somalia, Liberia, Chad and Angola have considered the federal option to salvage what is left of their war-torn countries. Ethiopia recently adopted a federal constitution in which, like the old USSR federation, grants the right of secession to the component ethnic nationalities,[2] in the bid to halt the long-drawn separatism of the Oromos, Tigreans and others opposed to Amhara domination.

But is federalism really a solution to the national question? The question is pertinent considering that not all divided multiethnic states have adopted the federal solution - in fact some of the most deeply divided of these states are not federal. So, when and under what (ideal or real) circumstances can federalism be a solution? Moreover, given the wide variety of governmental forms to which the term federal has been applied (Osaghae, 1997), which form is best suited to the demands and challenges of the national question? We would argue that, given its capacity to reconcile the contradictory forces of union and separation, federalism is and can be a solution to the national question depending, of course, on the nature of the question and how it is posed.

Federalism has proven to be a solution where, in spite of differences and competing claims to self-determination, the composite nationalities desire and have the will to cohere. It cannot be a solution and is not likely to work where the nationalities prefer to go their separate ways, as forced union is likely to create more problems than solve them. The workability of the federal solution also depends on the legitimacy of the federal arrangement. In operational terms, this means the extent to which the arrangement is accepted as just and equitable by the component nationalities. In classical federal settings where previously autonomous units come together to form a union, the question of legitimacy is less troubling, as the bargain preceding union would have afforded the federating units the opportunity to negotiate acceptable arrangements, although these are not usually enough to wipe out the sore point of many aggregative federations, namely, the problem of minorities.

By contrast, a federation like Nigeria's that came into being through the disaggregative process whereby a formerly unitary state is 'disaggregated', as it were, for the purposes of federation, experiences more serious legitimacy problems. The legitimacy question is somewhat inherent in disaggregative federations because the federating or constituent units are seldom coterminous with ethnic nationalities, thereby limiting the access of some groups to the right to self-determination and first-order federal bargain. Such federations (Nigeria and India offer good examples) face perennial problems of power and resource sharing, including the clamour for new states by groups wanting to actualise the right to self-determination.

It is against the foregoing background that this chapter examines the extent to which federalism has served as a solution to the national question in Nigeria where over four decades of federalism have neither resolved the national question, nor assured the survival of the Nigerian state. Could the continued - in fact increasing - threats to the survival of the state, such as the unprecedented uprisings by aggrieved nationalities in the 1990s, be taken as a suggestion that the federal solution has failed? Or is the problem that, as advocates of restructured federation argue, the wrong federal formula encompassed in the aberration called *military federalism* has been applied? If that is the case, what kind of federalism does Nigeria require?

The Nature and Dynamics of the National Question in Nigeria

One of the points made in the preceding section is that the ability of federalism to address the national question depends on the nature of the question and how it is articulated. To properly gauge the efficacy of the federal solution in Nigeria then, we need, first, to know the nature and dynamics of the national question. This is what this section is devoted to. We attempt to clarify the meaning and essence of the national question in Nigeria from a comparative African perspective and, on that basis, proceed to analyse the concrete manifestations and articulations of the question in Nigeria in historical perspective. The aim is to see what changes and transformations have occurred in the terrain of the national question and the implications they have for any attempt to resolve or address the problems arising therefrom.

Let us begin with a working definition of the national question. Briefly, it relates to the right to self-determination of nations, defined simply as "self-conscious ethnic groups" (Connor, 1973: p.3). Connor's definition is helpful because it avoids the debate over whether, in view of the (mostly uncompleted) reconstruction of ethnic identities within the context of the contemporary states, nations exist in Africa (Nzongola-Ntalaja, 1987),[3] as well as the controversy over the definition of peoples to whom the right to self-determination is ascribed in most human rights conventions, including the African Charter of Human and Peoples Rights.

Self-determination itself covers a range of related empowering and emancipatory group rights: to separate existence or, in the absence of this, free and voluntary choice of which state to belong to local political autonomy (self-maintenance) within a larger political territory; to language, culture, religion and other elements of group identity essential to the preservation of the group and held dearly by its members; to power and resource sharing in the state to which the group belongs; and finally, to equity and justice in relations with other groups and with the state.

These rights are not, as Shivji (1989: p.71) points out, "a standard granted as charity from above". They are the object of struggles "from below" by aggrieved groups, typically oppressed minorities and marginalised groups that are denied the rights (Osaghae, 1996),[4] although in counter-revolutionary fashion, power holding groups sometimes also seek to assert their right to self-determination to defend the status quo.[5] The struggle by aggrieved groups is usually difficult, and the likelihood of success quite low. This is because of the antipathy of the state towards self-determination and other supposedly state-threatening collective rights. According to Connor (1973: p.12), "Against a right to self-determination, the authorities raise the right and duty to preserve union, to stamp out rebellion, to insure domestic tranquility, and to defend the state's political and territorial integrity". It is understandable then why there is a tendency for the articulation and resolution of the national question to involve violence, war and even break-up of the state.

Against this working definition, what has been the nature of the national question in Nigeria? It has basically revolved around the equitable accommodation of the competing claims to self-determination, power and resources to the satisfaction of the several hundred ethnic nationalities, politico-administrative regions, and major religious groups (christian and muslim) despite inequalities in population, size, resource endowment and level of development. The origins of the national question lie, as many analysts have suggested, in the forced lumping together of the diverse groups by the British colonialists and the subsequent attempts, after independence, to force so-called national unity while keeping intact or in fact accentuating the extant inequalities and contradictions that have historically militated against peaceful co-existence.

The core of the national question then, consists of political mobilisation and struggles by dissatisfied and aggrieved groups to seek redress and exact more just and equitable accommodation, in the name of self-determination. These struggles have ranged from those by minority ethnic nationalities for separate states and more recently equitable resource and power sharing, to those by southern groups, principally the majority Yoruba and Ibo, to redress so-called northern domination through a shift of power to the south. It has also involved more localised but nationally consequential or induced conflicts between groups (such as those involving the Ijaw, Itsekiri and Urhobo in Warri over self-determination at the local government level) and struggles by Christians to uphold the secularity of the state against the counter-revolutionary mobilisation of hegemonic forces that has been organised around the ascendancy of Islamic interests (as in the country's membership of the OIC and attempts to introduce Sharia law at the federal level).

In the absence of democracy and the underdevelopment of its concomitant elements of accountability, consultation, consent, and reciprocity, no thanks to prolonged dictatorial rule by the military, the struggles have tended to be extra-parliamentary, uncompromising and violent. The civil war, revolts of the Niger Delta minorities, violent mobilisation by groups like the O'dua Peoples Congress, violent uprisings of fundamentalist Muslim sects, and the secessionist undertones of demands for self-determination by some aggrieved Southern groups in the late 1990s, are cases in point. The violent strategies have raised the stakes of the national question which have led to doubts being expressed about the survival of the country as presently constituted.

But as we argue on, it is misleading to regard such violence as suggesting that the groups no longer desire to belong to the Nigerian state. This is because violence represents not a first option, but a last-ditch recourse for groups seeking redress, after other (peaceful) strategies have failed to produce expected responses from the state (the likelihood of securing better hearing and responses is greater under civilian democratic governments which have multiple representative bodies than it is under authoritarian military governments). Even when aggrieved groups threaten secession, it is quite often the high point on a scale of redressive mechanisms. The Ogoni uprising of the 1990s, for example, was only the height of a clamour for redress that dated back to the late 1950s when oil exploration began in the country (Osaghae, 1995; Naanen, 1995). Indeed, one of the distinctive marks of the national question in Nigeria is that it has involved a low degree of separatism - *most groups would remain in the country if they can obtain more equitable accommodation.*

Having attempted to characterise the national question in Nigeria, let us deepen the examination by elaborating on what we consider to be its key defining elements. First, it is a question that has been accentuated by the inability of the postcolonial state to redress the structural inequalities inherited from the colonial regime. As is well known, that regime pursued policies of uneven development among ethnic groups and regions, and entrenched a system of ethnic ranking, stratification, and discrimination that virtually guaranteed the Fulani aristocracy and the northern system it controlled, political domination of the country, and the ethnic majority groups, domination in the regions and first-order competition for political power. The end-product of all this was a well entrenched system of unequal citizenship, notably between members of majority and minority groups, the North and South, and between Muslims and Christians.

Unequal citizenship resonated in the lopsided composition of key public institutions like the army, police, civil service, and universities, discriminatory practices against "non-indigenes" in their regions of domicile, and unequal access to state power and resources (Osaghae, 1990). Whatever hopes there were that the unity of purpose forged in the anti-colonial movement would force the postcolonial state to address these fundamental problems in the process of nation-building were dashed by the capture of state power by ethno-regional hegemons. Given the centrality of the state to development, resource allocation, and group status and power, it did not take long for marginalised, dominated and excluded groups to seek to emancipate themselves. This took the form of a struggle to reinvent, reconstruct (read as decolonise) and appropriate the state via a (re) negotiated social contract that is built on equity, justice and fairness (Laasko and Olukoshi, 1996). The instrumentality and tempo of the struggle came to depend in large part on how democratic or authoritarian the political regime was and the degree of material prosperity of the country, and how desperate the aggrieved groups were, as a consequence of these. Thus, the period of oil boom and relative prosperity, which also had less autocratic governments, did not witness the recourse to violence that characterised the articulation of the national question in the 1990s whose hallmarks were economic recession, ultra-authoritarianism and the struggles to overthrow military autocracy (Osaghae, 1998b).

The second element of the national question in Nigeria is that it evolved within the context of the modern Nigerian state which formally came into being as a colonial creation following the amalgamation of the northern and southern protectorates in 1914. This is without prejudice to the assertions of the right to self-determination that underlay the insurrections, secessionist movements, inter-group wars and mass migrations of the pre-colonial period. Some of these continued well into the colonial period, stoked as they were by the *divide et impera* policies of the British colonisers,[6] and had consequences for present-day realities. For example, ethnic groups with pre-colonial histories of political autonomy or struggles to assert autonomy, have tended to be more self-consciouness and assertive of the right to self-determination.

But, notwithstanding the historical relevance and continuities of pre-colonial dimensions of the national question, the question evolved and should be analysed within the context of the Nigerian state which is a wholly new experience, that elicits new competitions, orientations, and responses. This is because even the identities and boundaries claimed for some of the ethnic groups in the country today, especially the major ethnic groups were, and are still being, constructed in response to the stimuli elicited by the composition and power configuration of the Nigerian state. The Yoruba "nation" for example did not come into being in its present form, despite the Oduduwa myth of common origin of all Yorubas, until the 19th century. The same is true of the Ibo and Hausa groups as we know them today (Osaghae, 1986). Moreover, the configuration of groups in present-day Nigeria is different from that of the pre-colonial period when there was no common umbrella state. In this regard, it should be stressed that emergent Nigerian realities transformed powerful pre-colonial groups such as the Bini and Ijaw (who in fact lorded it over several Ibo sub-groups under King Jaja) into minority groups. Such transformations changed the complexion of the national question in important ways.

The rather discontinuous and eclectic manner in which the national question has been posed can partly be explained in these terms, as the difficulties and incompleteness of the process of constructing ethnic nationalities have kept the boundaries of self-determination in a state of flux. The frequent changes in the structuration of the federation, which have seen the phenomenal increase in the number of constituent units from three regions in 1946 to 36 states in 1996, is another factor that has complicated the process. In view of the foregoing, the answer to the question self-determination for who, has remained open-ended and unsettled.

For a long time, at least up until the Civil War (1967-70), it was the regions created by the colonisers, and for which new hegemonic identities were constructed by the elite of the major ethnic groups who held power in them, that were the claimants to self-determination. The high degree of autonomy enjoyed by the regions between 1954 and the early 1960s which elicited the forces of regionalism that kept the country deeply divided during the period, the threats by the Northern region in 1950 and 1953, and the Western region in 1953, to secede, and finally, the unsuccessful attempt by the Ibo-led Eastern region (as Biafra) to secede from the federation, were the high points of the era of regional self-determination.

Before regions took over the scene, self-determination belonged to the ethnic nationalities whose boundaries were sharpened by the Colonial Native Authority System. Even the British colonisers, for whom the idea of a Nigerian nation was a travesty, acknowledged this. In 1929, Governor Hugh Clifford affirmed "the consistent policy of the government of Nigeria to maintain and to support ... the right, for example, of the people of Egbaland... [or] of any of the great Emirates of the north ... to maintain that each one of them is, in a very real sense, a nation". To weld them into a single homogeneous nation (presumably without their consent), he argued, would deal a deadly blow "at the very root of self-government in Nigeria, which secures to each separate people the right to maintain its identity, its individuality and its nationality" (cited in Coleman, 1958:194). Although Clifford's assertions were meant to nullify the claims of the emerging nationalists at the time, who went as far as proposing (an Anglophone) 'West African nation', the essence of national self-determination was clear: that ethnic nationalities reserved the right to determine their political location. This point was taken up later in *The Freedom Charter* (1948) of the then National Council of Nigeria and Cameroons (NCNC). The charter prescribed a "Commonwealth of Nigeria and the Cameroons" whose constituent units were to be organised on a national and linguistic basis in actualisation of the right of ethnic nationalities to self-determination. Following the charter, the NCNC's affiliate ethnic (or tribal) unions transformed themselves into state unions to demand (autonomous) ethnic states. This was how movements by minorities, notably the Ibibios, Ijaws, Benin Delta, and various Middle-Belt minorities, for separate states originated (Coleman, 1958:390; and Vickers, 1997). The movements were also encouraged by the support given to the 'rights of nations' by the writings of avowed federalists like Chief Obafemi Awolowo. In 1947, Awolowo advocated a true federal constitution which granted autonomy to each group to manage its internal affairs, to ensure that each group, however small is entitled to the same treatment as any other group, however large" (Awolowo, 1947: p.54).

If the right of nations was honoured as the foregoing prescriptions had it, the resulting Nigerian federation and the national question would have been less contentious. But it was not, as administrative convenience and the wishes of the colonial Governor and other officials took the place of national and linguistic principles in the three-regional structuration of the federation. This created the anomaly that saw the separation of the Yoruba in Ilorin and Kabba provinces of the North from their kith and kin in the Western region, the Western Ibo of the West, later Mid-West, from their fellow Ibo in the Eastern region, and the strewing of the Ijaw across various parts of the Eastern and Western regions.

This set the pattern for the arbitrariness that came to characterise state creation exercises in the post-independence period, especially after 1976 when states and local government areas were created to serve largely neo-patrimonialist interests. The 1991 and 1996 exercises were particularly notorious in this regard. In 1991 for example, a Delta State was created in utter disregard of the wishes of the peoples of the old Delta province who had all along demanded the state. Even the wishes of the Ibo-speaking peoples of the old Bendel East, who turned out to be beneficiaries of the new state (at least they had Asaba as the capital city) for Anioma state were undermined in the process. There were other serious cases of arbitrariness and other anomalies in the composition of local governments, and this underlay the unprecedented spate of violent inter-group and communal conflicts that dominated the political scene in the 1990s.

Let us return to the implications of all this for the meaning of self-determination. For a long time, as we have said, what held sway was regional self-determination which in reality meant the self-determination of the major ethnic nationalities who quickly cashed in on the opportunities offered by the new structures to assert themselves. This left the stage for the strictly ethnic self-determination to the minorities who now had ample ground to demand separate states: they (and their cultures, religions and languages) were dominated, suppressed and discriminated against by members of the majority groups, and they were denied access to power and resources both in the regions and at the centre.

Ethnic self-determination was however submerged in the fervour of the anti-colonial movement. The ascription of the right to national self-determination in that movement to the state which represented the colonised peoples sort of delegitimised other struggles for self-determination, particularly struggles by ethnic groups. The latter were easily dismissed as subversive and treasonable.[7]

The post-independence period saw government trying to consolidate the sense of nationhood gained in the unity that was forged in the course of the anti-colonial struggle. But the temporary unity which papered over marked inequalities among the groups could only be sustained, and sub-national agitations prevented, for as long as the state embodied the common and shared aspirations of the different peoples and responded positively to demands for redress and redistribution by aggrieved groups. But it did not take long for anti-colonial coalitions to collapse, as the state was taken over by ethnic hegemons. This stirred self-determination agitations by members of disadvantaged and dominated groups.

The 1990s saw a revival of the assertion of the right to self-determination in the name of the ethnic nationality, an indication that the assimilationist nation-building project embarked upon by the post-colonial state had failed. Most of these were directed against the state, but there were others that resulted from deterioration in relations between and within ethnic groups as groups jostled to preserve or destroy extant configurations of power. The disaggregation and ventilation of ethnic differences through the many states and local government areas created in place of the old regions (12 in 1967, 19 in 1976, 21 in 1987, 30 in 1991 and 36 in 1996) had a lot to do with this revival.

Even major groups like the Ibo and Yoruba whose ethnicisation processes were generally regarded as complete, were not spared in the ravaging disaggregation. Indicators of the transformed ethnic terrain included the increases in intra-group conflicts such as those between the Ife and Modakeke in Osun state and the Aguleri and Umuleri in Anambra state, as well as inter-group conflicts (Hausa vs. Zangon-Kataf; Ijaw vs. Itsekiri vs. Urhobo; Tiv vs. Jukun; Ijaw vs. Ilaje; etc); autonomy-asserting redefinitions of subgroup identities; the spate of contestations over who or which organisation represented the group; and the multiplication of self-acclaimed 'minority' and 'marginalised' groups (by this time a minority or marginalised status conferred a strategic advantage on the group in the quest to exact resource redistribution and ethnic justice).

But it was the aggrieved historical ethnic minorities, especially those of the oil bearing Niger Delta, that took the lead in the new style ethnic re-assertiveness, as typified by the Ogonis (via the Ogoni Bill of Rights) and the Ijaws (via the *Kaiama Declaration*). Other groups, mostly re-defining themselves as marginalised or minority, were not left behind, as scores of ethnic mobilisational groups, similar to those of the 1940s and 1950s, such as the *Afenifere* and *Odua* Peoples' Congress (Yoruba) and *Ohaneze* (Ibo), emerged to make demands on behalf of the ethnic groups.

The character and scope of the "right of nations" demanded in the 1990s were however different from those of the 1950s and 1960s. While the latter revolved around the creation of separate states and had ethnic minorities as key actors, ethnic self-determination of the 1990s was more inclusive, materialist and prone to violence.[8] Demands for separate states (and local governments) persisted, but the greater accent was on so-called ethnic justice, which hinged on the elimination or correction of entrenched structures of domination and unequal access to power and resources through redistributive mechanisms, and the restoration of reasonable autonomy to the constituent units. This was the context within which demands for power rotation or shift from the north to the south, changes in the system of revenue allocation to give greater weight to the principle of derivation (rather than principles like population, equality, and need that did not favour the impoverished areas from which the bulk of the country's wealth was derived), and a restructuring of the federation to ensure that the states, redrawn to represent ethnic nationalities, would enjoy real fiscal and legislative autonomy, were made.

The shift in the character of the national question can be explained as an inevitable consequence of the movement from the building phase of state-building (in which the composite groups were still trying to establish the basis of association, given the dissaggregative nature of Nigeria's federal process) to the consolidation phase. The latter hinged on, centralisation which, unfortunately under the military, was carried to the extreme, thereby worsening an already bad situation (see below). State consolidation involved the assertion of central authority in crucial areas of the economy such as infrastructural development, taxation, planning, service delivery, external loans, and industrialisation. The state also asserted its supremacy in the political, social and cultural spheres, as attempts were made to effect national uniformities all round. All these (levelling) processes raised the stakes of the national question, and the efficacy of the federal solution came to depend largely on its ability to meet the new challenges.

By far the most vehement articulation of the national question in these terms involved the minorities of the oil-rich Niger Delta region, notably the Ogoni and Ijaw, whose situation amply reflected the contradictions and resultant injustices that bedevil the Nigerian state. Although the bulk of the country's wealth was derived from the region, and the people were subjected to environmental hazards of genocidal proportions against which the state offered no protection, the Niger Delta was one of the most impoverished regions in the country, lacking in basic infrastructure and social amenities, and its peoples belonged to the ranks of the most politically powerless and marginalised minority groups.

The minorities rose in the 1990s to demand, amongst others, the restructuring of the federation into largely autonomous ethnic nationality states based on the wishes of the people. The other demands included the vesting of states with powers to exercise some control over the resources found in their territories; changes in the system of revenue allocation to give greater weight to the principle of derivation and ensure that the communities from whose land oil is extracted are the direct beneficiaries of revenue allocated, especially where they have no states or local government areas of their own; the payment of bulk financial compensation for environmental degradation and other hazards from the oil companies and the state; and the enactment of new agreements with the oil companies to protect the interests of the impoverished communities.

The uprising of the Niger Delta minorities was part of an avalanche of grievances by other groups in the country that called into question the continued existence of the country. The milieu of democratisation, and in particular, the awakening of critical elements of civil society to issues of ethnic justice and accommodation politics, provided the enabling environment for this. In this connection, the annulment of the presidential election of 12 June, 1993 by the military government of General Ibrahim Babangida proved to be something of a landmark in the "coming of age" of the national question. The annulment seemed to confirm the fears long held by Southerners and Middle Belt minorities that Hausa/Fulani hegemony, acting in the name of the North, were not ready to relinquish the political power they had dominated since independence. This led to questioning of, and controversy over, the lopsided composition of critical government agencies like the military, police and security agencies, federal cabinet, and the federal public service and parastatals, as well as extant patterns of economic control and resource distribution, and what was perceived to be an attempt to *islamise* the country. Some of the more extreme responses to the explosive situation involved threats and plans of secession, but most groups were content to demand a restructuring of the federation along confederal lines to reduce the dangers of domination, rotation or shift of power from the north to the south, resource re-distribution, and a Sovereign National Conference of ethnic nationalities to freely and voluntarily re-negotiate the basis for the continued existence of the country that would be acceptable to all the groups.

This brings us to the third and final defining element of the national question in Nigeria. It is that although the claims and demands that make up the national question bother on the right to self-determination and they have been articulated in uncompromising terms and prone to violence, separatist tendencies of the secessionist type have been the exception, not the rule. When the Ogonis, Ijaws and other aggrieved groups such as the OPC rose against the state in the 1990s, it was to exact concessions and benefits, rather than to secede. As has already been pointed out, even when the threat of secession seemed to be a key instrument of the struggle for regional self-determination in the 1950s and 1960s,[9] it served more as a redress mechanism than an actual preparedness to secede (though the lesson of Biafra is that this may not always be the case). The notable exceptions, that involved actual separatism, have been the attempted secession by Biafra which led to civil war, the short-lived declaration of the independent Republic of the Niger Delta by Isaac Boro and his comrades, and the unsuccessful 1990 coup led by Major Gideon Orkar on behalf of the "well-meaning peoples of the Middle-Belt and the (dominated) south" against the internal colonialism of the Hausa/Fulani aristocracy whose core states - the bastion of domination - were to be excised from the federation if the coup succeeded (Ihonvbere, 1991; Jibo, 1993). For an exhaustive study of the mechanics of northern hegemonic rule as manipulated by the so-called *Kaduna Mafia*, see (Takaya and Tyoden, 1987). Space does not permit an elaboration of these landmark articulations of the national question, but it suffices to know that all three were last-resort recourse.

The Federal Solution to the National Question

On the basis of the preceding analysis of the complex national question in Nigeria it can be argued that federalism offers a viable framework for its resolution. This is because although the problematics and contradictions that underlie the national question are fundamental, and propel the centrifugal forces that have continually threatened the foundations of the country, virulent separatist agitations of the secessionist type which typify national question contestations in deeply divided societies are the exception, not the rule (federal solution, no matter how elegant cannot work well where the constituent groups basically prefer to go it alone as it were). This suggests that, in the final analysis, and notwithstanding the imperfections of the state, including the fact that it was created by colonial fiat, some minimum consensus exists on the rectitude of the Nigerian state. Even the most aggrieved groups generally seek redress for more equitable accommodation within the state in preference to break up or dissolution of the state.

For instance, in the *Kaiama Declaration*, which was acclaimed as one of the most important statements on the national question in the post-civil war era, the goal of the struggle for self-determination by the highly aggrieved Ijaws was to "ensure the continuous survival of the indigenous people of the Ijaw nationality within the Nigerian state" (see text of the Kaiama Declaration in The *Guardian*, 28 December, 1998: p.6). Similarly, the *Odua Bill of Rights* demanded, amongst others, the bringing together of the Yoruba people as a distinct federating unit within Nigeria, and the restructuring of the country on the basis of the equality of ethnic nationalities (*The Guardian*, 15 May, 1999: p.14).

But it is obvious that minimum consensus which presupposes greater reliance on coercion, cannot sustain a state for too long. It has to be translated into maximum consensus through the resolution of the problematics and contradictions inherent in the state to the satisfaction of the component groups in the country. This translation depends on the extent to which the composite groups are able to appropriate and feel belonging to the state which depends, in turn, on the extent to which the system is able to address contested issues of domination (of the minorities by the major groups in the regions, for example), and the political consequences of uneven size, population, resource endowment, and development. A federation that is built on or entrenches domination by one or a few ethnic nationalities, cannot last long, as the collapse of Nigeria's First Republic where the other regions were subjected to domination by the old northern region and the former USSR where Russia dominated, clearly show. All told, maximum consensus is *sine qua non* for the survival of the state.

To what extent has the federal formula, which was adopted in the first place as a means to this end, worked to bring maximum consensus about? This is the question that is addressed in this section. The argument advanced is that while the federal formula is suitable for resolving critical aspects of the national question, the specific forms of federalism that have been practiced in the country have been faulty, and, as a result, have had the unintended consequence of exacerbating the conflicts and tensions resulting from unresolved issues of social coexistence.

The Federal Formula

We shall begin with a brief elaboration on the origins of federalism in Nigeria. These lie not so much in the compelling federal character of the country, as in the attempt to establish a workable framework for holding the country together, and forging unity on that basis. Encouraged by the federal infrastructure already laid down by the British (which admittedly made federalism something of a *fait accompli*), the "founding fathers" of the Nigerian state saw federalism as the only system capable of holding together the diverse groups in the country, divided as they were by history, geography, language, religion, uneven development, and inequalities in size and resource endowment.

Obafemi Awolowo, the most avowed federalist of the founding fathers argued that "the constitution of Nigeria must be federal" because "any other constitution will be unsuitable, and will generate ever-recurring instability which may eventually lead to the complete disappearnce of the Nigerian composite state" (Awolowo, 1960: p.239). Similar arguments were made by other founding fathers. Nnamdi Azikiwe prescribed a Commonwealth of Nigeria to accommodate the cultural diversity and geographical configuration of the country. For Ahmadu Bello, federalism was the "**only** guarantee that the country will progress evenly all over" (Bello 1962: p.181, emphasis added). In his contribution to the debate on the future of the country in the legislative council in 1948, Tafawa Balewa, deputy leader of the Northern People's Congress and later Prime Minister of the federation, averred that "Nigeria's political future **may only lie** in a federation" (*Legislative Council Debates*, Daily Parts, 2nd Session, 10 March, 1948).

The founding fathers were not alone in the federalist advocacy. Organised groups like the London-based West African Students Union (WASU) and the Nigeria Society, as well as the principal political parties, all joined the federal bandwagon. Perhaps the most notable confirmation of the widespread appeal of federalism was the result of the referendum that heralded the Macpherson Constitution of 1951, in which the overwhelming support in all regions was for federalism. Given such unanimity, it was clear that anything short of a federal constitution would not work. It was therefore not surprising that the Macpherson constitution which tied the regions too closely to the centre and was therefore less federal than expected, collapsed almost as soon as it was introduced. It was in the aftermath of that collapse and the need to allow each region progress toward self-government at its own pace that a federal constitution was finally adopted in 1954.

While the appropriateness of the federal solution was not in doubt, the critical question was whether the resulting federal formula was capable of legitimating the Nigerian state by bringing about maximum consensus. In view of the instability and threats to the survival of the state that have continually bedevilled the country, the answer has to be an unqualified no. This is in spite of the efforts to correct the anomalies of the initial federal formula by moving from the region-centred trajectory to the nation-centred trajectory. The reason, we would argue, is because the flaws in the federal system are fundamental and subsisting rather than transient, and except they are acknowledged and addressed, the potential federalism has for resolving the national question cannot be actualised. It is to these that we now turn. What are the imperfections and flaws of the extant federal system that have so far prevented it from serving optimally as a framework for resolving national question issues in Nigeria? We discuss them under the headings that follow.

The Problem of Federating Units

First, as is the case with most disaggregative federations, the federating units have not been representative of the ethnic nationalities, thereby foreclosing the scope for asserting the right to self-determination by groups without states of their own. The major groups which controlled the erstwhile regions and continue to have distinct (ethnic) states have been the only fortunate groups in this respect. They were the major participants in the constitutional bargains of the 1950s which produced the original federal constitution that was based on the principle of regional autonomy, and have had pride of place in all subsequent phases of federalism.

All the others, principally the minorities and subjugated sub-groups of major groups, have not had a fair deal, and have had to struggle to overcome their second-order position. This partly explains why the mainstay of minority nationalism has been the quest to have their own states (and more recently local government units), with many of them insisting on this as a necessary condition for addressing their grievances. The value of states and local governments is two-fold. Firstly, they give the groups the much needed voice in national affairs, and by so doing, afford them greater (first-order) leverage in the federal bargain.

Secondly, "own" states and local governments entitle the groups to direct resource allocation and other benefits (such as political representation under the federal character principle) which are made to states and localities rather than ethnic groups. The (over) centralisation of allocatory powers in federal hands under military governments heightened the value of states in this regard. Indeed, one of the major sources of disaffection for Niger Delta minorities was precisely the fact that the actual communities from which oil was derived did not benefit directly from federal allocations. The OMPADEC was created to address the developmental needs of oil producing communities, but even this has not reduced the value of states. The groups desire to exercise some autonomy over their own internal affairs including, if possible, control of resources found in their areas.

The other dimension of the federating units flaw relates to the suggestion that the Nigerian federation is a British imposition (cf. Carnell, 1961), which is the essence of the argument that Nigerians themselves have never really negotiated or bargained the basis of their union.[10] Another variant of this argument attributes the survival of the state in the post-independence period to the force exerted by successive military governments to keep the country together, as in the civil war which was supposedly fought "to keep the country one", and the stipulation of the sanctity of the federation as a non-negotiable ("no-go area") in the constitutional conferences that usually accompanied tortuous transitions to civilian democratic rule.

But these views are only partially correct. Not only did Nigerians themselves strongly favour federalism, as we saw above, the federal constitution that was adopted in 1954 and the subsequent operation of federalism reflected bargains made by them. The bargains, which have been on-going considering that federal instrumentalities are expected to change in response to changes in the political society, spanned several constitutional conferences both in the colonial[11] and post-independence periods. These conferences ventilated and attempted to resolve key national question issues like representivity of government and its agencies, the problem of minorities, power and resource sharing, and uneven development. The value of these bargains for effective federal solution, to return to the point about "artificial" constituent units, was discounted by the fact that representation in the conferences was based on regions, states and localities rather than ethnic nationalities. In the ferment of the state-centred nation-building project of the post-independence era especially, this could very well have been done to discourage, or eliminate ethnic loyalties, and, in any case, the accent was on regional and later state self-determination. But the fact that the regions and states as they existed represented certain ethnic interests meant that the interests of unrepresented minorities were not well catered for. It also meant, in the numbers game of states, that a major group like the Ibo which had fewer states than the Hausa/Fulani and Yoruba, fellow major groups (some say this transformed the Ibo into a minority), was disadvantaged.

The plight of minorities is well illustrated by the bargain that led up to the adoption of a federal constitution in 1954. From proceedings at the 1950 (Ibadan) and 1953 (London) conferences, we know that regional autonomy, which was the mainstay of the federal bargain, would not have been enthroned if the minorities were well represented and/or their wishes were taken into account. The United National Independents Party (UNIP), the only party of minorities at the 1953 Conference, was forced to withdraw from the conference in protest, while the best minority leaders could do in 1950 was to write a minority report. It was not for nothing therefore that Busia (1967: p.115) observed that the resulting federal constitution was designed to *accommodate* the major groups and contain the minorities. The minorities were denied separate states because creating them would have eroded the basis of domination by the major groups in the regions. Even when the Willink Commission was appointed to enquire into the plight of minorities, creation of states was to be considered only as a last resort. Thus although the commission established the veracity of the fears of minorities arising from discrimination and neglect by members of the major groups, it failed to recommend the creation of separate states for them.

The creation of more states and local governments has however enhanced the status of many previously submerged groups and elevated them to the rank of federating units. More deliberate efforts on the part of federal authorities to expand the scope of representation has also improved the situation of groups that continue to be submerged. But fundamental problems remain. It is obvious for example that states and local governments cannot be created to the satisfaction of all groups, a point the Irikefe Panel on States Creation made quite well in its observation that even if a state was created for every family, the clamour for new states will remain for as long as bad governance and injustice persisted (Irikefe, 1976).

The bottom line, as we see it, is that even if states cannot be created for them, it should be possible for all ethnic nationalities to determine how they desire to be accommodated in the federation. If they have to be part of a larger state or region, they should have a say in determining which state. This way, the anomalies inherent in the creation of states and localities, notably the forced union of groups against their wishes (as was the case with the Delta State created in 1991) would be reduced, if not eliminated. This is perhaps the strongest point made by proponents of a Sovereign National Conference (SNC) where representatives of the various nationalities will negotiate the basis and their accommodation.[12]

The Absence of Constitutionalism and Democracy

Federalism, as a system of rules and rights, cannot thrive well in the absence of constitutionalism and democracy. The ground rules which govern relations between the different tiers of government, are meant to be respected, and no level of government, no matter how powerful it may be, can unilaterally change them. In particular, the powers that belong to the states which confer on them a measure of relative autonomy within their allotted spheres of jurisdiction, and according to federal theory are non-centralisable, must be protected. Where States lose these powers, they become mere agents of the federal government, and the system can hardly be regarded as federal. Democracy on the other hand is the bedrock of federalism. The efficacy of federalism is enhanced by a political culture that places value on popular sovereignty, pluralism, dialogue, tolerance, reciprocity and respect for human (individual and group) rights as instruments of equity and justice. In the absence of these, it will be almost impossible to assert state rights, self-determination will be meaningless, and hierachy and domination cannot be avoided (Osaghae, 1989).

These key solidifiers of the federal solution have been in very short supply in Nigeria. Most analysts of Nigerian politics attribute this to continuous undemocratic rule by the military whose principles of organisation - hierachical authority, unity of command, centralisation - contradict those of federalism. In addition, military governments have generally not operated within constitutional rules which they suspend on coming to power. Constitutional rules then give way to decrees that cannot be challenged in court, and it is under such circumstances that the ground rules of federalism are unilaterally changed and non-centralisable state powers are eroded. The suspension of political parties, legislative and other representative bodies, the decimation of the judiciary through the enactment of ouster clauses and scant regard for court rulings and judicial review, and the virtual absence of accountability (military governments have had nothing but disdain for the very civilian populace they govern), all of which disable the federal solution, complete the defederalising regime of military rule.

These severely limit the scope for self-expression and self-determination, especially as the military employs a basically repressive and intolerant approach to conflicts and redress-seeking mobilisation against the state in the name of keeping the nation-state together (it should be remembered that the military has usually intervened when the continued existence of the state is threatened). The wars declared on the Ogonis, Ijaws and other Niger Delta minorities, as well as the execution of Ken Saro-Wiwa and eight other Ogoni minority rights activists who dared to articulate the problems of the minorities and stand in defence of their rights, clearly illustrate this point. It is not surprising therefore that national question contestations have a tendency to be violent under military rule.

It is for reasons such as the foregoing, especially those of non-accountability and unconstitutionalism, that military rule has been susceptible to being used as an instrument of sectional domination.[13] Indeed, the strong anti-military movement in the South which was joined to the national question in the aftermath of the annulment of the 12 June 1993 presidential election was sustained by the increased perception of the military as an anchor of so-called Northern domination. The termination of military rule accordingly became a necessary condition for the resolution of the national question. But while it is true that the underlying contradictions between federalism and military rule on the one hand, and, on the other, what Nwabueze (1994: p.4) aptly terms "lawless autocracy, that is to say, a government not limited by law", have weakened the efficacy of the federal solution, the problems of constitutionalism and democracy are neither the creation of the military nor are they restricted to military governments. The problems are more structural and fundamental. As Chabal and Daloz (1998) have argued, the informalisation of politics and, in particular, the tendency to personalise power, engenders under-institutionalised and opportunistic elite politics. Constitutionalism and democracy can hardly grow under such circumstances.

Over-centralisation

As a system of multiple power centres, federalism is generally believed to offer a superior framework for managing conflicts than a unitary system. From a comparative study of conflict management in Uganda and Nigeria Barongo (1989) concluded that whereas in Uganda conflicts of a local nature easily assume country-wide significance because they escalate sooner or later to a point where state intervention becomes necessary, in Nigeria, several potentially nation destroying conflicts are deflected from the centre and resolved at the state or local levels. The difference, he argued, lay in federalism whose dispersal of power to constituent units reduces the potential local conflicts have of threatening the survival of the state, thereby complicating the national question.

By making the resolution of local conflicts the business of those involved, rather than inviting partisan state security and law enforcement agents (whom aggrieved groups tend to regard as occupation forces), the dangers of injustice and joining the fray of larger conflicts are reduced. Also, the deflection of conflicts to sub-national levels increases the likelihood that the complex nuances of the conflicts can be more contextually dealt with in a manner that recognises their differences. In a highly centralised unitary state on the other hand, the tendency is for conflicts to be dealt with in uniform ways through the use of catch-all formulas and therapies (Osaghae, 1998b).

At the time Barongo wrote, many scholars were still willing to excuse the devastating effects of over-centralisation, the overall consequence of prolonged military rule, on the grounds of consumating the self acclaimed superior nation building project of the military. The movement from the "divisive" region centred federation of the 1950s and 1960s to the "integrative" nation-centred federation of the post-civil war era was applauded for this reason. But in the name of checking divisionist tendencies, military governments destroyed the very essence of the federal solution through over-centralisation. States lost the fiscal and legislative capacity to function as autonomous centres of power; all that was left was administrative autonomy, but even this was consumed by the insistence on uniform national standards set by the federal government, which sometimes reduced states (and local governments) to the status of administrative agencies of the federal authorities (Osaghae, 1992). All major taxing and revenue collection powers were centralised, and states had to depend on the centre to discharge the most basic of functions such as payment of salaries. In the vertical allocation of revenue to the tiers of government, the federal government consistently had over 50 per cent, even with the increases in the number of states and localities.

Also, state competence in several areas was subordinated to federal might and abolished in areas like creation of local governments and university, education, the federal government even went as far as taking over primary education. Even in the few areas that remained under their control (such as waste and refuse disposal), state governments had to compete with local governments who seemed to have been empowered by federal military governments to check possible state excesses. Then there was the system of appointing non-indigenes as military governors in the states which, in popular perception, eroded the essence and basis of self-determination and political autonomy.

In the face of allegations of domination, such postings were sometimes seen as designed to perpetuate extant domination. The same interpretation was also given to the deployment of non-indigene police officers and personnel.

States increasingly lost whatever voices they previously had in sensitive national matters like the police and security forces and electricity generation and distribution. The knock that finally laid state autonomy to rest was the landmark argument by the Irikefe Panel in 1976 that "viability" was no longer a valid principle for states creation because the states derived and sustained their being from the federal government. By that argument which government accepted, states stopped being constituent units in the real sense of the world. They simply became extensions of the centre.

Over-centralisation had rather dramatic effects on the complexion of the national question. From autonomy-seeking self-determination the national question moved to equitable sharing self-determination. States were now sought more because they enhanced access to the national cake than for accommodating difference or asserting autonomy. This shift definitely heightened the stakes of the national question. This was the context in which issues of representation (in the military and federal public service especially) quota system, federal character, equitable revenue allocation, and creation of states and local governments, became the defining elements of the national question. With so much centralisation, Nigeria was no longer different from the Uganda studied by Barongo in 1989.

The grim zero-sum struggle to maximise the group's share of the national cake not only saw an increase in the number and complexity of inter-group conflicts, every one of such conflicts no matter how localised and isolated, now potentially threatened the very foundation of the state. Unfortunately, the solutions proffered by the federal authorities to equitable sharing self-determination which hinge on and strengthen central control - creation of more states and local governments, changes to revenue allocation formula, and consociational principles, notably power sharing, rotational presidency, and quota system have heightened, not reduced anxieties over domination. A more federal approach would have at the same time sought to counter-balance centralisation with state non-centralisation, which is the point those who demand a restructuring of the federation along confederal lines have made. This proposal is valid to the extent that it would enhance the federal solution, but it should be remembered that, as was pointed out in the earlier section, centralisation is an inescapable part of the process of state consolidation, especially where, as in aggregative federations, the centre has enjoyed imperial powers, including the power to create states themselves.

Conclusion

By virtue of the nature of the national question in Nigeria, particularly the fact that separatist agitation of the secessionist type is the exception rather than the rule, the relevance of federalism to its resolution is beyond question (cf. Adamolekun and Kincaid, 1991). It is significant that even in the 1990s when the question became far more vexing than ever before and the country's chances of survival as a corporate entity appeared slim, most aggrieved groups demanded a restructuring of the federation rather than a break-up (Amuwo et al, 1998). As was pointed out, if the only solution to the national question is for groups to go their separate ways, then federalism is not likely to be tenable or successful. The application of the federal solution in the old USSR in spite of the separatist inclinations of the constituent nationalities in the hope that the secession clause inserted in the constitution would provide a safety outlet for dousing the fire of agitations did not prevent the eventual collapse of what was in effect a forced union. Ethiopia has also adopted a similar clause, and structured the federation along ethnic lines to reinforce the federal solution. Only time will tell if this will work, but it is significant that neither ethnic structuration nor the secession outlet has reduced the spate of separatist agitations. If the example of the old USSR is anything to go by, the problem of Amhara domination, like that of Russian domination in the USSR is likely to remain a constant source of tension and separatist agitation.

Fears of domination were, and have continued to be, the major source of tension and separatist inclinations in Nigeria. The safety outlet in this case was not a secession clause, but a high degree of autonomy for the constituent units, in the days of the regions. The increased divisiveness that came with this (regionalism) and led to civil war forced a change of course to nation-centred federalism under the direction of military governments, ostensibly to save the federation. But poor political management and the erosion of democracy and constitutionalism, the poles on which federalism hang, and the consequent deepening of the crisis of the national question, have made a return to the principle of relative autonomy for the states a necessary condition for the workability of the federal solution to the national question.

All other instrumentalities and steps that have been introduced or taken in response to demands for more equitable power sharing and income redistribution – notably federal character principle, changes in the structure of revenue allocation, including the establishment of OMPADEC, rotational presidency and power shift from the north to the south – are expedient and even necessary, but they are derived from the region of over-centralisation, and are likely to sustain and extend, rather than diminish, centralisation which demonstrably raises the stakes of the national question. Such centrist devices in themselves are incapable of satisfying the demands for self-determination and self-expression. This is what the experience of the 1990s showed, as the so-called power shift from the North to South did not quieten the demands for restructuring the state along confederal lines – what some term true federalism. What is required is the restoration of the non-centralised powers of the state to counter-balance and limit the forces of possible over-centralisation which, given the disaggregative process of Nigeria's federalism, is not surprising.

In all this, the point that needs to be emphasised is that the federal solution, by design, is dynamic by being chameleonic, that is changing in accordance with changes in the political realities of the national question. In other words, it is perfectly in order – in fact it is a mark of the resilience of the federal solution in Nigeria – for the federal instrumentality to change from the regional autonomy trajectory to the imperial centre trajectory and back again to the regional autonomy trajectory as was demanded in the 1990s. The reality and demands may yet change when the need for unity becomes more urgent, and it is when the federal system proves incapable of adjusting accordingly, or more accurately, when the controllers of state power are impervious to change, that the federal solution cannot bring about the maximum consensus and legitimacy that are a necessary condition for the resolution of the national question.

Notes

1. This was a significant departure from the preference by Engels and the earliest Marxists for large territorial organisations rather than federalism. It was believed that the latter perpetuated traditional values and economic backwardness through regional division and isolation (see Engels, 1979). Influenced by Lenin, the central party in the USSR later accepted federation as 'lone of the transitional forms on the road to complete unity" (cited in Smith, 1996: p.5; also see Szporluk, 1973).

2. The rationale for the right to secession is well explained by Lenin in the light of its extension to ethnic nationalities in the old USSR. The logic was:

    If nations were not given this right, then, among peoples whose national consciousness was emerging as a political force, it would encourage a combative nationalism which would run counter to the establishment of [a strong state]. In an oft-quoted analogy, Lenin noted that 'the right of divorce is not an invitation for all wives to leave their husbands'. Lenin believed that even if small nations seized the opportunity to declare themselves states, they would soon realise the benefits of being part of a larger territorial unit and would opt for reincorporation (Smith, 1996: p.5).

3. Once members of the ethnic group become conscious of their corporate interests and act on that basis to make demands that bother on self-determination in the name of the group, the group can be regarded as a nation.

4. Recent studies of the national question, especially those set in the postmodernist paradigm have expanded the scope of marginalised groups to include gender, class, youth, and other categories. While such expansion helps to deepen our knowledge of untenable power relations that underlie national question contestations, the fact that these categories generally lack a territorial back-up for the claim to self-determination, means that in the final analysis the notion of self-determination relation to them is different from that of nations. Nations can become states, but women and men cannot. In this study, these other expanded categories are excluded from the analysis.

5. A good example is the insistence by the Afrikaners in South Africa on their right to self-determination which the right-wing believes can only be satisfied by the creation of a separate state *(volkstaat)*. As the authors and beneficiaries of apartheid, the objective of self-determination in this case is to protect the privileges enjoyed by members of the group.

6. Colonial intervention however produced a mixed picture. While various Mid Western groups like the Esan, Ika and Urhobo were finally able to assert their autonomy from the imperial Benin empire, others like the Middle Belt minorities who had all along managed to ward off or at any rate challenge Sokoto Caliphate Islamic over-lordship were delivered to new forms of internal colonialism.

7. The state-supremacist notion of self-determination, coupled with the decision of the founding fathers of the Organisation of African Unity (OAU) to maintain the boundaries inherited from the colonial powers, legitimised the inclination of post-colonial governments towards suppression of all forms of (supposedly counter) assertions of self-determination, in the name of holding the state together. However, some would argue that in the case of Nigeria at least, this was not really the case because, almost

from the beginning, the nationalist movement was divided along ethno-regional lines, and this made the assertion of the right of all Nigerian peoples, as opposed to ethno-regional peoples, a contested issue indeed, independence was delayed because the regions found it difficult to agree on a date.

8.　The impetus for the more violence-prone agitations of the 1990s was provided by a combination of global forces in favour of minority and environmental rights, the desperate levels of economic decline in Nigeria which saw every group making last-ditch efforts to appropriate what was left of the diminishing national cake, and the contradictions of the seemingly unending democratisation process which sharpened the national question.

9.　Several instances can be cited. The Northern region threatened to secede in 1950 if the allocation of parliamentary seats and revenue allocation was not based on the per capita principle, and again in 1953 over the self-government in 1956 motion in parliament. In 1953, the Western region also threatened to secede if Lagos was not made a part of the region. The 1960s saw several threats by the Eastern region which actually attempted to secede as Biafra in 1967. Finally, at the height of the political crisis that engulfed the country and ultimately led to civil war, virtually all the regions, with the exception of the minorities' Mid-West, threatened secession.

10.　The Kaiama Declaration states for example that it was through British colonisation that the Ijaw nation was forcibly put under the Nigerian state" (*The Guardian*, 28 December 1998: p.6).

11.　There is an unfortunate tendency to underrate the importance of the conferences held in the colonial period on the grounds that only the colonisers could annul the continued existence of the country. This is really unfortunate because even at that stage, the survival of the country depended more on the wishes and preferences of the people. A foreign press agency captured the importance of these conferences when it observed on the eve of the landmark Ibadan General Conference of January 1950 that "The African politicians... [will debate]... the constitutional change which according to some observers may ultimately split the country into two" (Reuters Press, quoted in *West African Pilot*, 10 January 1950).

12.　The colonial period conferences took place in 1950, 1953, 1954, 1956, 1957, 1958, and 1959. The post-independence period has so far witnessed the ad hoc constitutional conference of 1966 which gave General Yakubu Gowon the mandate, as it were, to fight Eastern secessionists to keep the country together, and the conference of 1994 which was convened at a time the country appeared set for disintegration, in addition to a number of constitution drafting committees and constituent assemblies.

13.　For example, appointments which perpetuate sectional domination are justified on the grounds that they are military postings, and traditional rulers who lack popular support and are agents of the state are propped up as representatives of ethnic nationalities to rubber stamp hegemonic agendas.

References

Adamolekun, L. and Kincaid, J. (1991), 'The Federal Solution: Assessment and Prognosis for Nigeria and Africa', *Publius*, Vol. 21, No. 4.

Amuwo, K., Agbaje, A., Suberu, R. and Herault, G. (eds), (1998), *Federalism and Political Restructuring in Nigeria.* Ibadan: Spectrum Books.

Awolowo O. (1947), *Path to Nigerian Freedom* London: Faber.

—— (1960) Awo: *The Autobiography of Chief Obafemi Awolowo.* Cambridge: Cambridge University Press.

Barongo, Y. (1989), 'Ethnic Pluralism and Political Centralisation: The Basis of Political Conflict' in K. Rupesinghe (ed), *Conflict Resolution in Uganda* Oslo: PRIO.

Bello, A. (1962), *My Life*, Cambridge: Cambridge University Press.

Carnell, F. G. (1961), 'Political Implications of Federalism in New States', in U.K. Hicks et al (eds), *Federalism and Economic Growth in Underdeveloped Countries.* London: Allen and Unwin.

Coleman, J. (1958), *Nigeria: Background to Nationalism.* Berkeley: University of California Press.

Connor, W. (1973), 'The Politics of Ethnonationalism', *Journal of International Affairs,* Vol. 27, No. 1.

Embree, A. T. (1973), 'Pluralism and National Integration: The Indian Experience', *Journal of International Affairs*, Vol. 27, No 1.

Engels, F. (1979), 'The Movements of 1847', in K. Marx & F. Engels, *Collected Works*, Vol. 6, Moscow: Progress Publishers.

Friedrich, C. J. (1968), *Trends in Federalism in Theory and Practice*, London: Pall Mall.

Ihonvbere, J. (1991), 'A Critical Evaluation of the Failed 1990 Coup in Nigeria', *Journal of Modern African Studies*, Vol. 29, No.4.

Irikefe (Panel on States Creation) (1976), *Federal Military Government's Views on the Report of the Panel on the Creation of More States.* Lagos: Federal Ministry of Information.

Jibo, M. (1993), *Tiv Politics since 1959* Zaria: Ahmadu Bello University.

Laasko, L. and Olukoshi, A. O. (1996), "The Crisis of the Post-Colonial Nation-State.Project in Africa, in A. O. Olukoshi and L. Laasko (eds), *Challenges to the Nation State in Africa.* Uppsala: Nordiska Afrikainstitutet.

Naanen, B. (1995), 'Oil-Producing Minorities and the Restructuring of Nigerian Federation: The Case of the Ogoni People', *Journal of Commonwealth and Comiparative Politics*, Vol. 33, No.1

Nwabueze, B.O. (1994), *Nigeria : The Political Crisis and Solutions.* Ibadan: Spectrum.

Nzongola-Ntalaja (1987), 'The National Question and the Crisis of Instability in Africa' in E. Hansen (ed), *Africa: Perspectives on Peace and Development*, London and New Jersey: Zed and United Nations University.

Okpu, U. (1977), *Ethnic Minority Problems in Niqerian Politics, 1960-1965*, Uppsala: University of Uppsala.

Olukoshi, A. O. and Laasko, L. (eds), (1996), *Challenges to the Nation-State in Africa.* Uppsala:

Nordiska Afrikainstitutet.

Osaghae, E. E. (1986), 'On the Concept of the Ethnic Group in Africa: A Nigerian Case', *Plural Societies*, Vol. 16, No.2.

— (1989) 'Federalism and Democracy: An Old Romance Revisited in the Light of the Nigerian Experience' in J. 'Bayo Adekanye ed. Institutions and Processes of Democratisation in Nigeria Calabar: Proceedings of the Nigerian Political Science Association Conference.

— (1990), 'The Problems of Citizenship in Nigeria' *Africa*, Vol. xlv, No.4.

— (1992), 'The Status of State Governments in Nigerian Federalism', Pub.Uus: *Journal of Federalism*, Vol. 22, No.3.

— (1994), *Ethnicity and its Management in Africa: The Democratisation Link.* Lagos: Malthouse.

— (1995), 'The Ogoni Uprising: Oil Politics, Minority Agitation, and the Future of the Nigerian State', *African Affairs*, Vol. 94.

— (1996), 'Human Rights and Ethnic Conflict Management: The Case of Nigeria', *Journal of Peace Research*, Vol. 33, No.2.

— (1997), 'The Federal Solution in Comparative Perspective' *Politeia*, Vol. 16, No.1.

— (1998a), *Crippled Giant: Nigeria Since Independence.* London and Bloomington: C. Hurst and Indiana University Press.

— (1998b), 'Managing Multiple Minority Problems in a Divided Society: The Nigerian Experience', *Journal of Modern African Studies*, Vol. 36, No.1.

Sawer, G. (1969), *Modern Federalism.* London: C.A. Watts.

Shivji, I. G. (1989), *The Concept of Human Rights in Africa.* Dakar: CODESRIA.

Smith, G. (1996) 'The Soviet State and Nationalities Policy' in G. Smith (ed), *The Nationalities Question in Post-Soviet States*, 2nd ed. (London & New York: Longman).

Szporluk, R. (1973), 'Nationalities and the Russian Problem in the USSR: An Historical Outline', *Journal of International Affairs*, Vol. 27, No.1.

Takaya, B.J. and Tyoden, S.G. (eds), (1987), *The Kaduna Mafia: A Study of the Rise, Development and Consolidation of a Nigerian Power Elite*, Jos: Jos University Press.

Vickers, M. (1997), *Ethnicity and Sub-Nationalism in Nigeria: Movement for a Mid-West State.* London: Hillfield Press.

Wheare, K. C. (1967), Federal Government. London: Oxford University Press.

12 Conclusion: The National Question in Comparative Perspectives

SAID ADEJUMOBI
ABUBAKAR MOMOH

It is apparent from the foregoing study that the national question raises more questions. What answers are sought is a function of several possibilities and options. This study has not been geared toward social policy as such although many of its conclusions have implication for policy science.

As it relates to the various contributions in the book, there are two broad remarks to be made particularly as it relates to certain thematic areas. The first is methodological. The approaches or perspectives to the study have varied. There are various perspectives that have been employed from the structural to the institutional to the political economy and class analytical approach. The issues identified range from social to political and economic. The role of the military, religion, ethnicity, language and uneven development in various ways and how they have been factored into the understanding of the national question in Nigeria. The weight of any of these variables is a function of the circumstances and agencies in the fore of pushing them.

The second thematic issue relates to historical (re)construction. The historical account of what is "Nigeria", how it came to be what it is; what factors are responsible for certain occurrences and what social forces should be held accountable for this, have also been highly contentious issues. There is the crucial question whether Nigerians are "compatible" people as such; whether the amalgamation of Nigeria in 1914 "was a mistake", whether what took place in 1914 was a "unity of states" rather than a "unity of peoples" and so on. It is however clear that issues of uneven development, injustice, domination and favouritism have all been mentioned as factors that affect the resolution of the National Question in Nigeria. The manifestation of each of these factors take different dimension from one state to the other from one ministry to the other and from one institution to the other (including the military institution). The state's response to the national question through federal character, zoning of offices and the use of quota system in various public institutions have not

245

helped matters, it merely further compounds them. Hence the "federal solution" has become part of the national question. Part of the basis for this relates to the role of the military in Nigeria's political life. As Suberu and Agbaje note "... military influence is crucial to an understanding of the paradoxes, pathologies and irregularities that currently plague the Nigerian system of federalism" (1998: p.335). Even under the current civilian dispensation of President Olusegun Obasanjo, it is yet to be seen whether the government intends to take a just and democratic attitude to the resolution of the national question. This could be gleaned from the total destruction of the oil-producing community of Odi, the near indecisive attitude of the government toward the killings in Kaduna over the Sharia debacle and so on. But the other aspect of all this is, what is the solution of the people to the crisis of the nation-state in Nigeria and the national question? We dare to say that the voices of the toiling people have been missing in the entire discourse of the national question. Do the toiling people of Sokoto State believe they are different from those of Delta State? Will the toiling people of Kano State with over 500 fuel stations accept a situation where the people of Bayelsa State have only one fuel station even though the latter is an oil-producing state? Do the toiling people have information about the living and social conditions elsewhere in the country other than in their areas of domicile? Who then holds brief for them? Why are they not consulted for their opinion over sensitive matters? Why is their opinion not seen to matter? Endless questions arise. The benefit of different methodological and historical account is that it provides us a basis on which to carry out an enriching comparative analysis.

What constitutes the national question differs in time and space and reflects a fundamental issue of social existence, more often with a national dimension which fragments a nation-state, yet for which the state and its people are bound to search for an acceptable consensus or solution. It may be the issue of ethnic nationalities, the minority question, the land question, the question of race, gender imbalances or social inequalities. In recent times, the first issue, that is, the nationality question has been at the core of political crisis in many parts of the world.

The twilight of the 20th century witnessed a remarkable attack on the nation-state both in theory and practice. Modern nation-states, multinational in character have shown less homogeneity, resilience and consociational tendencies such as disintegrating practices, separatist agitation, intense ethnic and civil strife threaten the political fabric of many countries. There is a gradual privatisation of the instruments of violence and the democratisation of anarchy by many constituent groups. The armed space hitherto monopolised by the state has seen the crowding-in of ethnic militias, rag-tag communal "armies" and mercenary soldiers, who take up arms on behalf of aggrieved ethnic or communal groups either in the search for self determination or in order to redress perceived imbalances in the geo-political distribution of scarce resources-wealth and power. The fall-out of the cold war and the democratisation process in most parts of the Third World gave vent to this development.

The phenomenon of ethnic nationalism and the political crisis it provokes assumes a global dimension. From the Philippines to Sudan, United Kingdom to Nigeria, Burundi to Fiji, Rwanda to India, the nationality question is a recurring decimal, albeit in various forms and degrees. The political management of this phenomenon also differs among countries, so is the level of violent outburst that result from it. Between 1989 – 1998, there were 101 internal armed conflicts in the world, mostly ethno-political in nature (Cf. Wallenstein and Sollenberg, 1999: p.593). In Africa, armed agitation by ethnic nationalities has become the language of political expression. In 1999, there were eighteen armed conflicts in Africa, with eleven countries under the threat of severe political crises (Adedeji, 1999: p.5). Today, virtually all countries in Africa are under the constant threat of violent political explosion of an ethnic bent.

The tenor and morphology of those conflicts usually take into account local peculiarities. In Zimbabwe for example, a constellation of ethnic and racial factors have found expression around the land question. The land question is a major national issue in Zimbabwe today, just as it is in many southern African countries that experienced settler-colonialism. Zimbabwe's compromised independence negotiation with the British tempered the ability of the post-colonial government to redistribute land and promote transparent governance (Ihonvbere, 2000: 16). As a result, land ownership has assumed a racial dimension. Most of the black and landless Zimbabwean peasants, work as farm labourers on the white dominated commercial agricultural farms. Although the issue is racial in nature, the current struggle for land redistribution in Zimbabwe is a class question. The urge to redress social and class inequalities is predicated on a bankrupt colonial logic of racial superiority and class distinction. Robert Mugabe's sudden awakening and support for the process is obviously to gain political capital, yet the issue is real and transcends him. Criminalising the genuine agitation of the Zimbabwean people for land redistribution as the western media did is to trivialise a major national issue in Zimbabwe. Also, to interpret the problem in strictly racial or personality terms is to blur or detract from its import. Confronting and resolving the land question in Zimbabwe (as in most other southern African countries) within the parameters of constitutional rule is a necessary step to promoting social cohesion, peace, stability and security in that country.

In Nigeria, while the national question is premised mainly on the nationality issue, its anatomy is multi-formed and multi-dimensional. This ranges from the issue of minorities, to revenue allocation, the military, the oil question, to language. The preceding chapters have exhaustively analysed the various dimensions of the national question in Nigeria.

It may be useful in this concluding part of our analysis to unravel how the introduction of civil rule in Nigeria since May 1999 has impacted on the national question (precisely on the nationality question) and the direction of the nation's political future. To pose the question quite sharply: will Nigeria survive as a single entity? If so, under what condition(s)?

Since the transition to civil rule in May 1999, there has been a deepening crisis of the national question in Nigeria. First there has been a dramatic increase in the level and intensity of inter-group conflicts, of ethnic, communal and religious nature. Inter-communal conflicts have occurred in most parts of the country, which include the Ijaw-Ilaje conflict in Ondo State, the Ife-Modakeke in Osun State and the Ndiabo-Edere – Okun Ibokun communal clashes in Rivers State. Inter-ethnic conflicts have erupted in major Nigerian cities such as Lagos, Kaduna, Sagamu, and Ibadan. While religious conflicts premised mainly on the introduction of the Sharia legal code in some of the northern states of the country such as Sokoto, Kaduna, Niger, Kano and Zamfara States have unleashed anarchy in some of those states. The crisis has been most profound in Kaduna, where there has been colossal loss of lives and property. This religious conflict also assumes an ethnic bent. Most of the victims of the Kaduna religious mayhem are mostly Christians from the eastern part of the country. This development has provoked reprisals from the easterners against the northerners living in the eastern part of the country.

A disturbing trend in most of these conflicts is the seemingly organised fashion that they now assume. Sophisticated weapons such as AK47 rifles are increasingly and freely used even during communal clashes. These crises have proved very daunting for the Obasanjo civilian administration to handle. President Olusegun Obasanjo after one year in office in May 2000, admitted that the greatest challenge to his regime is the issue of inter-group conflicts and violence. While some argue that the issue is a logical hang-over from military rule, and that the military should must take full responsibility for it, others contend that it portends the disquieting feelings of the people about the current structure of the Nigerian federation and the imbalances that characterise it.

However, the development of inter-group conflicts evokes high level of physical insecurity for the people, especially those who live and work in areas outside their ethnic domain. As a result, a wave of emigration has occurred, of people living outside their ethnic zone back to their ethnic domains. More than ever before, since the end of the civil war in 1970, Nigeria's federal system is under enormous stress with the internecine conflicts among ethnic and religious groups.

The second trend about the national question is that the debilitating political situation in the country has provided a window of opportunity for separatist agitation by some ethnic-based civil society groups. In the south-eastern part of the country, a group which calls itself the "Movement for the Realisation of the Sovereign state of Biafra" (MASSOB) has been engaged in political mobilisation to actualise the aborted dream of a Biafran state. It has been making trenchant, yet unsuccessful call for self-determination by the people of eastern Nigeria. It has created new signs and symbols, flag and map for the new dream. Also, public demonstrations have been organised by the group to press home its demand. However, the agitation is yet to gather the necessary political clout from a broad segment of the society in the eastern states. The political elite, the business class, labour and the traditional rulers have all distanced themselves from the move.

In other parts of the country while the demand is not for self-determination, the call centers on the loosing up of the Nigerian federation to allow for regional autonomy based on ethnic contiguity. Most ethnic groups now harbour and promote lumpen youth elements, that serve as their ethnic militias. These groups are ostensibly formed to defend the interest of their ethnic constituencies. They include the Odua Peoples Congress (OPC), the Arewa Peoples Congress (APC), the Egbesu Boys, and so on. The inability of the state to engineer and lead the process of political change in re-negotiating the social pact amongst Nigeria's ethnic nationalities has elicited a dangerous wave of militant ethnic nationalism.

The restructuring of the Nigerian federation (with its elements of over-centralisation of power and resources at the centre) is the most crucial issue that the new civilian administration will have to confront and resolve. Indeed, some have suggested that the present civilian administration is a transitional arrangement whose task is to carry out the process of restructuring of the Nigerian federation. As Wole Soyinka notes "we merely warn this government to avoid the delusion, the self-destructive pitfall of imagining that the present arrangements, under which the Nigerian people have consented to give it qualified support, is the ultimate answer to the productive yearnings of the people". It is "a transition to an authentic popular representation that will usher in a firm structure of democracy". According to Soyinka, the present arrangement "as defined, structured, and operated, cannot hold. Not while the relations of the centre to the parts are so acquisitive, unbalanced and exploitative" (*The Guardian*, November 3, 1999).

A national consensus seems to gravitate towards the issue of the restructuring of the Nigerian federation, although there are different views on the approach and strategy to it. Perhaps a strategic, yet simple approach to it is through a process of constitutional engineering that should be inclusive, just and democratic. This approach if properly managed will checkmate the demand for a sovereign national conference which the civil society has insisted upon, and will achieve the same purposes as the latter. However, the nation's political leadership (both the presidency and the national assembly) is marred in confusion, political bickering and pettiness on the issue of constitutional redesign for the country. Hence their efforts in this regard are short sighted and run at cross-purposes. While the president set up a "technical committee" to undertake a review of the 1999 constitution foisted by the military, shortly thereafter, the National Assembly also set up its own committee made of its members to do the same work. In both cases, the approach was hazy, poorly organised, and the committees' highly unrepresentative of the broad interests of the Nigerian society.

It is important that the process of constitution making especially for a plural society like Nigeria should be seen as a political process, rather than strictly a legal or technical issue. It must not be treated as a sensitive, technical or secluded process, to be dominated and driven by the political elite of lawyers and politicians (see, Ihonvbere, 2000: p.34). The body to undertake the constitutional redesign process (i.e. the constitutional commission) must be fairly representative, credible, and seen to be legitimate. The process itself must be simple, open and highly inclusive. And the product (i.e. the draft constitution) must be devoid of bogus, complex, and confusing language or *legalese* (Ihonvbere, 2000: p.34). Ultimately, the draft constitution must be subjected to the test of popular will before it is adopted and become a constitution for the country. It is only through this process that a new constitution can meet the political yearnings and aspirations of the Nigerian people for a re-mapping of the political structure and governance arrangement of the country.

Beyond constitutional engineering, there must a renewed commitment to constitutionalism, a process by which constitutional rule and the rule of law would be well entrenched and institutionalised in the society. It is only through this process that the constitution can become a living document to be protected by all and sundry (see, Adejumobi, 2000). The present political situation in Nigeria is a complete negation of this. The political leadership engages in wanton violation of the law. For example, public holidays are declared arbitrarily by presidential fiat.[1] Criminal law makers who forged certificates and were convicted by the court of law are given questionable presidential pardon,[2] and erstwhile corrupt public officials who miscreantly peculated national wealth and who have been duly exposed by the media and human right groups have been given political cover by the new civilian regime.[3] Democracy cannot grow in a lawless society; neither can a leadership engaged in "double standards" build public confidence and trust.

Whether Nigeria survives or not and in what shape or form it will possibly do so, are issues of political conjecture. However, germane to the process of its survival is the initiative, creativity, and ingenuity of the political leadership at anticipating, initiating and managing a process of an inevitable political change that will centre on the re-negotiation of the social pact between Nigeria's ethnic nationalities and between the citizens and the state. In that process, the views, feelings and interests of the toiling people should be taken into account otherwise the exercise will remain endangered. All over the world, the toiling people have been both the victims and agency in the crisis resulting from the national question.

Notes

1. The Obasanjo administration declared May 29, 2000, as a public holiday, which it called the "democracy day". The day chosen was the one-year anniversary of the regime in power. This was by presidential fiat, without recourse to the National Assembly. This situation led to a boycott of the ceremony by the senate president and the speaker of the House of representatives, insisting quite rightly that as lawmakers, they cannot be part of an illegality. Indeed, most civil society groups have criticised both the illegality of the decision and the choice of a date as "democracy day" for Nigeria. According to them, if any day is to be so designated as "democracy day" in Nigeria, it should be "June 12", when Nigerians decisively decided through the electoral process to terminate military rule, and when the struggle for democracy took a new, and decisive turn.

2. The President, General Olusegun Obasanjo (rtd) gave a questionable presidential pardon to Salisu Buhari, the former speaker of the House of Representatives, who was duly found guilty and convicted for forging certificates. Buhari was subsequently removed as speaker and lost his seat in the House of Representatives. However, apart from the presidential pardon now granted him by Obasanjo, there are current deft political manoeuvrings to reinstate him back in the House of Representatives.

3. Some of the erstwhile public office holders who have been accused of corruption like Michael Ani, the former finance minister under the Abacha regime, and General Babangida, the former military dictator, have remained untouched by the Obasanjo administration. Indeed, some of them have been given public appointments under the new regime. This is why many Nigerians are increasingly being critical and cynical about the vaunted anti-corruption crusade of the Obasanjo regime.

References

Adedeji A (1999), (ed), *Comprehending and Mastering African Conflict: The search for Sustainable Peace and Good Governance*. London: Zed Books.

Adejumobi S, (2000), *'Between Democracy and Development in Africa: What Are the Missing Links?'*, paper presented to the World Bank Conference on 'Development Thinking in the New Millennium'. Paris, France, June 26-28.

Ihonvbere J, (2000), 'Towards a New Constitutionalism in Africa' *CDD Occasional Paper Series 4*. London: Centre for Democracy and Development (CDD).

Soyinka W, (1999), cited in Laolu Akande, 'Soyinka Faults Sharia, Brings Home Radio Kudirat' *Guardian Newspaper*, November 3.

Suberu, Rotimi T. and Adigun Agbaje (1998), 'The future of Nigeria's Federalism' in Kunle Amuwo et al (eds), *Federalism and Political Restructuring in Nigeria*, Ibadan: Spectrum Books and IFRA.

Wallenstein P. and M. Sollenberg, (1999), 'Armed Conflict', *Journal of Peace Research*. Vol. 36, No.5.

Appendices

Appendix 1

Matters in the Exclusive Legislative List

1. Accounts of the Government of the Federation and of offices, courts and authorities thereof, including audit of those accounts.
2. Arms, ammunition and explosives.
3. Aviation, including airports, safety of aircraft and carriage of passengers and goods by air.
4. Awards of national titles of honour, decorations and others dignitaries.
5. Bankruptcy and insolvency.
6. Banks, banking, bills of exchange and promissory notes.
7. Borrowing of moneys within or outside Nigeria for the purposes of the Federation or of any state.
8. Census, including the establishment and maintenance of machinery for continous and universal registration of births and deaths throughout Nigeria.
9. Construction, alteration and maintenance of such roads as may be declared by the National Assembly to be Federal Trunk Roads.
10. Citizenship, naturalisation and aliens.
11. Commercial and industrial monopolies, combines and trusts.
12. Control of capital issues.
13. Copyright.
14. Currency, coinage and legal tender.
15. Customs and excise duties.
16. Defence.
17. Deportation of persons who are not citizens of Nigeria.
18. Diplomatic, consular and trade representation.
19. Drugs and poison.
20. Designation and securities in which trust funds may be invested.

21. Election to the offices of president and vice-president or Governor and deputy Governor, and any other office to which a person may be elected under this constitution, including election to the Local Government Council.

22. Evidence.

23. Export duties.

24. Exchange control.

25. External affairs.

26. Extradition.

27. Fingerprints, identification and criminal records.

28. Fishing and Fisheries other than fishing and Fisheries in rivers, lakes, waterways, ponds and other inland waters within Nigeria.

29. Immigration into and emigration from Nigeria.

30. Implementation of treaties relating to matters on this list.

31. incorporation, regulation and winding-up of bodies corporate, other than co-operative societies, Local Government Councils and bodies corporate established directly by any law enacted by a House of Assembly of a state.

32. Insurance.

33. Labour, including trade unions, industrial relations; conditions; safety and welfare of labour; industrial disputes; prescribing a national minimum wage for the federation or any part thereof; and industrial arbitrations.

34. Legal proceedings between Government of states or between the Government of the federation and Government of any state or any other authority or person.

35. Maritime shipping and navigation, including-

    a)   Shipping and navigation on tidal waters;

    b)   Shipping and navigation on the River Niger and its affluents and on any such other inland waterways as may be designated by the National Assembly to be an International waterway or to be an inter- state waterway;

    c)   Lighthouses, lightships, beacons and other provisions for the safety of shipping and navigation;

    d)   Such ports as may be declared by the National Assembly to be Federal ports (including the constitution and powers of ports authorities for Federal ports).

36. Meteorology.

37. Mines and Minerals, including oil fields, oil mining, geological surveys and natural gas.

38. National parks being such areas in a state as may with the consent of the Government of that state be designated by the National Assembly as national parks.

39. Naval, military and air forces, including any other branch of the armed forces of the Federation.

40. Nuclear energy.

41. Passports and visas.

42. Patents, trade marks, trade or business names, industrial designs and merchandise marks.

43. Pensions, gratuities and other like benefits payable out of the Consolidated Revenue Fund or any other public funds of the Federation.

44. Police and other security services established by law.

45. Posts, telegraphs and telephones.

46. Powers of the National Assembly, and the privileges and immunities of its members.

47. Prisons.

48. Professional occupations as may be designated by the National Assembly.

49. Public debt of the Federation.

50. Public holidays.

51. Public relations of the Federation.

52. Public services of the Federation, including the settlement of disputes between the Federation and officers of such service.

53. Quarantine.

54. Railways.

55. Regulation of political parties.

56. Service and execution in a state of the civil and criminal processes, judgements, decrees, orders and other decisions of any court of law established by the House of Assembly of that state.

57. Taxation of incomes, profits and capital gains, except as otherwise

prescribed by this Constitution.

58. The establishment and regulation of authorities for the federation or any part thereof-

    a) To promote and enforce the observance of the Fundamental objectives and Directives Principles of State policy contained in this Constitution;

    b) To identify, collect, preserve or generally look after ancient and historical monuments and records and archaeological sites and remains declared by the National Assembly to be of National significance or national importance;

    c) To administer museums and libraries other than museums and libraries   established by the Government of a state;

    d) To regulate tourist traffic; and

    e) To prescribe minimum standards of education at all levels.

59. The formation, annulment and dissolution of marriages other than marriages under Islamic law and customary law including matrimonial causes relating thereto.

60. Trade and commerce, and in particular-

    a) Trade and commerce between Nigeria and other countries, including import of commodities into and export of commodities from Nigeria, trade And commerce between the Federal Government and the state and trade and commerce between the states;

    b) Establishment of a purchasing authority with power to acquire for export or sale in World markets such agricultural produce as may be designated by the National Assembly;

    c) Inspection of produce to be exported from Nigeria and the enforcement of grades and standards of quality in respect of produce so inspected;

    d) Establishment of a body to prescribe and enforce standards of goods and commodities offered for sale;

    e) Control of the prices of goods and commodities designated by the National Assembly as essential goods or commodities; and

    f) Registration of business names.

61. Traffic on Federal trunk roads.

62. Water from such sources as may be declared by the National Assembly

to be sources affecting more than one state.

63. Weight and measures.

64. Wireless, broadcasting and television other than broadcasting and television provided by the Government of a state; allocation of wavelengths for wireless, broadcasting and television transmission.

65. Any other matter with respect to which the National Assembly has power to make laws in accordance with provisions of this constitution.

66. Any matter incidental or supplementary to any matter mentioned in this list.

Appendix 2

Matters in the Concurrent Legislative List Item

1. Subject to the provisions of this constitution, the National Assembly may be an act make provisions for-

    a)   The division of public revenue-

        I.   Between the Federation and the states,
        II.   Among the state of the Federation and the States.
        III. Between the States and Local Government,
        IV.   Among the Local Government in the States; and

    b)   Grants or loans from and the imposition of charges upon the consolidated Revenue Fund or any other public funds of the Federation or for the imposition of charges upon the revenue and its relates to a matter with respect to which the National Assembly is not empowered to make laws.

2. Subject to the provisions of this Constitution, any House of Assembly may make provisions for grants or loans from and the imposition of charges upon the revenue and assets of that state for any purpose notwithstanding that its relates to a matter with respect to which the National Assembly is empowered to make laws.

3. The National Assembly may make laws for the Federation or any part thereof with respect to such antiquities and monuments as may, with the consent of the State in which such antiquities and Monuments are located, be designated by the National Assembly as National Antiquities or National Monuments, but nothing in this paragraph shall preclude a House of Assembly from making Laws for the State or any part thereof with respect to Antiquities and Monuments not so designated in accordance with the foregoing provisions.

4. The National Assembly may make laws for the Federation or any part thereof with respect to the archives and public records of the Federation.

5. A House of Assembly may, subject to paragraph 4 hereof, make laws for that State or any part thereof with respect to archives and public record of the Government of the State.

6. Nothing in paragraph 4 and 5 hereof shall be construed as enabling any laws to be made which do not preserve the archives and records which are in existence at the date of commencement of this Constitution, And which are kept by authorities empowered to do so in any part of the federation.

7. In the exercise of its powers to impose any tax or duty on-

    a) capital gains, incomes or profits of persons other than companies; and

    b) documents or transactions by way of stamp duties, the National Assembly may, subject to such conditions as it may prescribe, provide that the collection of any such tax or duty or the administration of the law imposing it shall be carried out by the Government of a State or other authority of a State.

8. Where an act of the National Assembly provides for the collection of tax or duty on capital gains, incomes or profit or the administration of any law by an authority of a State in accordance with paragraph 7 hereof, it shall regulate the liability of persons to such tax or duty in such manner as to ensure that such tax or duty is not levied on the same person by more than one State.

9. A House of Assembly may, subject to such conditions as it may prescribe, make provisions for the collection of any tax, fee or rate or for the administration of a law providing for such collection by a Local Government Council.

10. Where a Law of a House of Assembly provides for the collection of tax, fee or rate or for the administration of such law by a Local Government Council in accordance with the provision hereof it shall regulate the liability of a persons to the tax, fee or rate in such manner as to ensure that such tax, fee or rate is not levied on the same person in respect of the same liability by more than one Local Government.

11. The National Assembly may make laws for the federation or any part thereof with respect to-

    a) electricity and the establishment of electrical power stations;

    b) the generation and transmission of electricity in or to any part of the Federation;

    c) the regulation of the right of any person or authority to damn up or otherwise interfere with the flow of water from sources in any part of the Federation;

    d)   the participation of the Federation in any arrangement with another country for the generation, transmission and distribution of electricity for any area partly within and partly outside the Federation;

    e)   the promotion and the establishment of a National grid system; and

    f)   the regulation of the right of any person or authority to use, work or operate any plant, apparatus, equipment or work designed for the supply or use of electrical energy.

12.   A House of Assembly may make laws for the State with respect to-

    a)   electricity and the establishment in that State of electric power stations;

    b)   the generation, transmission and distribution of electricity to areas not covered by a national grid system within that state; and

    c)   the establishment within that State of any authority for the promotion and management of electricity power stations established by the State.

13.   In the foregoing provisions of this item, unless the context otherwise requires, the following expressions have the meanings respectively attached to them-

"distribution" means the supply of electricity from a station to he ultimate consumer;

        "management" includes maintenance, repairs or replacement;

        "power station" means an assembly of plant or equipment for the creation or generation of electrical energy; and

        "transmission" means the supply of electricity from a power station to a sub-station or from one sub-station to another sub-station, and the reference to a "sub-station" herein is a reference to an assembly of plant, machinery or equipment for distribution of electricity.

14.   The National Assembly may make laws for the establishment of an authority with power to carry out censorship of cinematograph films to prohibit or restrict the exhibition of such films and nothing herein shall-

    a)   preclude a House of Assembly from making provision for a similar authority for that State; or

    b)   authorise the exhibition of a cinematograph film in a State without sanction of the authority established by the law of that State for the censorship of such films.

15. The National Assembly may make laws for the Federation or any part thereof with respect to-

   a) the health, safety and welfare of persons employed to work in factories, offices or other premises or inter-state transportation and commerce including the training, supervision and qualification of such persons;

   b) the regulation of ownership and control of business enterprises throughout the federation for the purpose of promoting, encouraging and facilitating such ownership and control by citizens of Nigeria;

   c) the establishment of research centres for agricultural studies; and

   d) the establishment of institutions and bodies for the promotion or financing of industrial, commercial and agricultural projects.

16. Subject to the provisions of this Constitution a House of Assembly may make Laws for the State with respect to industrial, commercial or agricultural development of that State.

17. Nothing in the foregoing paragraphs of this item shall be construed as precluding a House of Assembly, from making Laws with respect to any of the matters referred to in the foregoing paragraphs.

18. For the purpose of the foregoing paragraphs of this item, the word "agricultural" includes fishery.

19. The National Assembly may make Laws to regulate or co-ordinate scientific and technological research throughout the Federation.

20. Nothing herein shall preclude a House of Assembly from establishing or making provisions for an institution or other arrangement for the purpose of scientific and technological research.

21. A House of Assembly may, subject to paragraph 7 hereof, make Laws for the imposing and regulation of Stamp Duties on documents, or transactions.

22. The National Assembly may make laws for the Federation or any part thereof with respect to statistics so far as the subject matter to relate to-

   a) any matter upon which the National Assembly has power to make laws; and

   b) the organisation of a co-ordinated scheme of statistics for the Federation or any part thereof an any matter or not it has power to make laws with respect thereto.

23. A House of Assembly may make Laws for the state with respect to statistics and on any other matter other than that referred to in sub-paragraph (a) of paragraph of this item.

24. The National Assembly may make laws for the Federation or any part thereof with respect to trigonometrical, cadastral and topographical surveys.

25. A House of Assembly may, subject to paragraph 24 hereof, make Laws for the State or any part thereof with respect to trigonometrical, cadastral and topographical surveys.

26. The National Assembly shall have power to make Laws for the Federation or any part thereof wit respect to university education, technological education or such professional education as may from time to time be designated by National Assembly.

27. The power conferred on the National Assembly under paragraph 26 of this item shall include power to establish an institution for the purpose of university, post-primary, technological or professional education.

28. Subject as herein provided, a House of Assembly shall have power to make Laws for the State with respect to the establishment of an institution for purposes of university, professional or technological education.

29. Nothing in the foregoing paragraph of this item shall construed so as to limit the powers of a house of Assembly to make Laws for the State with respect to technical, vocational, post-primary, primary or other forms of education, including the establishment institutions for the pursuit of such education.

Appendix 3

Functions of Local Governments

1. The main functions of a Local Government Council are as follows-

   a) the formulation of economic planning and development schemes for the local Government Area;

   b) collection of rates, radio and television licenses;

   c) establishment and maintenance of cemeteries, burial grounds and homes for the destitute or infirm;

   d) licensing of bicycles trucks (other than mechanically propelled trucks), canoes, wheel barrows and carts;

   e) establishment. Maintenance and regulation of slaughter houses, slaughter slabs, markets, motor parks and public conveniences;

   f) construction and maintenance of roads, streets, street lightings, drains, parks, gardens, open spaces, or public facilities as may be prescribed from time to time by the House of Assembly of a State;

   g) naming of roads and streets and numbering of houses;

   h) provision and maintenance of public conveniences, sewage and refuse disposal;

   i) registration of all births, deaths and marriages;

   j) assessment of privately owned houses or tenements for the purpose of levying such rates as may be prescribed by the House of Assembly of a State;

   k) control and regulation of-
      i. Out-door advertisement and hoarding.
      ii. Movement and keeping of pets of all descriptions.
      iii. Shops and kiosks.
      iv. Restaurants, bakeries and other places for sale of food to the public.
      v. Laundries; and
      vi. Licensing, regulation and control of the sale of liquor.

2. The functions of a Local Government shall include participation of such Local Government in the Government of a State as respects the following matters, namely

a) the provision and maintenance of primary, adult and vocational education;

b) the development of agriculture and natural resources, other than the exploitation of minerals;

c) the provision and maintenance of health services; and

d) such other functions as may be conferred upon a Local Government by the House of Assembly of the State.

Bibliography

ZEN M. FALEIYE

ACARTSOD (1990), 'Ethnicity, Citizenship, Stability and Socio-Economic Development in Africa'. Proceedings of the Regional Conference held in Tripoli, Libyan Arab Jamabiriya, 5-9 August 1989.

Adamolekun, L. (1991), 'The Federal Solution: Assessment and Prognosis for Nigeria and Africa'. *Publius*, Vol.21, No.4.

Adejuyigbe, Omolade (1970) 'The Ethnic Nations of Nigeria'. Paper read at a Seminar, Linguistics Department, University of Ibadan.

Adekanye, J.B (1979), 'Military Organisations in multi-ethnical segmented societies' in Marret C. and C. Leggon (eds), *Research in Race and Ethnic Relations*. Greenwich Press Inc.

_____ (1994), 'Structural Adjustment, Democratisation, and Rising Ethnic Tension in Africa'. *Development and Change*. Vol.26, No.2.

_____ (1996), 'Rwanda/Burundi: Uni-ethnic dominance and the cycle of armed ethnic formations'. *Social Identities*. Vol.2, No.1

Adeleye, R.A, (1971), *Power and Diplomacy in Northern Nigeria, 1804-1906: The Sokoto Caliphate and Its Enemies*. London: Longman.

Ajayi, J.F Ade, and Robert S. Smith, (1962), *Yoruba Warfare in the Nineteenth Century*. Ibadan: Cambridge University Press.

Ake, Claude, (1993), 'What is the Problem of Ethnicity?' *Transformation*. No.22.

Akintoye, S.A. (1971), *Revolution and Power in Yoruba. 1840-1893, Ibadan Expansion and the Rise of Ekiti Parapo*. London: Longman.

Akinyele, R.T. (1992), 'Safeguarding Nigeria's ethnic minorities: The Relevance of the American Approach to Minority Problems'. *Nigerian Journal of American Studies*, Vol. 11, July.

Amuwo, K., et.al.(1998), (eds), *Federalism and Political Restructuring in Nigeria*. Ibadan: Spectrum Books.

Anifowose, R. (1982), *Violence and Politics in Nigeria: The Tiv and Yoruba Experience*. New York: NOK.

Anikpo, M. (1991), *Trade, Class and Ethnic Identity*. Enugu: ABIC Publishers.

Ayoade, A.A. (1986), 'Ethnic Management in the 1979 Nigerian Constitution'. *Publius*, Vol.16, No.2, Spring.

Bach, D (1997), 'Indigeneity, Ethnicity and Federalism' in Diamond, L., et.al. (eds), *Transition Without End*. Ibadan: Vintage Press.

Balogun, S.A. (1970), Gwandu emirates in the Nineteenth Century with Special Reference to Political Relations: 1817-1903). Ibadan, Nigeria: Unpublished M.A. Thesis, Department of History, University of Ibadan.

Balogun, I. (1978), *Religious Understanding and Cooperation in Nigeria*. Ilorin: University Press.

Barongo, Y. (1989), 'Ethnic Pluralism and Political Centralisation: The Basis of Political Conflict' in K. Rupesinghe (ed), *Conflict Resolution in Uganda*. Oslo: PRIO.

Barth, F. (1969), (ed), *Ethnic Group and Boundaries*. Boston, Mass.: Little Brown and Company.

Bascon, W. (1969), *Civilisation and the Yoruba of South-western Nigeria*. New York: Holt, Rinehart and Winston.

Coleman, J. (1958), *Nigeria: Background to Nationalism*. Beckley: University of California Press.

Conner, W. (1973), 'The Politics of Ethnonationalism'. *Journal of International Affairs*, Vol.27, No.1.

Cornell, F.G. (1961), 'Political Implications of Federalism in New States', in U.K. Hicks et.al. (eds), *Federalism and Economics Growth in Underdeveloped Countries*. London: Allen and Unwin.

Diamond, L. (1988), *Ethnicity and Democracy in Nigeria*. London: Macmillan.

Dietz, H. (1991), 'Conclusion', in H. Dietz, J.Ellan and M. Roumani (eds.) *Ethnicity, Integration and the Military: U.S Special edition on Armed Forces and Society*. Colorado: Westview.

Dudley, B. (1973), *Instability and Political Order*. Ibadan: University Press.

Egwu, S.G. (1998), *Structural Adjustment, Agrarian Change and Rural Ethnicity in Nigeria*. Uppsala: The Nordic Africa Institute.

_____ (1998), *Democracy at Bay: Ethnicity and Nigeria's Democratic Eclipse, 1986-1995*. Jos: African Centre for Democratic Governance.

Ekechi, F. (1971), *Missionary Enterprises and Rivalry in Igboland, 1857-1914*. London: Frank Cass.

Ekekwe, E. (1986), *Class and State in Nigeria*. Zaria: Longman.

Enloe, C. (1980a), *Police, Military and Ethnicity: Foundations of State Power*. New Brunswick, NJ: Transaction Press.

_____ (1980b), *Ethnic Soldiers*. Athens: University of Georgia Press.

Erikson, Erik (1968), *Identity, Youth and Crisis*. New York: W.W. Norton.

Fishman, J.A. (1997), 'Language and Ethnicity: The View from Within', in Coulmas, E. (eds), *The Handbook of Sociolinguistics*. Oxford Blackwell Publishers.

Friedrich, C. J. (1968), *Trends in Federalism in Theory and Practice*. London: Pall Mall.

Gites, H. (ed), (1979), *Language and Ethnic Relations*. Oxford: Pergamon Press.

Ihonvbere, Julius (1999), 'Federalism, Power sharing and the Politics of Redistribution'. Paper presented at the International conference on 'Consolidating Democracy: Nigeria in Comparative Perspective' organised under the auspices of AEGIS, the European Network of African Studies, Portugal, September 21-25.

Jega, M. (1999), The Nigerian Federal System: Problem and Prospects', in Lidija R. Basta and Jibrin Ibrahim (eds), *Federalism and Decentralisation in Africa:*

The Multicultural Challenges. Institute of Federalism, Fribourg, Switzerland.

Jinadu, L. A. (1985), 'Federalism, the Consociational State and Ethnic Conflict in Nigeria'. *Publius*, Vol.15, No.2, Spring.

Kukah, M.H. (1994), *Religion, Politics and Power in Northern Nigeria*. Ibadan: Spectrum Books Limited.

Kymlicka, Will (1995), *Multicultural Citizenship*. Oxford: Clarendon Press.

Lenin, V.I. (1975), *On the National and Colonial Questions: Three Articles*. China: Foreign Languages Press.

Madiebo, A. (1980), *The Nigerian Revolution and the Biafran Civil War*. Enugu: Fourth Dimension Publishers.

Mafeje, A. (1997), *Ethnicity and Inter-Class Conflicts in Africa* (Mimeo).

Mare, G. (1993), *Ethnicity and Politics in South Africa*. London: Zed Press.

Mazrui, A. (1978), *Soldiers and Kinsmen: The Making of a Military Ethnography*. London: Sage Publication.

McHenry, D. (1986), 'Stability of the Federal System in Nigeria: Elite Attitudes at the Constituent Assembly toward the Creation of States'. *Journal of Federalism*, Vol.16, No.2, Spring.

Mkandawire, Thandika (1994), 'Adjustment, Political Conditionality and Democratisation in Africa', in Giovanni A. Cornia and Gerald K. Helleiner (eds), *From Adjustment To Development in Africa: Conflict, Controversy, Convergence, Consensus?* New York: St Martins Press.

Nnoli, O. (1978), *Ethnic Politics in Nigeria*. Enugu: Fourth Dimension.

Nwankwo, A. (1984), *Civilianised Soldiers: Army-Civilian Government for Nigeria*. Enugu: Fourth Dimension Publishers.

Okamura, J.Y. (1981), 'Situational Ethnicity'. *Ethnic and Racial Studies*, Vol. 4, No.4.

Okeke, O. (1992), *Hausa-Fulani Hegemony*. Enugu: Acena.

Okonjo, G. (1967), 'Strangers Communities: The Western Ibo', in P.C Lloyd, A.L Mabogunje and B. Awe (eds), *The City of Ibadan*. Cambridge University Press.

Onah, J.K. (1998), 'The Impact of Oil on Nigeria's Revenue Allocation System: Problems and Prospects for National Reconstruction' in Kunle Amuwo et.al (eds), *Federalism and Political Restructuring in Nigeria*. Ibadan: Spectrum.

Onimode, Bade (1994), 'Towards a Fuller Understanding of Ethnicity in Africa: Bringing Rural Ethnicity Back', in *Between State and Civil Society in Africa* (Dakar: CODESRIA).

Osaghae, E. (1986), 'On the Concept of the ethnic Group in Africa: A Nigerian Case'. *Plural Societies*, Vol.16, No.2.

_____ (1989), 'Federalism and Democracy: An Old Romance Revisited on the light of the Nigerian Experience', in J. Bayo Adekanye (ed), *Institutions and Processes of Democratisation in Nigeria*. Proceedings of the Nigerian Political Science Association Conference.

_____ (1990), 'Do Ethnic Minorities Still Exist in Nigeria?'. *Journal of Commonwealth and Comparative Politics*. Vol. xxiv, No.2.

_____ (1994), *Ethnicity and Its Management in Africa: The Democratisation Link*. Lagos: Malthouse.

_____ (1995), 'The Ogoni Uprising: Oil Politics, Minority Agitation and the Future of the Nigerian State'. *African Affairs*, Vol.94.

_____ (1996), 'Human Rights and Ethnic Conflict Management: The Case of Nigeria'. *Journal of Peace Research*, Vol.33, No.2.

Otite, O. (1971), 'Modernising MidWestern Nigeria in Urban Agglomerations' in *The States of the Third World: Their Political, Social and Economic Role*. Brussells: INCIDI.

_____ (1990), *Ethnic Pluralism and Ethnicity in Africa*. Ibadan: Shaneson Ltd.

Sanda, A.O. (1974), 'Ethnicity And Intergroup Conflicts: Some Insights From Non-Elite Actors in a Nigerian City'. *Nigerian Journal of Economic and Social Studies*, Vol.16, No.3.November.

_____ (1974), 'The Dynamics of Ethnicity Among the Yoruba'. Unpublished Ph.D. Thesis, University of Califonia, Los Angeles.

_____ (1976), *Ethnic Relations in Nigeria*. Ibadan: The Caxton Press (West Africa) Limited.

Sen, Y. (1991), 'The Middle Belt in Nigerian Politics: A Futuristic Analysis'. Paper presented at Service for S.D.P Chairmen, Jos.

Smith, Anthony, D. (1981), *The Ethnic Revival in the Modern World*. Cambridge: Cambridge University Press.

Szparlvk, R. (1973), 'Nationalities and the Russian Problem in the USSR: An Historical outline'. *Journal of International Affairs*, Vol.27, No.1.

Takaya, B.J. and Tyoden, S. Gwanle (1987), *The Kaduna Mafia: A Study of the Rise, Development and Consolidation of a Nigeria Power Elite*. Jos: Jos University Press.

Tyoden, S. Gwanle (1993), *The Middle Belt in Nigerian Politics*. Jos: AHA Publishing House Ltd.

Usman, Y. Bala (1992), *Katsina State in the Nigerian Federation: The Basic Realities*. Kaduna: Dansa Publications Limited.

Vickers, M. (1997), *Ethnicity and Sub-Nationalism in Nigeria: Movement for a Mid-West State*. London: Hillfield Press.

Waziri, I. (1985), 'Towards Understanding the Ethnic Question in Nigeria and Fika Local Government Area'. *Democrat Weekly*, April 2.

Wright, S. (1991), 'State Consolidation and Social Integration in Nigeria: The Military Search for the Elusive', in H. Dietz (ed), *Ethnicity, Integration and the Military*. US Special Edition on Armed Forces and Society. Colorado, Westview.

Index

271